Questions
Women Asked

Questions
Women Asked

Historical Issues, Timeless Answers

Simonetta Carr

Reformation Heritage Books
Grand Rapids, Michigan

Questions Women Asked
© 2021 by Simonetta Carr

Reformation Heritage Books
3070 29th St. SE
Grand Rapids, MI 49512
616-977-0889
orders@heritagebooks.org
www.heritagebooks.org

Printed in the United States of America
21 22 23 24 25 26/10 9 8 7 6 5 4 3 2 1

Unless otherwise indicated, all Scripture quotations are taken from the King James Version, which is in the public domain.

Scripture quotations designated NKJV are taken from the New King James Version®. Copyright © 1982 by Thomas Nelson. Used by permission. All rights reserved.

Library of Congress Cataloging-in-Publication Data

Names: Carr, Simonetta, author.
Title: Questions women asked : historical issues, timeless answers / Simonetta Carr.
Description: Grand Rapids, Michigan : Reformation Heritage Books, [2021] | Includes bibliographical references.
Identifiers: LCCN 2020058484 (print) | LCCN 2020058485 (ebook) | ISBN 9781601788382 (paperback) | ISBN 9781601788399 (epub)
Subjects: LCSH: Women in Christianity—History. | Christian women—Religious life—History.
Classification: LCC BV639.W7 C3273 2021 (print) | LCC BV639.W7 (ebook) | DDC 248.8/43—dc23
LC record available at https://lccn.loc.gov/2020058484
LC ebook record available at https://lccn.loc.gov/2020058485

For additional Reformed literature, request a free book list from Reformation Heritage Books at the above regular or email address.

To the women who have shaped my life, especially my mother, Luciana Negrini, who taught me to raise questions; my daughter Renaissance Carr, whose questions always challenge me to grow in wisdom and understanding; and my granddaughters Charlize, Micaela, and Cate Carr, who just gave me a big book of questions to try to answer.

Contents

Preface

Questions are important. Sometimes they help us understand the person who is posing them. Sometimes they help us understand ourselves and bring to light similar queries that have fluttered in our minds. Quite often, they spark new questions and generate new discussions.

The women included in this book span most of the history of the church. I have chosen thirty-one inquisitive women who have either posed or examined a variety of puzzling questions, striving to find biblical answers. Of course, each woman included in this collection asked more questions than the one featured in her chapter. Readers are encouraged to explore the resources listed at the end of each chapter and to do more independent studies.

Each chapter ends with a section titled "Food for Thought," which can be used for private reflection or for group studies. Rather than endorsing wholesale every conclusion the women in this book have made, I encourage readers to use the questions in this book as a springboard for a deeper consideration of important issues.

Finally, a note about names: while today's editorial rules require that both men and women be referred to by their last names, I have chosen to use the first names of these women so that readers can view them as close friends.

Acknowledgments

I want to thank everyone who has encouraged me to pursue this project, especially my friends and excellent authors Glenda Mathes and Janie Cheaney, who have supported me with prayer and advice; and my friend Kris Moberly, who has read every chapter of this book and brought up new and interesting questions.

I can't even begin to describe the forbearance of the scholars who have patiently replied to my relentless questions. By now, they probably dread receiving an email from me. But this book couldn't have come about without their help.

Following the order of the chapters they edited, I want to thank Philip Cary, scholar-in-residence at Templeton Honors College, Eastern University, and author of several books on Augustine of Hippo and on church history, for reading my chapters on Macrina and Monica; medieval scholar Travis Baker, who has read my chapters on Dhuoda and Christine de Pizan; Michael Haykin, professor of church history and biblical spirituality and director of the Andrew Fuller Center for Baptist Studies at the Southern Baptist Theological Seminary, who has read my chapters on Anne Dutton and Anne Steele; Justin Skirry, professor of philosophy at Nebraska Wesleyan University and author of *Descartes: A Guide for the Perplexed*, who has read my chapter on Elisabeth of the Palatinate; and E. Wyn James, emeritus professor of the School of Welsh at Cardiff University and editor of *Flame in the Mountains: Williams Pantycelyn, Ann Griffiths and the Welsh Hymn*, who has read my chapter on Ann Griffiths and has educated me on the fascinating story of Welsh Methodism.

All these have generously and patiently given their time to correct my misgivings and to provide valuable suggestions. I will be forever grateful.

As always, I am also thankful for the encouragement and support of Dr. Joel Beeke, Jay Collier, Annette Gysen, David Woollin, and all the staff at Reformation Heritage Books, who have welcomed this idea and brought the book to completion.

Last but certainly never least, I thank my husband, Tom, who has patiently listened to my frequent recounting of the discoveries I made in my research and has supported me with his interest and encouragement.

How Can I Understand Scripture Correctly?

MARCELLA OF ROME (ca. 325–410)

Marcella became a widow after seven months of marriage. As an attractive noblewoman in her midthirties, she had no shortage of suitors. Even a consul, Neratius Cerealis, asked insistently for her hand. He was much older than she and promised her honors and guidance. Marcella's mother, Albina, who was also a widow, saw it as a golden opportunity.

Marcella was not interested. She lived in the days of the great hermits and early monastic communities. The life story of the desert monk Anthony and his struggle with demons, written by the Egyptian bishop Athanasius, was a best seller, especially among young believers who thought Constantine's edict of toleration of Christians had made life too easy and convenient for followers of Christ.

MARCELLA'S COMMUNITY OF FAITH

The extreme life choice to retreat from the world made exasperated parents sigh in frustration. "Incomprehensible!" an upstanding citizen of Antioch said about one of these young, restless people. "How could the son of respectable middle-class parents with a good education and excellent prospects for a steady comfortable life leave his home to go off and join a company of dirty vagrants!"[1]

---

1. John Chrysostom, *Against Those Who Oppose the Monastic Life*, as

And yet this was the type of life Marcella wanted for herself. She was still a teenager when she heard Athanasius speak about Egyptian monks like Anthony and Pachomius and the monasteries they established or promoted.[2] She later heard similar stories from Peter, bishop of Alexandria, who stayed in Rome between 373 and 378. She was enticed. In the end, her choice was not as drastic. Instead of traveling to the desert, she lived a simple life of prayer and meditation at home.

Because of this, she refused every suitor, even when Albina insisted on the importance of marrying into financial security. Marrying for money seemed illogical to Marcella. "If I wanted to marry and didn't wish to devote myself to perpetual chastity," she told her mother, "I would look for a husband—not an inheritance."[3]

On the contrary, she readily renounced her fancy clothes, jewelry, and riches in order to donate her money to the poor. Albina could only persuade her to compromise a little. If Marcella had to give her wealth away, she should at least keep it in the family and give it to some cousins who could use it. She complied. Gradually, Albina accepted and even adopted her daughter's choice.

Soon, other women joined them: first Paola and her daughters Eustochium and Blesilla, and then Sofronia, Asella, Principia, Leah, Feliciana, and Marcellina. Marcella's large domus on the outskirts of Rome in a quiet country area known as Aventino provided an ideal place for a religious community. Some women lived with her, and others, like Paola, stayed in their homes, but they all met together to pray, sing psalms, read Scripture, and perform charitable work. Managing a community of women who looked to her as a mother in the faith was a large responsibility for Marcella, who faced it by

---

quoted in Robert Wilken, *The First Thousand Years* (New Haven, Conn.: Yale University Press, 2012), 108.

2. Marcella probably heard Athanasius speak during his exile in Rome (339–346).

3. As quoted in Jerome to Principia, Letter 127.2, *Sancti Eusebii Hieronym Epistulae*, part 3, ed. Isidoer Hilberg (Leipzig: G. Freytag, 1918), 146; my translation.

devoting herself to a serious study of Scripture. When in 382 a young Christian presbyter named Jerome (340–420) arrived in Rome from Antioch, she insisted on meeting him.

MARCELLA AND JEROME

Fiery, skillful, and determined, Jerome attracted both loyal followers and fierce critics. Marcella had heard of him as a famous ascetic and exegete, well versed in Hebrew, Greek, and Latin, and decided to ask him some questions she had pondered for a while. At first Jerome shunned her. He was a firm believer in chastity as a holier form of life, so he avoided, out of "modesty," any eye contact with women.[4] But Marcella didn't give up easily. She kept insisting "in season and out of season,"[5] until she gained his attention. Her overall question was, How can I understand Scripture correctly?

It was imperative that she did. The Christian church was still establishing certain areas of its doctrine, and the formulation of different views demanded that Christians engage in a careful investigation of Scripture. Marcella's position of influence over the women in her circle made this investigation particularly urgent. Besides, there were several other teachers trying to enlist her support, and she had to weigh their doctrines in order to decide whether they were based on Scripture.

Initially, Jerome's replies were short and simple. *Not sufficient*, she thought. She persisted in her inquiries, both in person and by letter, not "for argument's sake but to learn the answers to those objections which might, as she saw, be made."[6]

---

4. Jerome, Letter 127.7, trans. W. H. Fremantle, G. Lewis, and W. G. Martley, vol. 6, *Nicene and Post-Nicene Fathers*, Series 2, ed. Philip Schaff and Henry Wace (Buffalo, N.Y.: Christian Literature, 1893).

5. 2 Tim. 4:2, quoted in Jerome, Letter 127:7.

6. Jerome, Letter 127:7. An example of Marcella's questions can be found at "Letters of St. Jerome," Letter 59, Church Fathers, New Advent, http://www.newadvent.org/fathers/3001059.htm. Other women at that time also asked Jerome questions. See https://epistolae.ctl.columbia.edu/letter/1290.html.

QUIETING JEROME'S SPIRITS

Jerome had a fiery personality and didn't take criticism well. He was particularly furious with those who criticized his translation of the Gospels
as inconsistent with the original Greek. Where could he vent his resent-
ment? In a letter to Marcella, of course—even though he stopped midway
to explain he could easily imagine her reaction.

"I know that as you read these words you will knit your brows," he
wrote, "and fear that my freedom of speech is sowing the seeds of fresh
quarrels; and that, if you could, you would gladly put your finger on my
mouth to prevent me from even speaking of things which others do not
blush to do."[a]

---

a. Jerome, Letter 27.2.

Many of her questions regarded the interpretation of Hebrew
words, particularly the names of God and words related to worship,
such as *ephod, therabim, selah,* and *hallelujah.* Eventually, she realized she had to learn the language and applied herself to it until she
was able not only to interpret it but to sing the Hebrew psalter without a trace of a foreign accent. This is notable in more ways than one
because the study of Hebrew was a rare discipline in those days, let
alone for a woman.

Jerome's interaction with Marcella—and subsequently her
friends—didn't escape the disapproval of those who thought he was
wasting his time with insignificant women. Some people even found
his friendship with them scandalous. He retorted by pointing to the
women who assisted Jesus and had the privilege of seeing His resurrected body sooner than the male disciples. Also, he recognized
Marcella's high level of education, so much that in a letter to her he
apologized that his Latin was not up to her standards.

Jerome remained in Rome until 385 at the service of Pope Damasus I. For a while, there were great expectations that Jerome would
become his successor, but when Damasus died, the choice fell on the
deacon Siricius. One substantial reason for this change of plans was

Jerome's encouragement of extreme forms of asceticism. He was particularly accused of having exercised undue influence on the young Blesilla, who died from excessive fasting. He ended up returning to Antioch. From there, he traveled throughout the Holy Land and parts of Egypt.

COMMITMENT TO ROME

By the time Jerome left, Marcella had acquired such a wealth of biblical knowledge that both men and women in Rome sought her advice. She gave it freely but made sure to give credit for the answers to Jerome. She did so partially out of social correctness, partially out of respect for 1 Timothy 2:12, and partially (according to Jerome) to avoid embarrassing the men who had not solved those issues on their own.

Jerome continued to encourage Marcella to join him across the Mediterranean as her disciples Paola and Eustochium had done. The two women wrote Marcella a long letter trying to make her feel guilty for letting them go by themselves: "You were the first to set our tinder alight; the first, by precept and example, to urge us to adopt our present life. As a hen gathers her chickens, so did you take us under your wing. And will you now let us fly about at random with no mother near us? Will you leave us to dread the swoop of the hawk and the shadow of each passing bird of prey?"[7]

Their words suggest that Marcella had reacted with harshness, perhaps showing some irritation at their insistence: "Separated from you, we do what we can: we utter our mournful plaint, and more by sobs than by tears we adjure you to give back to us the Marcella whom we love. She is mild, she is suave, she is sweeter than the sweetest honey. She must not, therefore, be stern and morose to us, whom her

---

7. Jerome, Letter 46.1., vol. 6, *Nicene and Post-Nicene Fathers*, Series 2, ed. Philip Schaff and Henry Wace (Edinburgh: T&T Clark, 1893), Christian Classics Ethereal Library, https://ccel.org/ccel/schaff/npnf206/npnf206.i.html.

winning ways have roused to adopt a life like her own."[8] The women quoted a long list of Scripture passages, from Genesis to Revelation, as evidence of the special spiritual benefits attached to the Holy Land—especially to Jerusalem.

Paola and Eustochium's anticipation and list of Marcella's rebuttals suggest that they had probably discussed these things before. Marcella didn't share their views on these "holy" places, looking to the Jerusalem to come rather than the earthly one. She had her own independent views and didn't follow Jerome as closely as others did.

In any case, she stuck to her decision. Along with any theological convictions, at about sixty years old, she might have been feeling the weight of her years, and there was plenty to do in Rome. Eventually, even Jerome recognized she was needed where she was. After all, it was because of her efforts that he had "the joy of seeing Rome transformed into another Jerusalem."[9]

FIGHT AGAINST HERESY

Normally, Marcella shunned polemics. At the end of the fourth century, however, when some theological disagreements degenerated into what Jerome called "a tornado of heresy,"[10] she felt compelled to raise her voice.

The catalyst had been a translation by Rufinus of Aquileia (345–411) of two controversial books: one, *On First Principles*, by a theologian named Origen of Alexandria (ca. 184–253); and the other, an *Apology for Origen* by Pamphilus of Cesarea. Today, Origen is often remembered as a key figure in the battle against heretics who denied the inspiration of the Old Testament. Despite his resort to interpreting the Old Testament by allegory, he was important in establishing the literal text of the Bible. He was brilliant in many ways, and sometimes his brilliance led to attempts to explain Christian truths that went beyond what is found in Scripture. Such

---

8. Jerome, Letter 46.1.

9. Jerome, Letter 127.8.

10. Jerome, Letter 127.9.

attempts appear to have led him into a belief in a universal salvation and the preexistence of the human soul before the creation of the body. Since at that time writings could easily be misattributed, it's hard to know how many of these ideas were really his and how many were simply accredited to him after his death.

By the time Rufinus published his translations in Rome, the doctrines he included were already viewed with suspicion in large parts of the Western church. Rufinus's claim that the text of *On First Principles* had been modified by heretics and that his version was an attempt to reflect Origen's true thoughts didn't help. In fact, it infuriated Jerome, who thought Rufinus was trying to make Origen's doctrines more acceptable.

Marcella shared these concerns. Together with her cousin Pammachius, an old friend of Jerome, and other friends, she brought the matter to the bishop of Rome. The details of the controversy are murky, and there was apparently a great deal of misunderstanding between Jerome and Rufinus, who never received Jerome's letter of reconciliation. In any case, Marcella emerges as an important and resilient voice in the defense of orthodoxy.

MARCELLA'S DEATH

Few people could have predicted what happened next. In 408, Alaric, king of the Goths, besieged the "eternal city" of Rome, departing only after receiving large quantities of precious goods. Since Emperor Honorius refused to meet Alaric's conditions, the king attacked the city again in 410, this time thoroughly sacking it and destroying large parts of it. By that time, the Romans had been starved for so long that they could offer little resistance.

The Goths invaded Marcella's property. She was probably in her seventies by this time. According to witnesses' accounts, she didn't show any fear. Refusing to believe that Marcella had chosen a life of poverty, the raiders asked where she had hidden her goods. When they couldn't find them, they beat her brutally. Frustrated by the lack of spoils, they went after Marcella's young disciple Principia, but Marcella defended her with her life. In the end, the Goths relented and left Marcella's home. She died a few months later, possibly as a result of the attack.

Marcella is remembered as a woman with an insatiable love for God's Word and a desire to interpret it correctly, protecting others from wrong interpretations. At a time when Christian doctrine was still in its formative stage, she found an answer to her quest for proper understanding by studying the original Scriptures and consulting teachers she trusted—always comparing the two and drawing well-informed and careful conclusions.

FOOD FOR THOUGHT

- A careful scrutiny of Christian teachings was imperative at a time when doctrines were still being formed. Are things the same or different today? Discuss some differences and similarities.

- Not every Christian can embark on a study of the biblical languages. What can be a valid alternative? Do you think it's important to find a church where the pastor is trained in Hebrew and Greek? Why or why not?

- Marcella had to learn how to properly exegete Scripture because of her responsibilities to other women in her community and because she received many requests from preachers who wanted her support. What are other reasons a woman should embark in a serious study of Scripture? Do you see a difference between men and women in this responsibility? If so, explain the difference.

- How can a Christian learn to properly exegete and apply Scripture?

- Given the historical context, what were some advantages and disadvantages of living a semimonastic life like Marcella's? Why do you think it was particularly attractive to young people? What are some ways in which young Christians today choose a more radical path than their parents?

• What are some reasons for Marcella's decision to stay in Rome? Was there any spiritual benefit in moving to the Holy Land? Are there still some places to which Christians attach a special spiritual meaning? What are they?

• Few people enjoy polemics, but there are times when Christians need to stand up against serious misinterpretations of the Bible. What are some misconceptions that are particularly dangerous today?

FOR FURTHER RESEARCH

The only information we have about Marcella is in Jerome's letters, which can be found in vol. 6 of *The Nicene and Post-Nicene Fathers*, Series 2, ed. Philip Schaff and Henry Wace (Edinburgh: T&T Clark, 1893), Christian Classics Ethereal Library, https://ccel.org/ccel /schaff/npnf206/npnf206.i.html. His letters have also been revised and edited for the New Advent website by Kevin Knight (http://www .newadvent.org/fathers/3001.htm).

2

How Should a Christian Live in This World and Have Hope for the Next?

MACRINA THE YOUNGER (ca. 327–379)

After her future husband died suddenly before their marriage, twelve-year-old Macrina refused to consider any of her numerous suitors. Failing to see a substantial difference between a betrothal and a marriage, she believed her union with her husband-to-be was already sealed. According to her brother Gregory, who wrote a biography of her life, she thought it was "absurd and unlawful...not to keep faith with the bridegroom who was away" since, "thanks to the hope of the resurrection," he was only absent, not dead.[1]

As the oldest daughter, she continued to help her widowed mother, Emmelia, in her household duties, including raising the other eight children. She especially devoted herself to her brother Peter, becoming to him, in Gregory's words, "father, teacher, tutor, mother, giver of all good advice."[2] Eventually, Peter became a bishop, as did his brothers Basil, known as "the Great," and Gregory.

MACRINA'S COMMUNITY

Like other young men and women of her time, Macrina was drawn to an ascetic life, with a renunciation of the material attractions of

---

1. Gregory of Nyssa, *Life of St. Macrina*, ed. W. K. Lowther Clarke (London: Society for Promoting Christian Knowledge, 1916), 25, http://www.tertullian .org/fathers/gregory_macrina_1_life.htm.
2. Gregory of Nyssa, *Life of St. Macrina*, 37.

this world and a commitment to prayer and charitable work. Her enthusiasm was contagious. When Emmelia moved the family from their home in Caesarea of Cappadocia, in today's Turkey, to their estate near Annesi, Pontus (about thirty miles west on the southern coast of the Black Sea), Macrina persuaded her to turn the place into a religious community where the family and other like-minded people could live together. Emmelia was used to radical choices. She had grown up during the Great Persecution of 303–311, when her father died as a martyr. In keeping with her daughter's vision, she freed all her slaves so that everyone in the community could live on equal terms.

Over time, the community became well known for its radical generosity. For example, in 369, during one of the worst droughts in the region, Macrina did more than feed those who knocked at her doors. Together with her brother Peter, she searched the area for children who were abandoned by their starving parents and adopted them, taking them into her home.

By the time Macrina's brother Basil returned from Athens, where he had gained a reputation as a skilled orator, his home was a far cry from the original wealthy domus of his youth. According to Gregory, Basil's success had made him rather smug and arrogant, and Macrina had no hesitation in pointing it out while encouraging him to pursue a humble life in service of others. Basil had already been attracted to the monastic life, particularly through the writings of the monk Eustathius of Sabaste, but Gregory only mentions Macrina's intervention, which probably had a deeper and more personal impact on Basil's life.

Eventually, after visiting newly founded monastic centers in Egypt and Syria, Basil concluded that the model of religious community Macrina had founded at home—an ordinary life of housework, prayer, and service to others—was more congenial to a true Christian life than isolation and withdrawal from the world. "How will [a Christian] give evidence of his compassion," he asked, "if he has cut himself off from association with other persons? And how will

THE REVOLUTIONARY NATURE OF CHRISTIAN COMMUNITIES

In a day when charities abound, it's difficult to understand how revolutionary Macrina's and Basil's communities were in their day. While charity was certainly extolled by some Greco-Roman philosophers and applied in some measure by the Roman government, the idea of giving of one's properties and time without expecting anything in return was still generally alien.

In 361 Emperor Julian found Christian charity to be a major obstacle to his plan of leading the empire back to its pagan traditions. The poor and needy, who constituted the majority of the population, flocked to Christian institutions, where they received acceptance, love, and assistance. In response, he tried to teach his pagan priests to do the same but didn't live long enough to see his dream come true.

In any case, Christians like Macrina and Basil who built charitable institutions had to overcome centuries of public indifference, as demonstrated in the pleading sermons given by Basil, his brother Gregory, and other preachers of their times, aimed at shaking the wealthy from their complacency and denouncing the hoarders and profiteers.

he exercise long-suffering, if no one contradicts his wishes?"[3] These questions could easily have come from Macrina's lips. In fact, Basil modeled his monasteries on Macrina's community, formalizing her vision in two books of instructions for their members.

After becoming bishop of Caesarea, Basil continued his charitable activities. Through a persistent program of fund-raising, he was able to build a large complex of facilities, which included a hospital and convalescent home, a home for orphans and the elderly, and the first hospital ever built for lepers.

---

3. Basil of Caesarea, *The Long Rules*, in *Ascetical Works*, vol. 9 of The Fathers of the Church—A New Translation, ed. Ludwig Schopp (Washington, D.C.: Catholic University of America Press, 1969), 251.

MACRINA'S INFLUENCE

The hagiographic nature of Gregory's biographical work *The Life of Macrina* has led some scholars to doubt its historical accuracy, but this is the Macrina he wanted us to know: a strong, resolute woman who was firmly committed to the welfare of others and the glory of God and an active participant in the ongoing exchange of ideas that characterized the lives of Basil, Gregory, and their friend Gregory of Nazianzus—commonly known as "the three Cappadocians."

Gregory found particular comfort in Macrina in 379 when Basil died as a result of a prolonged illness. At a highly emotional time, it was only natural that Gregory would visit their family's pillar of strength. Two decades earlier, Macrina had given courage to their mother, Emmelia, after the fatal fishing accident of their young brother Naucratius. Gregory knew she would have some words of comfort for him too.

He could also count on her to be honest—even blunt—as she had been two years earlier when she chided Gregory for his whining after Emperor Valens exiled him from Nyssa, where Gregory was bishop. "You are renowned in cities and peoples and nations," she had told him then. "Churches summon you as an ally and director, and do you not see the grace of God in it all? Do you fail to recognize the cause of such great blessings, that it is your parents' prayers that are lifting you up on high, you that have little or no equipment within yourself for such success?"[4]

Seeking comfort at the death of Basil, Gregory found that Macrina was just as spirited as before. In spite of a serious illness that had left her bedridden—in fact, close to dying—she welcomed her brother with affection, donning her usual role of mother and teacher.

ON THE RESURRECTION

Gregory could not hide his heavy heart or the questions that had been plaguing him for a while. He started out protesting against the biblical exhortation not to grieve as those who have no hope (1 Thess.

---

4. Gregory of Nyssa, *Life of St. Macrina*, 17–19.

4:13). Death is dreadful and seems to leave us all on equal ground. We turn our heads at the sight of a dead body and build all kinds of protections around our lives, he explained. We all share the same feelings of astonishment, confusion, and impotence when death robs us of a loved one. So how can Christians not grieve as others do?

Macrina knew that Gregory had not traveled back home to find answers to abstract questions, so she went straight to the heart of his query: "Why, what is the special pain you feel…in the mere necessity itself of dying?… Surely what alarms and disturbs your mind is not the thought that the soul, instead of lasting forever, ceases with the body's dissolution!"[5]

She had hit the nail on its head. Gregory confessed, "rather audaciously,"[6] that he felt compelled by Scripture to believe in the eternal life of the soul but couldn't find a rational explanation for it. If the soul exists within the body, how can it keep on living without it after death? And where does it live? What is a soul, anyhow? Is it made of corruptible elements like the body? Is it even real?

Seeing that some of Gregory's objections stemmed from Greek philosophy, Macrina repudiated the "pagan nonsense"[7] of the Stoics and Epicureans of her day, who believed there was nothing besides material, sensible realities. Equally faulty were the teachings of the Greek philosopher Plato, who saw human life as a conflict between virtuous impulses and irrational passions ("the Platonic chariot and the pair of horses of dissimilar forces yoked to it"[8]) and death as liberation of the soul from the weighty shell of the body.

---

5. Gregory of Nyssa, *On the Soul and Resurrection*, vol. 5, *The Nicene and Post-Nicene Fathers*, Series 2, trans. William Moore and Henry Austin Wilson, ed. Philip Schaff and Henry Wace (Buffalo, N.Y.: Christian Literature, 1893), paras. 3, 5.

6. Gregory of Nyssa, *On the Soul and the Resurrection*, para. 6, rev. and ed. Kevin Knight, Fathers of the Church, New Advent, http://www.newadvent.org/fathers/2915.htm (*NPNF*[2], vol. 5).

7. Gregory of Nyssa, *On the Soul and the Resurrection*, para. 7.

8. Gregory of Nyssa, *On the Soul and the Resurrection*, para. 35. This is a reference to Plato's allegory of the rational mind as a charioteer that tries to

To Macrina, all these popular Greek philosophies had to be shunned. "We must neglect all before and since their time," she said, "whether they philosophized in prose or in verse." Instead, "we will adopt, as the guide of our reasoning, the Scripture."[9]

To answer Gregory's questions on how human bodies will rise again, incorruptible—especially those that have returned to dust or have been eaten by wild animals—she quoted the apostle Paul's main treatment of the resurrection in 1 Corinthians and his example of a seed that dies in the ground in order to sprout into a new plant (15:35–37). "The Divine power, in the superabundance of Omnipotence," she said, "does not only restore you that body once dissolved, but makes great and splendid additions to it, whereby the human being is furnished in a manner still more magnificent."[10]

At the same time, the resurrected body will retain the same elements of the one we have now. "For if the identical individual particle does not return and only something that is homogeneous but not identical is fetched," Macrina explained, "you will have something else in the place of that first thing, and such a process will cease to be a resurrection and will be merely the creation of a new man." In other words, resurrection is not a creation of a new body that *looks* just like the old one.

The conversation continued to move from topic to topic, from the existence of God to the value of emotions. In particular, Macrina pointed out the practical, present effects of the doctrine of the resurrection as the only grounds for hope and the only reason to attempt a life of virtue. If there is no resurrection, we might as well seek "the pleasure of the moment only," she said.[11]

In the end, she returned indirectly to her initial question to Gregory: Why does the inevitable fact of dying cause you so much pain? *Why do you fear death?* After all, "as to the how and the when

---

bring its chariot, pulled by two horses with opposite inclinations, toward enlightenment.

9. Gregory of Nyssa, *On the Soul and the Resurrection*, para. 34.

10. Gregory of Nyssa, *On the Soul and the Resurrection*, para. 85.

11. Gregory of Nyssa, *On the Soul and the Resurrection*, para. 7.

of [man's] dissolution, what do they matter to the Resurrection?" Man's doubts and objections cannot prevent God's power to arrive at His end or goal.

"And His end is one, and one only; it is this: when the complete whole of our race shall have been perfected from the first man to the last…to offer to every one of us participation in the blessings which are in Him, which, the Scripture tells us, 'eye has not seen, nor ear heard, nor thought ever reached.'"

Macrina died soon after this discussion, leaving her brother doubly bereaved but comforted in the hope she had strengthened. Now more than ever, he was convinced that Basil, Naucratius, their parents, loved ones, and Macrina herself would not cease to exist nor be dissolved into a unified soul, as some philosophers taught, nor become completely unrecognizable. They would be the same people, but "raised in incorruption…in glory…[and] in power" (1 Cor. 15:42–43).

FOOD FOR THOUGHT

- Most of us are not attracted to monastic lives, but there are other ways in which Christians today isolate themselves from the world, resting in the safety of their Christian communities and gravitating toward those who share their ideas. But, as Basil said, "How will [a Christian] give evidence of his compassion if he has cut himself off from association with other persons? And how will he exercise long-suffering, if no one contradicts his wishes?" Do you think some Christians today tend to avoid the type of experiences that produce this compassion and long-suffering? If so, how, and what can they do to prevent it?

- Some Christians are accused of focusing so much on the hereafter that they neglect to help those in need. As a reaction, some go to the opposite extreme and stress service to others above a thorough knowledge of Scripture. What can we learn from the example of Macrina and her family?

- A Platonic view of death as a liberation of the soul from the bondage of the body is very prevalent today, even among Christians. How is a biblical understanding of the resurrection of both body and soul particularly comforting to dying believers and those who care for them? How was the same understanding troubling to the Greeks who believed in the inferior and detrimental nature of the body?

- Some people believe that Gregory's dialogue with Macrina in *On the Resurrection* was only a literary device. They find it hard to imagine that a theologian of Gregory's caliber could have serious doubts on a basic scriptural teaching and, much more so, that he would have discussed them with his sister. But theologians are human beings and can benefit from scriptural reminders and discussions with other believers. Besides, a study of theology is not restricted to a few people. Describe a time when a discussion with other believers has helped you to clarify your understanding of the Bible. Do you think all believers can benefit from studying Christian doctrines? Why or why not?

- Commenting specifically on the resurrection of the body, John Calvin wrote, "There is nothing that is more at variance with human reason than this article of faith. For who but God alone could persuade us that bodies, which are now liable to corruption, will, after having rotted away, or after they have been consumed by fire, or torn in pieces by wild beasts, not merely be restored entire, but in a greatly better condition. Do not all our apprehensions of things straightway reject this as a thing fabulous, nay, most absurd?"[12] What do you think about his last question? What should we do when our rational mind finds some scriptural teaching "absurd"? How does Christ's bodily resurrection guarantee that we will also rise incorruptible?

---

12. John Calvin, *Commentary on Corinthians* (1 Cor. 15:35), vol. 2, Christian Classics Ethereal Library, https://ccel.org/cce/calvin/calcom40/calcom40 ?queryID=422447&resultID=1118.

• Like many theologians, Macrina found it useful to include reason and logic in her examination of Scripture. This is actually what Paul did in 1 Corinthians 15, by bringing up the examples of a seed and of different types of creation. Occasionally, however, the examples given by both Macrina and the Cappadocian Fathers fell into speculation. What caution would you offer to those who want to use similes and metaphors to explain biblical truths? Why can we trust the metaphors used by Paul in his letters?

FOR FURTHER RESEARCH

For more information about Macrina's life, see Gregory of Nyssa, *Life of St. Macrina*, ed. W. K. Lowther Clarke (London: Society for Promoting Christian Knowledge, 1916).

For the description of Macrina's conversation with Gregory on the human soul and resurrection, see Gregory of Nyssa, *On the Soul and the Resurrection*, in volume 5 of *The Nicene and Post-Nicene Fathers*, Series 2, trans. William Moore and Henry Austin Wilson, ed. Philip Schaff and Henry Wace (Buffalo, N.Y.: Christian Literature, 1893).

3

Will My Son Be Lost?

Augustine was a difficult teenager, the kind who keeps parents up at night. The restlessness he later described in his *Confessions* was already evident at a young age, especially to his mother, Monica. As a Christian, she was terrified by the unbearable thought that he might be lost forever. But she never gave up. She upheld him constantly in prayer, followed him with her thoughts, pleaded for help, and crossed land and sea to be near him.

PATIENT WIFE, ANXIOUS MOTHER

Born in Tagaste, in the Roman region of Numidia (today's Souk Ahras, Algeria), Monica was raised in a Christian home. She was still young when her parents gave her in marriage to Patricius, a government officer. He was a pagan, was prone to bursts of anger, and demanded Monica's obedience while he philandered as he pleased. Aware of her limited choices, she learned to live patiently with his moods and self-indulgent lifestyle. Because of this, she escaped the beatings that other women, more vocal in their objections, suffered in a society that provided no protection for wives. Her gentle attitude won over even her mother-in-law. According to Augustine, Monica's meekness was a strong contributor to Patricius's conversion to Christianity, which happened around the end of his life. He died in 371, when Monica was forty.

She couldn't, however, maintain the same level-headedness with Augustine. She had raised him as a Christian, and his youthful wavering was troubling and unexpected. Her apprehension grew when, at the age of seventeen, he moved to the big city of Carthage, in today's Tunisia, to study. Patricius had high ambitions for his talented son, and Tagaste couldn't offer the level of education the young man needed. Monica was both anxious and hopeful. Somehow, she thought Augustine's studies would help him learn more about God.

In Carthage Augustine encountered new ideas and experimented with new freedoms—what a mature Augustine, in hindsight, called temptations, seductions, and false paths. "A cauldron of unholy loves…sang" all around him, as he discovered the theater and other forms of entertainment that, in his day, were often obscene.[1] Later in life he regretted that his parents didn't arrange a marriage for him at that time to keep him stable and away from temptations. Instead, they were concerned about his career and considered a wife "a clog and hindrance" to their ambitions for him.[2]

It was in Carthage that he began living with a woman who became his concubine and gave him a son, Adeodatus ("given by God"). While Augustine's sex life was probably not as promiscuous as he makes it sound in his *Confessions* (concubinage was a respectable arrangement in his society, and he apparently stayed faithful to the same woman), it was not what Monica had hoped.

Monica's predictions were correct to a point. Augustine's philosophical studies gave him a love for wisdom. But rather than finding it in the Bible, he discovered it in Cicero, one of Rome's greatest philosophers. Cicero's masterful language made the old Latin translation of the Bible available at that time look coarse and unrefined. Because of this, Augustine began to despise the Bible and to search for more.

---

1. Augustine, *The Confessions* 3.1, trans. Edward B. Pusey (Oxford: John Henry Parker, 1853).

2. Augustine, *Confessions* 2.8, trans. Pusey.

Carthage had a lot to offer to those who looked for "higher" religious knowledge. Heresies proliferated. Augustine became particularly attracted to a group known as the Manicheans, who gave a simpler explanation for the problem of evil than what he had found in the Bible—a dualistic struggle between two equivalent forces of good and evil. After all, saying that evil is just as powerful as good eliminates the question of why God allows it in this world. The Manicheans' language was also more impressive than that used by the simple priests Augustine knew in Tagaste and sounded more authoritative.

MONICA'S TEARS

Monica was devastated. If Augustine's youthful passions troubled her, this heresy overwhelmed her. The Manicheans were an extreme and illegal sect that found enlightenment in revelations that were alien to Scripture. His eternal state was at stake. Will he be lost forever?

Gone was the poise she exhibited with Patricius. Her reactions oscillated from anger to despair. Once, she refused to let Augustine live with her. His new beliefs were too blasphemous for her. But her heart could never let him go, and eventually she took him back.

She cried rivers of tears, "which gushed forth and watered the ground beneath her eyes wherever she prayed." She wept "more bitterly than ever mothers weep for the bodily death of their children."[3] Eventually, she visited the local bishop, pressuring him to talk to her son. The bishop refused, a reaction that Augustine in later years deemed wise. He didn't think Augustine was ready for discussions, being "puffed up with the novelty of [his] heresy."[4] He knew this by experience since he had been in the same shoes many years earlier. "Leave him alone," he told Monica. "Simply pray for him to the Lord. He will find out for himself, through his reading, how wrong these beliefs are, and how profoundly irreverent."[5]

---

3. Augustine, *Confessions* 3.19, trans. Pusey.

4. Augustine, *Confessions* 3.21, trans. Pusey.

5. Augustine, *Confessions* 3.21, trans. Maria Boulding (New York: New City Press, 1997).

This reasoning was not enough for Monica. The same woman who could wait patiently for Patricius's conversion was now frantic about Augustine's. How could she leave him alone? She knew God was in control, but everything in her being screamed for action. Finally, frustrated by her insistence, the bishop dismissed her: "Go away now, but hold on to this: it's inconceivable that he should perish, a son of tears like yours."[6] Monica found comfort in the bishop's words and took them as "an oracle from heaven."[7]

She had further confirmation in a dream that she had around the same time. She saw herself standing on a wooden ruler, "overwhelmed with grief," when a young man, cheerful and smiling, asked her the reason for her sorrow. "She replied that she was mourning [Augustine's] ruin."[8] The man told her that Augustine would be right where she was. At that very moment, Augustine appeared in the dream, standing with her on the ruler. Excited, she related the dream to Augustine, who interpreted it to mean that his mother would become as enlightened as he was. "No, no," she insisted, "what was said to me wasn't, 'Where *he* is, you are too,' but 'Where *you* are, he is too.'"[9] In the end, both the dream and the bishop's words proved to be right. In 383 Augustine abandoned Manichaeism nine years after he had first embraced it.

MONICA IN ITALY

Energized by this success, Monica continued to pray that Augustine would dismiss the heretical teachings that had charmed him. After all, he seemed to be maturing, holding a respectable position as a teacher in Carthage. But her tranquility was about to be shaken. In 385 he announced he had been offered a better career in Rome. It promised higher pay and more opportunities for advancement. Also,

---

6. Augustine, *Confessions* 3.21, trans. Boulding.
7. Augustine, *Confessions* 3.21, trans. Boulding.
8. Augustine, *Confessions* 3.21, trans. Boulding.
9. Augustine, *Confessions* 3.20, trans. Sarah Ruden (New York: Modern Library, 2017), emphasis added.

he had heard that Roman students were more disciplined than the wild and vexing Carthaginian youth.

Monica didn't take well to the idea. The 170 miles that separated Tagaste from Carthage had been hard enough to accept, but a whole sea? She tried to persuade him to stay. When she couldn't argue any longer, she begged him to take her with him.

But thirty-year-old Augustine was not ready to bring his mother along. Resorting to a lie, he told her he had to see a friend and asked her to go back home. When she refused, he suggested she wait in a nearby chapel, where she could spend some time in prayer. She was still praying while he boarded the ship. "And what was she begging of you, my God, if not that you should not allow me to sail?" a remorseful Augustine wrote later. "But in your deep counsel you hearkened to her true wish."[10] This was a key moment in the story. While Monica wept, God was answering her true prayer—not her earthly desire to be near her dear son but her spiritual desire that he would be made right with God.

Unaware of God's plans, Monica followed her son to Italy. By the time she arrived, he had moved to Milan, the most important city in Italy at that time, where he held a good position at the imperial court. She was understandably proud of his accomplishments and encouraged him to make a difficult decision: leave the concubine who was still living with him.

In the eyes of an ambitious parent, a concubine was acceptable for a simple teacher, but in order to advance in his career—especially in Italy—Augustine had to marry into an influential family. Augustine questioned Monica's advice. He wondered if she had any evidence that God approved of that decision, but she could come up with only personal feelings. In the end, he agreed to make the break, leaving the woman he had loved for fifteen years and keeping Adeodatus with him. Later, he described his mother's advice and his decision to

---

10. Augustine, *The Confessions* 5.8.15, trans. Philip Burton, Everyman's Library (New York: Alfred A. Knopf, 2001).

accept it as products of the sin of ambition he was now sharing with his parents: a disordered and misdirected desire for honor and power.

Leaving his concubine was painful. Augustine felt as though she was being torn from his side and that he was betraying the mother of his son. "My heart, which clave to her, was racked, and wounded, and bleeding," he said. "And she went back to Africa, making a vow unto You [God] never to know another man, leaving with me my natural son by her." In doing so, he said, she behaved more honorably than he did. In his later years, Augustine wrote that a man who leaves a woman with whom he had been living, even if not in the bond of marriage, and marries another, commits adultery.

As it turned out, Monica's chosen bride could not contract the marriage for two years, and Augustine, unable to subject himself to the same commitment made by his concubine, ended up with another woman. He found this lack of self-control deeply humiliating.

In the middle of this emotional turmoil, he started to attend the services at the cathedral in the center of Milan led by Bishop Ambrose (ca. 340–397), one of the most influential churchmen in the Latin-speaking world. Ambrose was a well-read man who could discuss theology on the level Augustine had come to expect. Augustine respected Ambrose and treated him as a father in the faith.

Eventually, Augustine left his high position and moved with Monica and Adeodatus to the nearby country town of Cassiciacum into a villa a friend had placed at their disposal. A few other young men joined him, including his brother, Navigius.[11] He was baptized in April 387, on the eve of Easter day. He also renounced any plans to advance his career and pursue marriage. Instead, he decided to return to North Africa and start a Christian community.

---

11. Augustine might have had other siblings. We know only about Navigius and a sister who ran a female monastery after her husband died.

MONICA'S VIRILE FAITH

Finally free from her anxiety over her son, Monica participated fully in the life of the community he had started in Cassiciacum—a group of young men preoccupied with theological and philosophical questions. In some ways, it was like living with a bunch of first-year seminarians.

"My mother kept us company," Augustine said, "woman in outward form but endowed with virile faith, uniting the serenity of an elderly person with a mother's love and Christian devotion."[a]

Monica's personality comes through in the small interventions Augustine describes in his writings, such as her witty replies, her protest at being included in theological discussions, and her complaint when a young man kept singing a psalm while on the toilet—an improper place for sacred songs, she thought.

Often, her lucid common sense brought clarity to the men's convoluted debates. For example, when they tried to determine if it's proper to say that a man "has God" while he is still searching (since he's at least doing the right thing), she interjected a factor they had not considered: everyone has God. The question is, do they have Him as a friend or as an enemy?

This discussion was part of a longer conversation that had started during Augustine's birthday and lasted three days, centered on the subject of happiness. Monica had her opinion: unhappiness comes from lack. The men found her claim easy to disprove since a man can have everything and still be unhappy for fear of losing what he has. But their objection served only to prove her point. "His fear of losing shows he lacks wisdom," she said, "so he's still wanting." This time, her comment raised a "unanimous cry of admiration."[b]

At the end of the debate, it was Monica who summarized, in simple words, their general conclusion: "A happy life is the perfect life to which we are led by a firm faith, cheerful hope, and fervent love."[c]

---

a. Augustine, *Confessions* 9.8, trans. Boulding.

b. Augustine, *De Vita Beata* 4.27, S. Aurelii Augstini Opera Omnia, Sant' Agostino, https://www.augustinus.it/latino/felicita/index2.htm; my translation.

c. Augustine, *De Vita Beata* 4.35.

MONICA'S DEATH

In the fall of 387, Monica, Augustine, Navigius, Adeodatus, and a few friends left Cassiciacum and traveled south with the intent of sailing back to Numidia. They stopped in Ostia, near Rome, where they waited for a ship.

It was then that Monica, wearied by travels, contracted a high fever that proved to be fatal. She yielded compliantly to death, with the conviction that she had done what she was meant to do. She had lived to see the conversion of her son. "My God has fulfilled this wish," she said, "filled it to overflowing…. So what am I doing here?"[12] She told her sons to bury her in Ostia, without needless scruples. It didn't matter where her body was laid.

In his *Confessions*, Augustine described his pain at her death. "I let go the tears I'd held in, letting them run out as freely as they wanted, and out of them I made a bed for my heart."[13] He devoted many paragraphs in praise of his mother's virtues. She had been to him a picture and a tangible expression of God's relentless love for sinners.

He was not blind to her shortcomings, from a youthful attraction to wine to her worldly ambitions. His relationship with her had been marred with mutual frustration, obstinacy, and tension. She had not been a perfect mother, but she had been the instrument God had chosen and had kept faithful to her calling.

FOOD FOR THOUGHT

- Monica's story is often cited as an example of how God answered the prayers of a mother. In some ways, however, her anxiety became overbearing, and Augustine agreed with the bishop's advice of letting her son sort things out on his own. What do you think? Can we agree with this advice in every situation? Why or why not?

---

12. Augustine, *Confessions* 9.26, trans. Ruden.
13. Augustine, *Confessions* 9.33, trans. Ruden.

- What did the bishop mean when he said, "It's inconceivable that he should perish, a son of tears like yours"? Did he mean that Monica's tears could influence her son's salvation? Does the earnestness of our prayers have anything to do with God's answers? Explain your answer. Later in life, Augustine explained this event by saying it was God's gift that she was what she was. "Assuredly You were near, and were hearing and doing in that method in which You had predetermined that it should be done."[14] In other words, Monica's tearful prayers worked in the salvation of her son because God had predestined her by His grace to be the means that would lead Augustine to that salvation. If that's true, do you think Monica's prayers could have failed? Explain your answer.

- Why do you think Monica found it easier to trust God for her husband's salvation than for her son's?

- Not all of Monica's prayers were answered verbatim. When Augustine left her in the chapel by the sea, she simply prayed that God would stop him from leaving. God didn't answer that specific prayer, but, in the long run, as Augustine later noted, He "hearkened to her true wish" not because it was her true wish (our true wishes can be sinful or opposed to God's plan), but because of *what* she was wishing: Augustine's eternal salvation. What answers can we be absolutely sure will be granted when we pray? Why is it important to trust God's wisdom and goodness in our prayers?

- Monica was often torn between two contrasting concerns: she wanted Augustine to ground his faith solidly in Christ, but she was also concerned about his career. At times, this second concern took priority—for example, when she refused to arrange a marriage for him and when she asked him to leave

14. Augustine, *Confessions* 5.9.17, rev. and ed. Kevin Knight, Fathers of the Church, New Advent, https://www.newadvent.org/fathers/110105.htm (*NPNF*[1], vol. 1).

his concubine in order to marry into an influential family. How can our society's emphasis on success and status skew a parent's perspective?

- How are parents symbols of God's relentless love for His children? Can this love be evident in spite of the parents' shortcomings?

FOR FURTHER RESEARCH

Most of the information about Monica is contained in Augustine's *Confessions*, which is available in many translations.

How Can I Nurture a Son Who Lives Miles Away?

DHUODA OF UZÈS (ca. 800–843)

In 841, Dhuoda's world fell apart. William, the son she had nurtured and loved for fourteen years, left for Aachen, about six hundred miles north of her residence in Uzès, to live at the Frankish court. It was a sudden decision made by Dhuoda's husband, Bernard of Septimania, in order to prove his allegiance to the new king, Charles the Bald. What's more, Bernard took their six-month-old son with him to the western region of Aquitaine, about three hundred miles away from Dhuoda, allegedly for the baby's safety. She didn't even know the child's name because he hadn't yet been baptized. Scholars tell us he was named Bernard after his father.

Dhuoda and Bernard were married in 824 at the palace at Aachen, where William was born. Sometime after that, Dhuoda moved to her husband's properties in Uzès, in the south of France, while Bernard spent most of his time away in service to the king.

Dhuoda's second pregnancy was the result of one of Bernard's visits. She was used to her role of single mother and had devoted much time to William's education. Like most noblewomen at that time, she also worked to maintain her husband's estate and to preserve his reputation. This last duty became increasingly difficult after 830 when, at the height of Bernard's career, he was accused of having relations with Judith, wife of Emperor Louis the Pious.

This accusation might have been fabricated by Louis's three oldest sons. Louis had divided his kingdom so they could all have assigned territories, but the birth of a new son, Charles the Bald, and the subsequent redistribution of lands caused a rebellion. Bernard, who had a high position at court and was in charge of the young child, became an easy target.

After a year in voluntary exile, Bernard returned to court but never rose to the same position. His siblings met a worse end in the conflict among Louis's sons. One of Bernard's brothers was blinded and exiled; another beheaded; and a sister, the nun Gerberga, was accused of sorcery and drowned. Dhuoda was fully aware of all this when she watched her son leave for Aachen.

DHUODA'S *MANUAL*

A mother's work is never done, and Dhuoda refused to let the separation put an end to her calling. Deprived of her children and fretful about their future, she set her mind to write William a long letter, asking him to share it with his brother as soon as the little one could understand. In the end, her letter turned out to be an actual book—an instruction manual in twenty-seven chapters—written over the course of fifteen months.

She took her task seriously. She researched her subjects and added frequent quotes—mostly from the Bible but also from several authors in her book collection, such as Augustine of Hippo, Alcuin of York, and Gregory of Tours. She might have owned copies of their single works or, most likely, anthologies (*florilegia*), which were common in the ninth century. Moving back and forth between poetry and prose, gravity and playfulness, she included prayers, theological lessons, word games, and some medieval interpretation of numbers.

Dhuoda knew her limitations. She was not a theologian; rather, she compared herself to a little puppy that gathers crumbs under her master's table—in her case, gleaning thoughts from God's Word for herself and her son.

THE CAROLINGIAN RENAISSANCE

Stories of violence and intrigue—such as those filling the imperial court and personally affecting Dhuoda's family—have fueled many misunderstandings regarding the Middle Ages as a dark era of ignorance, cruelty, and strife. In reality, things were not better in antiquity nor during the acclaimed sixteenth-century Renaissance.

In fact, the eighth century saw a renaissance of its own. Since this cultural revival began mostly with Charlemagne (in Latin, Carolus Magnus), it is commonly known as the Carolingian Renaissance.

One of Charlemagne's first moves was to call to his court some of the best scholars in Europe in order to educate his court and organize schools throughout the empire. These scholars were led by the English Alcuin of York (735–804), who wrote textbooks and created a standardized curriculum for all schools following the classical trivium and quadrivium.

Believing that religion is the foundation of culture, Charlemagne and Alcuin emphasized preaching and catechizing. Most likely the high level of education and the knowledge of Scripture Dhuoda exhibited were a product of this emphasis on both academic and religious instruction.

In a way, writing was to Dhuoda's benefit as much as to William's, as it eased her "anxiety and desire to be useful" to him.[1] She was not present with her son to give advice and instruction but could pray he would read her reminders. She found encouragement in Paul's example of one man planting and another watering, while God gives the increase (1 Cor. 3:6–8). The knowledge of God's sovereignty permeates her book.

DHUODA'S INSTRUCTIONS

Dhuoda's first chapter is all about God and His attributes of omnipotence, omnipresence, omniscience, majesty, excellency, wisdom, goodness, and mercy. This knowledge of God gave her comfort, as

---

1. This is my translation of the Latin version as found in Dhuoda, *Le Manuel de Dhuoda*, ed. Edouard Bondurand (Paris: A. Picard, 1887), 50.

"He surrounds like an impregnable rampart and places a crown like a shield."[2]

Her book included instructions for William to continue his studies, respect the king, be kind to the poor, be patient in adversity, seek wisdom, remain chaste until marriage, and glorify God in all things. Every chapter is filled with Scripture passages, which she quoted verbatim or as she remembered them.

Dhuoda devoted several pages to the importance of filial duty, urging William to respect his father, support him in his old age, and pray that he might get along with others. Concord was, at that time, more than a cherished ideal. It meant the difference between life and death. She exhorted William to pray for everyone, friends and enemies alike.

After God and his father, the king was to come next in William's loyalty. The young man was to serve the king faithfully and obediently. Knowing the temptations that lurked at a royal court, Dhuoda encouraged William to fight them and to cultivate the gifts of the Spirit. If he sinned, he should ask God for forgiveness and make amends.

Among William's duties, Dhuoda listed the care of his brother, asking William "to teach, nurture, and love him, rousing him to go from good to better."[3] As soon as little Bernard was able to read, William should show him Dhuoda's handbook so that when "weighed down with the cares of this world," they would remember God, "who reigns in the heavens."[4]

She included specific instructions on prayer with examples to imitate and meditations on the Psalms, recognizing that all virtues come from God. She listed what could be proper objects of William's prayer: the church, the king and other leaders, his father, his enemies, and also the sick, the afflicted, the poor, and those who are traveling.

She didn't offer herself as a role model. In her prayers, she admitted, she was "lukewarm and lazy, fragile and always tending toward

---

2. Dhuoda, *Le Manuel*, 68. Reminiscent of Pss. 5:12 and 91:4.
3. Dhuoda, *Le Manuel*, 71.
4. Dhuoda, *Le Manuel*, 71.

the abyss" and didn't particularly find pleasure in praying. Her trust, however, was not in her prayers' length, quality, or quantity, but "in Him who grants to His faithful permission to pray."[5]

DHUODA'S LOVE

Dhuoda reassured her son that she would always be there for him as long as she lived, but death is a common reality. In spite of her young age (given the common age of marriage in her times, she was probably between thirty and thirty-five), she believed she would not live long. She hinted at ill health, and life expectation was low in those days. In any case, the book would remain for him not only as a reminder but also as a "mirror," reflecting her image of mother, which she believed played an irreplaceable role: "My son, you will have instructors who can teach you many loftier and more useful things," she wrote, "but you will not find in their books the same fervent, heartfelt love that I, your mother, have for you."[6]

Every page of Dhuoda's manual rings with concern for her son's soul, from her opening chapter, in which she entreats her "beautiful and lovable" son to learn about God and "plead with Him, treasure, and love Him,"[7] to her final exhortation: "Farewell, noble boy. May you always flourish in Christ."[8]

A PAINFUL ENDING

The story didn't end as happily as one may wish. In 844 Charles the Bald executed Bernard for treason. Whether this action was justified, William felt compelled to take revenge for his father and allied with some of Charles's enemies. He died in 850, either executed by Charles or killed in flight; the circumstances are not clear.

Apparently, Dhuoda's younger son, Bernard, emulated William's attempts to vindicate their father. He also failed, but his punishment

---

5. Dhuoda, *Le Manuel*, 78.
6. Dhuoda, *Le Manuel*, 71.
7. Dhuoda, *Le Manuel*, 70.
8. Dhuoda, *Le Manuel*, 248.

seems to have been limited to a demotion. Probably Dhuoda, who complained of ill health while writing the book, died before all this took place.

Ultimately, we can hope William and Bernard committed their souls to the Christ their mother loved, recognizing Him as their true "guardian, captain, companion, homeland, way, truth, and life."[9] Dhuoda knew this is ultimately all that counts.

FOOD FOR THOUGHT

Like the women we have met so far, Dhuoda was a creature of her time. She mentioned prayers for the dead, and her advice to William was based on the concept of meritorious obedience. Still, there is much we can learn from her love for God, her regard for Scripture, and her commitment to her family.

- Dhuoda believed that mothers have a unique role in their children's lives—one for which no books or teachers can substitute. Do you agree or disagree, and why? In what ways does a mother impact her children's lives more than anyone else?

- Dhuoda stayed faithful to her calling as mother in spite of the physical distance from her sons. But the book benefited her by reducing her anxiety. Discuss a time when you had a similar experience, when staying faithful to your calling gave you peace, knowing God would take care of the rest.

- There is a difference between keeping faithful to one's calling and just keeping busy. The latter is often promoted as a way to keep the mind occupied during periods of anxiety, but it can only go so far. Understanding our calling and doing what we know God wants us to do gives a different type of peace. Describe a time when you noticed this difference in your life.

---

9. Dhuoda, *Le Manuel*, 70.

- Dhuoda believed that the results of her prayers didn't depend on their length or quality but on God, "who grants to His faithful permission to pray." How did this attitude help her commit her sons to the Lord?

FOR FURTHER RESEARCH

For an excellent translation of the *Handbook*, see *Dhuoda, Handbook for Her Warrior Son*, ed. Marcelle Thiebaux (Cambridge: Cambridge University Press, 1998).

5

The Fullness of My Sins Who Can Explore?

KASSIA (ca. 810–865)

Around the year 830 in Constantinople, the Byzantine Empress Euphroshyne organized a bride show to find a wife for her newly crowned sixteen-year-old son Theophilos. This was a common matchmaking system of her times. Kassia—possibly twenty at that time—was one of the contenders. According to the story, she was the first one Theophilos approached with what could possibly go down as the worst pickup line in history: "Through a woman, evils came to man."

Kassia's answer was quick: "Through a woman, better things began."

If the references were theological, she was right. If sin came into the world through Eve, Christ, the only remedy to sin, came through Mary. In any case, Theophilos was not impressed with the answer and chose another contestant, Theodora, as his bride.

Many speculations have been made about the feelings of this potential couple. According to a legend, Theophilos later regretted his choice and expressed his love to Kassia. At any rate, given that Theophilos and Kassia took opposite sides in a major theological debate of their times—the legitimacy of images in worship—their union might have created great difficulties.

This debate had been heated for some time, with defenders of images (iconodules) claiming that images reminded Christians of

Christ's incarnation, and opposers (iconoclasts) maintaining that only Scripture can correctly represent Christ as both God and man.

Some Byzantine emperors had issued a ban on icons. The first ban lasted from 726 to 805, and the second from 814 to 842, ending with the death of Theophilus. During these bans, images were destroyed and iconodules were persecuted. Kassia sided with the iconodules, helping those who were persecuted, including a man who had been imprisoned for his beliefs. Like many others, she suffered beatings for her convictions.

THE HEINOUSNESS OF SIN AND THE GREATNESS OF GOD'S MERCY

In 843, after the ban on icons, Kassia founded a convent in Xerolophos, Constantinople's seventh hill, and became its abbess. Along with leading other nuns in devotions and good works, she encouraged learning and music. Coming from an aristocratic family, she had probably received a good education in many academic areas, including theology, philosophy, and literature.

Today, she is mostly known as a poet, composer, and hymnographer. In fact, she is the only woman whose works are included in the Byzantine hymnals. Her talents were encouraged by others, including the renowned abbot Theodore the Studite, who corresponded faithfully with her and was greatly impressed by her knowledge and wisdom. Most of what we know about her life is gathered from her letters.

Her most famous poem, often known as the "Hymn for Holy Wednesday," is also included in Anglican hymnals. It recounts the story of the sinful woman who anointed Jesus's feet not long before His arrest and crucifixion (see Matt. 26:6–13; Mark 14:3–9; Luke 7:36–50).

> O Lord, the woman fallen among manifold sins,
> Perceiving Thy divinity
> Assumes the office of myrrh-bearer
> And, mourning, beareth myrrh to Thee before the day of Thy
>   burial,

Saying, Woe is me, for night is about me
The sting of passion twilight and moonless dark,
Even love of transgression.
Accept, I entreat, my tears' fountains,
Who in vapours aloft drawest the waters of Ocean.
Bow down, I pray, and give ear to my heart's bitter groanings,
Thou who didst bend the heavens, emptying Thee of Thy glory.
I will kiss Thy undented feet,
And will wipe them dry again
With the curling locks of my head,
The feet whose dread sound Eve in Paradise
Heard in her ears, and hid for terror.
The fulness of my sins, and the abysses of Thy judgments
Who can explore, Soul-saver, Deliverer mine!
Turn not Thy sight from Thy servant,
Thou whose compassion is infinite.[1]

This hymn is a fine sample of Kassia's poetic mastery and sensibility. In the biblical account, Jesus rebuked the Pharisees for condemning this woman when she had gone far beyond the simple acts of courtesy to guests that they should have exhibited: customary washing of feet, a kiss, and anointing the head. Instead, she had washed His feet with her tears, dried them with her hair, kissed them, and anointed them with the most expensive oil.

But the woman's actions had an even deeper, prophetic meaning, Jesus said. They were an early anointing for His burial. And Kassia went even further. She suggested that the woman had perceived Christ's divinity.

Kassia employed a set of contrasting images to evoke powerful reflections. The woman's downward flow of tears is offered to the One who draws the ocean's water up to the sky. Her hope that Christ might bend down and listen to her sighs is grounded on the knowledge that He had come down to our level, emptying Himself of His

---

1. Kassia, "Hymn for Holy Wednesday," in *The Scottish Review*, ed. Alexander Gardner (London: Paisley, 1898), 32:311.

glory (Phil. 2:7), and is reinforced by the beautiful image of heaven bending at His incarnation.

Kassia's correlation of Christ's feet with the footsteps of God in the garden of Eden after man's first rebellion (Gen. 3:8) strengthens both her affirmation of Christ's divinity and her confidence in His pardon: instead of running from His feet, as Eve did, the woman is now allowed to wash them, stroke them, and kiss them.

Kassia ended the poem with one last powerful contrast between the fullness of the woman's sins and the abysses of God's judgments on one side, and God's infinite compassion on the other. No matter how numerous and extensive her sins or how abysmal God's judgments, His compassion, being infinite, surpasses them all.

OTHER WRITINGS

The empathy and sensitivity Kassia displayed in the "Hymn for Holy Wednesday" seems to negate the common belief that she was a strict abbess—a belief that is based on her collection of short and blunt proverbs and maxims.

Kassia's second-most-famous hymn is about Christ's incarnation, which she perceived as the greatest event in human history. Once again Kassia employed parallelism, both in words and in music. If Augustus brought much of the Western world under his rule, Kassia said, Christ did much more. He crushed the gods of idolatry and brought the gospel to all nations, making of all nations His people. Just as Augustus registered many populations into the Roman Empire, Christ ascribed the faithful to His name.

Most likely, Kassia wrote more than the 49 hymns and 261 poetical works that are in existence today. Of her hymns, 23 were incorporated into what became the Triodion and the Menaion, liturgical books of the Eastern Orthodox Church. Translations in English are still scarce, but what is available is definitely worth reading.

FOOD FOR THOUGHT

- Some critics have doubted that Kassia could feel so much empathy for an adulterous woman and describe so earnestly her feelings if she had not fallen into the same sin. But there is nothing in Theodore's letters, which seem to date as far back as 816, to even slightly support this supposition. What might account for these critics' opinion? Can a conscience awakened by God's Spirit understand the struggles of sinners in different situations? Can you think of other examples of this empathy in your life, or in the writings of another author?

- Think of other examples in the Bible or church history of men and women who came to understand the heinousness of sin without committing what the world would consider outright crimes (for example, Augustine of Hippo's conviction after stealing some pears from his neighbor).[2]

- Kassia didn't simply lament "the sting of passion twilight and moonless dark" but something more frightful—"even love of transgression"—showing that she understood the pervasive and addictive nature of sin. (This realization is also present in Augustine's *Confessions*.) What was the woman's only hope in Kassia's poem? On what did she ground her confidence of receiving pardon?

- Most Protestants oppose the use of images in worship. Do some research on both sides of the argument. What are your conclusions? Do you think this is an important issue for the church and for individual believers? If so, why?

- How can poetry help a reader to investigate events, objects, and feelings that we might otherwise consider in passing? List other benefits of reading poetry. How can you apply these observations to your study of the Psalms?

---

2. Augustine of Hippo, *The Confessions*, trans. E. B. Pusey, book 2, https://www.gutenberg.org/files/3296/3296-h/3296-h.htm.

FOR FURTHER RESEARCH

The main resource on Kassia is Antonia Tripolitis, *Kassia: The Legend, the Woman, and Her Work* (New York: Garland, 1992).

Articles about Kassia are available on the internet, including musical renditions of her hymns.

6

Is the Woman a Faulty Creation of God?

CHRISTINE DE PIZAN (ca. 1364–1430)

Christine de Pizan was the first professional woman writer in France, if not in Europe. She is normally seen as an early feminist rather than as a theologian and mother. But many of her writings are based on her study of Scripture and the church fathers, and her questions about the role of women were triggered by her struggles as a single mother in a dangerous and cruel world.

CHRISTINE'S EARLY LIFE

Christine's life started out joyful. Her father, Tommaso di Benvenuto da Pizzano, was an esteemed physician and astrologer at the University of Bologna. Her mother was the daughter of a counselor of the Republic of Venice, where Tommaso transferred in 1357 and where Christine was born about eight years later.

Soon after Christine's birth, Tommaso moved to Paris, France, on invitation by King Charles V, who appreciated his skills as both a physician and politician. Tommaso's family joined him later. Taking advantage of the cultural opportunities and the impressive library he found there, Tommaso was careful to give Christine a thorough education.

At fifteen years of age, Christine married Etienne Castel, the royal secretary, a man she described as handsome, "kind and fair."[1]

---

1. Christine de Pizan, Ballad 9, PoemHunter.com, https://www.poemhunter .com/poem/ballad-ix/.

Their union brought her much happiness and produced three children: two boys and one girl.

Things began to change in 1380 when King Charles died, leaving the throne to his underage son. Because of this, the court was troubled by contests for power. Tommaso kept his position, but his salary decreased. His health also began to fail until he died, sometime before 1389, leaving his family in debt. But the greatest turnabout of Christine's life was the sudden death of her husband in 1390 due to the plague. He was thirty-four, and Christine was twenty-five.

A SINGLE MOTHER IN A CRUEL WORLD

Overnight she became a single mother, responsible for the care of her children, her aging mother, and a niece. Since in those days most husbands didn't share economic matters with their wives, she was unprepared for her new task and ignorant of the household's financial situation. This led creditors to demand more than was due and debtors to ignore their obligations. When an investor she had trusted with some of her funds pretended he was robbed and disappeared, the courts turned a deaf ear. She lost additional money on lawsuits that she invariably lost.

In spite of these financial problems, Christine found time to write, something she had always loved to do. Many of her writings were just songs of lament over the death of her husband. In what is probably her best-known poem from that time, "Seulete suy" (I am alone), she described herself as "left without a friend," "lost beyond compare," "abandoned by all," "harshly humiliated," and "threatened by all sorrows."[2]

---

2. Christine de Pisan, poem 11, in *Oeuvres poétiques*, vol. 1 (Paris: Librairie de Firmin Didot et Cie, 1886), Project Gutenberg, https://www.gutenberg.org /files/18061/18061-h/18061-h.htm.

SEEING GOD IN ADVERSITIES

Writing is rarely a solid means of support, and Christine's popularity didn't immediately mark the end of her financial troubles. In her autobiography, she employed a common writing technique of her times to describe how she came to accept her trials as wise acts of her omniscient God.

As the philosopher Boethius[a] did in the early sixth century, she imagined the intervention of personified Philosophy, who rebuked her for attributing the painful events in her life to Fortune: "Because with respect to the death of the king and others, it is God who had ordained that they take place at that time as being to their benefit, as He does with all things. And if it had been better to leave them alive, He would have done so. And although God's judgments may seem astounding to you, it is not up to you to boldly dispute them. Being omniscient, He knows exactly what He is doing."[b]

Philosophy encouraged Christine to think of those who suffered or had suffered much more than she did, to the point of losing every earthly good, including health and limbs. "What shall we say about them and others who experience various tribulations in many forms? That they are unhappy, unfortunate, and hated by God? No, on the contrary!... Instead, they are the most blessed, since they come closest to the life of Jesus Christ in this world in every tribulation for your example."[c] In the end, Christine was able to count her blessings, including her excellent education, her good children, and a beautiful marriage she had enjoyed while it lasted.

---

a. Christine mentions Boethius in her book,

b. Christine de Pizan, *The Book of the City of Ladies and Other Writings*, ed. Rebecca Kingston and Sophie Bourgault, trans. Ineke Hardy (Indianapolis, Ind.: Hackett, 2018), 16–17.

c. De Pizan, *Book of the City of Ladies*, 16–17.

With time, some French aristocrats noticed her talents and asked her to write poetry on commission, some for private use, and some to be read aloud. Soon, she was able to turn writing into a profession—something unusual for a woman of her day. In fact, she openly attributed her success to her female voice, which was seen as an oddity. By the time she wrote her autobiography, she had written fifteen major volumes and some minor works. Her writings included advice on ethics, politics, as well as military tactics and diplomacy, and explored ways in which Christian men and women could best contribute to the common welfare.

WOMAN AS GOD'S IMAGE-BEARER

Christine's most famous book is *The Book of the City of Ladies*. It begins with a woman named Christine, who picked up a book by Matheolus of Bologna that turned out to be a long invective against marriage, depicting women as a source of suffering for men. Christine put it down, but it was too late. The author had implanted a thought in her mind that she couldn't chase away.

She began to wonder: Is the woman a faulty creation of God? Most of the things Christine heard and read from men of her time seemed to answer affirmatively. Even the Greek philosopher Aristotle, so well esteemed during her time, saw women as deficient human beings.

"I concluded that God had created a vile creature when He fashioned woman," her protagonist says. "Indeed, I was astonished that such a worthy craftsman could have produced such an abominable creature.... Oh, Lord, how can this be?"[3]

While mulling over these thoughts, Christine sees three personified virtues: Reason, Righteousness, and Justice. Reason helps Christine understand that the woman "was created in the image of God" as much as man, and, "How can anyone dare slander the vessel that bears such noble imprint?... And if anyone says that it was a woman, Lady Eve, who caused man's fall from Paradise, I would say that man gained more through Mary than he lost through Eve."[4]

Far from being created from vile material, the woman was not even made from dust. She was created from the body of man. Like many authors before her, Christine emphasized that Eve was taken from Adam's side to be his companion, and not from his foot to be his slave nor from his head to be his superior. She agreed that men

---

3. De Pizan, *Book of the City of Ladies*, 22.
4. De Pizan, *Book of the City of Ladies*, 37.

and women were created differently and played different roles in life, but they were both God's image-bearers and worthy of respect.

Christine based her defense of the dignity of women on both Scripture and the example of virtuous women in church history. She even took a Latin proverb that men used to slander women ("God made women to weep, talk, and spin") to show how Christ had compassion on the tears of many women, including Mary, Martha, Mary Magdalene, and later Monica, mother of the great theologian Augustine. And Christ used Mary Magdalene's speech to bring the first announcement of His resurrection and the Samaritan woman's speech to proclaim the coming of the Messiah to her town.

In other works, Christine explained how deeply a faulty view of the nature of women could affect the cultural and ethical makeup of her time. She specifically criticized the typical love stories of her day, especially the thirteenth-century best seller *Le Roman de la Rose* by Jean de Meun.

These were usually stories of men who finally achieved the seemingly unattainable object of their desires. The trouble was, this object was usually a married woman—a quest that should have been discouraged rather than glorified. Besides, this type of writing depicted all women as superficial, weak, and manipulative, perpetuating false stereotypes.

Christine's works include practical suggestions for promoting the well-being of women. In *The Book of Three Virtues*, she explained how women can serve God in their individual callings. While remaining faithful to the medieval belief that the contemplative life of withdrawal from the world represents a higher calling, a teaching that was later refuted by the Protestant Reformers, she admitted it was not her calling and that the active life of serving others for the love of God rendered a greater service to the world. She then gave practical examples of how women can serve God in their specific situations, exercising prudence in their decisions.

CHRISTINE AS A MOTHER

A manuscript in the Bibliothèque Nationale of Paris shows a minia-
ture of Christine teaching her son Jean from an open book. This goes
along with her educational views, which she outlined in *The Treasure
of the City of Ladies,* a follow-up to her first book: "The wise lady who
loves her children dearly will be diligent about their education. She
will ensure that they will learn first of all to serve God, and to read
and write, and that the teacher will be careful to make them learn
their prayers well."[5]

She described Jean as "clever and a good singer."[6] As time passed,
she, like many educated parents with unreliable financial prospects,
wondered how to send him to college. In 1396 the English John Montague, Earl of Salisbury, a poet and admirer of Christine's poems,
offered to take thirteen-year-old Jean under his wings and educate
him in England. Christine saw this as a wonderful opportunity. One
wonders if she knew that Montague was a Lollard (a follower of a
religious movement related to John Wycliffe) who criticized the corruption of the Roman Catholic Church and promoted the Vulgate
translation of the Bible. In any case, her emphasis on Scripture and
on the importance of Christian ethics in both life and society were
not far from the Lollards' teachings.

Christine wrote two booklets to encourage her son to love
God and live well. One of the poems addressed to him starts with
this admonition:

> Love God with all your might
> Fear Him and strive to serve Him.[7]

But the situation in England changed quickly. In 1399, Henry IV
seized the throne from his cousin King Richard II and executed many

---

5. Christine de Pizan, *The Treasure of the City of Ladies*, trans. Sarah Lawson (London: Penguin Classics, 2003), 42.

6. Christine de Pizan, *The Vision of Christine de Pizan*, trans. Glenda
McLeod and Charity Cannon Willard (Cambridge: D. S. Brewer, 2005), 106.

7. Christine de Pizan, *Oeuvres poétiques de Christine de Pisan*, ed. Maurice
Roy, vol. 23, issue 3 (Paris: Librairie de Firmin Didot, 1896); my translation.

of Richard's counselors, including Montague. He then expressed his desire to keep Jean in his service and invited Christine to join him. But England was then hit by the plague, and she had no desire to leave France. She looked for other patrons for Jean and found one in Philippe le Hardi, Duke of Burgundy. Eventually, Jean became a secretary and notary for King Charles VI of France.

Christine's last work was a long poem about Joan of Arc, a woman who, in Christine's view, used her God-given ability for the good of her country. Christine finished the poem in 1429 and died a year later, probably at the convent of Saint-Louis de Poissy.

FOOD FOR THOUGHT

- Christine had a hard time managing her household because her husband had never disclosed financial matters with her. I have personally seen this happen with my mother-in-law. Are things the same or different today? Explain why you think it is or is not important to keep both spouses aware of important matters regarding the home. The justice system and men in general dismissed Christine's pleas and took advantage of her situation as an inexperienced woman. Explain why you think this is or is not happening in our society. If you think it is, what can be done to remedy this problem?

- How can the church help widows and single parents?

- How does remembering that God decrees everything that happens and He is both powerful and good help us to face difficulties and trials?

- Philosophy asked Christine, "What shall we say about them and others who experience various tribulations in many forms? That they are unhappy, unfortunate, and hated by God?" Her answer was no. And yet some Christians today would answer yes. The so-called prosperity gospel teaches that Christians can have a happy and prosperous life simply by claiming these blessings and those who don't receive them must examine their faith or prayer life. What are your opinions in this regard? What does Scripture say about this?

- Christine pointed out that a view of women as lesser creatures was not Christian, but pagan. How much dignity does the Bible confer on women? Find some verses to confirm your answer.

- Christine criticized some common maxims of her day and especially romance novels in which adultery was glorified and women were considered gullible objects of desire. While sexism is strongly combated in our society, especially since the Me Too movement, many people don't realize that some attitudes, such as the glorification of adultery and the acceptance of pornography, end up hurting the dignity of women. Give some other examples of these problems. What can be done to alert our society about them?

- Christine didn't just condemn men's unbiblical attitudes toward women. She also held women up to high ethical standards. In order to fight stereotypes that depicted women as weak, superficial, and manipulative, women had to prove them wrong in their own lives. Do you agree with her assessment? Find some Bible verses that exhort all believers to avoid giving others an occasion for slander.

- The Reformers contested the medieval view that the contemplative life of withdrawal from the world represents a higher calling. Do you think they were right, and why?

- While defending the dignity of women as individuals made in the image of God and insisting that "they are not a different race or a strange breed,"[8] Christine recognized the obvious differences between men and women and their different roles in the home and society. What are your opinions on this?

---

8. De Pizan, *Treasure of the City of Ladies*, 172.

FOR FURTHER RESEARCH

For Christine's most famous work, see Christine de Pizan, *The Book of the City of Ladies and Other Writings*, ed. Rebecca Kingston and Sophie Bourgault, trans. Ineke Hardy (Indianapolis, Ind.: Hackett, 2018), which includes also some excerpts from other writings.

For Christine's follow-up to this work, see Christine de Pizan, *The Treasure of the City of Ladies*, trans. Sarah Lawson (London: Penguin Classics, 2003).

For a review of Christine's theological thought, see Margaret Marion Gower, "The Heart of Peace: Christine de Pizan and Christian Theology" (thesis, Harvard University, 2015), https://dash.harvard.edu/bitstream /handle/1/23845469/GOWER-DISSERTATION-2015.pdf?sequence=6 &isAllowed=y.

7

Should We Speak against Injustice?

ARGULA VON GRUMBACH (ca. 1492–ca. 1554)

The news of the trial of eighteen-year-old Arsacius Seehofer circulated quickly through Ingolstadt, Germany. He was an instructor at the town's university who had been accused of following evangelical beliefs. This occurred in 1523, two years after the Diet of Worms condemned Martin Luther as a heretic.

Luther, still outlawed, had just published a German translation of the New Testament that was selling quickly. The message of the gospel as an announcement of salvation in Christ for all who believe was spreading rapidly throughout Europe. Overtaken by these developments, exponents of the Roman Catholic Church tried hard to contain the damage.

Seehofer was an easy target and his punishment a fit occasion to set an example for others. In an abusive, public mockery of a trial, he was forced under terror of the stake to deny his newly found convictions and was sent to a remote cloister for indefinite confinement.

AN UNLIKELY DEFENDER

From the nearby town of Dietfurt, Argula von Grumbach, a thirty-one-year-old mother of four, listened to the news with apprehension and outrage. "How in God's name can you and your university expect to prevail," she asked, "when you deploy such foolish violence against the word of God; when you force someone to hold the gospel in their hands for the very purpose of denying it…and use imprisonment and even the threat of a stake to force him to deny Christ and his word? Yes, when I reflect on this, my heart and all my limbs tremble."[1]

How could they even call it a trial? On what did they base their accusations? What's more, she wondered why no one had come to the student's defense. If the men were silent, she concluded, she had to speak out.

In a move that was unprecedented in her day, she challenged in writing the university's faculty, which included the famous John Eck, who had disputed with Luther in 1517. She suggested that the trial be held in German, allowing the community to participate, and that Scripture be the only standard. She even offered to appear before the faculty in person to defend Seehofer and argue against his charges.

Quite predictably, her letter was dismissed. News of her challenge, however, began to spread around Germany. In Nuremberg, some Lutheran friends of Argula decided to print her letter, which ended up being reprinted fourteen times in a single year. In the meantime, she wrote seven more pamphlets on similar pressing issues. Between 1523 and 1524, about twenty-nine thousand copies of her writings were distributed in Germany—an impressive number at that time. Her gender played an undoubted role in this wave of notoriety, as the wounds to the mighty university faculty were all the more conspicuous when inflicted by a woman. Her supporters compared her to Deborah, Esther, Judith, and the women who accompanied Jesus.

Argula knew her limitations. She was not trying to become a Reformation "star." She described herself as one of the foolish people whom the Lord had made wise. Being a woman, she didn't have the kind of theological training the faculty had received. She didn't know biblical languages and could only quote the Coburg Bible her father had given her as a child and Luther's recent translation. For these and other reasons, she didn't insist on an inherent right to speak, but

---

1. Peter Matheson, *Argula von Grumbach: A Woman's Voice in the Reformation* (Edinburgh: T&T Clark, 1995), 76.

rather on her responsibility as a Christian. She found confirmation in the words of Jesus: "If these should hold their peace, the stones would immediately cry out" (Luke 19:40).

She must have counted the cost, mainly the opposition of her husband, the knight Friedrich von Grumbach, who was Roman Catholic, and the repercussions her action could have on her children. Also, the threats the faculty had hurled against Seehofer could easily have turned against her. As she was writing, the Roman Catholic Church was circulating pamphlets hailing the news of the first executions of Lutherans at Brussels. Still, she was ready to face death if that was God's will.

WHEN SILENCE IS NOT AN OPTION

Her dismay was largely caused by general indifference to the Bible. While the church based its judgments on traditions and papal decrees, few church authorities seemed willing to compare their claims with the Scripture she had read and loved from youth. "What do Luther or Melanchthon teach you but the word of God?" she asked.[2]

She was quite disappointed by both clergy and nobility, both equally selfish and corrupt, and by their casual dismissal of any idea that contrasted with their mindsets. The local preacher, the learned Georg Hauer, whom she didn't mention by name, exemplified this attitude by crying out against Lutherans, "*Kentzer, Kentzer!*" (heretic, heretic), without attempting to engage Luther's writings and compare them with Scripture. "I could say that much myself, no doubt," she said, "and I have never been to university."[3]

She was also appalled by the use of force in imposing religious convictions, which are a matter of conscience. If she was wrong, she was willing to be instructed, as long as it was done "by writing, and not by violence, prison, or the stake."[4] But if persecution had to come, "if Christians are to be martyred in this town, just as they

---

2. Matheson, *Argula von Grumbach*, 76.
3. Matheson, *Argula von Grumbach*, 79.
4. Matheson, *Argula von Grumbach*, 90.

were in Jerusalem…even if I were dead already," she said, "the word of God would not be wiped out, for it abides forever. I am persuaded too, that if I am given grace to suffer death for his name, many hearts would be awakened."[5]

FACING THE MUSIC

Argula was not martyred nor threatened with death but was persecuted in other ways, perhaps equally painful, as most of her town and a large part of Germany turned against her. References to her gender were prominent in the insults she endured not only in person but in writings. The clearest example of these is found in an anonymous satirical poem published in nearby Landshut, which concluded with the scurrilous suggestion that she might have been overtaken by young Seehofer's good looks:

> Are you in heat, perhaps
> For this eighteen-year-old chap?[6]

Even her relatives rose against her since she had sullied her family's honor. The most vocal was her high-ranking cousin, Adam von Thering, recipient of one of her letters, who suggested her husband should wall her up—a practice not uncommon for unruly Bavarian wives. If he was not up to the task, a relative should step in. Argula replied he should not worry about that. "He [Friedrich] is doing far too much to persecute Christ in me."[7]

What she meant is not clear, but we can only imagine her husband's distress when, due to her actions, he lost his respected and well-paid position as guardian, or high-ranking governor, of Dietfurt. Still, she felt her loyalty to Christ and His word was to trump any other allegiance.

> May God teach me to understand
> How to conduct myself towards my man,

---

5. Matheson, *Argula von Grumbach*, 120.
6. Matheson, *Argula von Grumbach*, 167.
7. Matheson, *Argula von Grumbach*, 145.

she wrote in a 556-line reply to the insulting poem from Landshut.

> But should he ever wish to force me
> From God's word, compel or coerce me
> I should think that counts for nought.[8]

Her husband's demotion meant a loss of income for their family—another painful trial of faith for a mother. Even in the face of this hardship, Argula believed that defending the gospel should take priority over any other concern. Quoting Matthew 6:28–34, she chose to trust God to provide for her family.

Overall, however, Friedrich must not have been too opposed, given that he didn't apply the extreme measures he was legally allowed to use, and allowed their children (Georg, Hans-Jörg, Appolonia, and Gottfried) to be tutored by Lutheran sympathizers. Argula leaned on these tutors to play a fatherly role when her husband died in 1530.

AFTERMATH

Argula limited her public writings to the crucial years when she felt compelled to protest. After 1524, she limited her advice to personal visits and private correspondence, nurturing her family and influencing the area where she lived. In the meantime, she stayed in touch with other Reformers, including Luther, who became a close confidant.

When she visited Luther during his stay at the Castle of Coburg at the time of the Diet of Augsburg, which he was legally forbidden from attending, they discussed many things, from theology to breastfeeding. After Argula left, he sent his wife, Katherine von Bora, her recommendations for weaning their little girl Lenchen gradually, by taking away one breastfeeding session at a time.

Argula's most noticeable intervention was at the 1530 Diet of Augsburg, where she promoted harmony between the differing Protestant views of the Lord's Supper. She remarried in 1533, but her new husband died three years later. This added to a string of painful

---

8. Matheson, *Argula von Grumbach*, 192.

events in her life, including serious problems caused by her second son, a bout of the plague that nearly killed her daughter, and constant financial woes.

Her troubles continued until her death in 1554, compounded by ill health and by the widespread mistreatment of widows. To survive, she wrote countless letters to influential people and became involved in some legal disputes. In spite of these adversities, her faith remained strong, and she continued to be held in great esteem by the Protestant community.

In fact, realizing how common her situation was in her day, she built a network of support for other widows and spoke strongly against the indifference of men to their plight, as well as against other evils, such as male violence against women and the toleration of male infidelity.

As for Seehofer, he escaped from the Ettal monastery, went on to Wittenberg, and served as a teacher and Lutheran pastor until his death.

FOOD FOR THOUGHT

- In her letter to the rector and faculty of the University of Ingolstadt, Argula said she was aware of Paul's admonitions in both 1 Timothy 2:11 and 1 Corinthians 14:34 about women being silent, but she appealed (among other arguments) to Matthew 10:32, which exhorts everyone—men and women—to confess Christ before all; and to Joel 2:28–29 about women prophesying. She also brought up the biblical examples of Deborah, Jael, Esther, and Judith, who stood up to save their people. What are your views? Explain why you think Argula was right or wrong in speaking out against the injustice done to young Seehofer and to the gospel. What is the difference, if any, between speaking out as a disciple of Christ in your daily life and preaching in a church?

- Argula's decision to speak out was particularly difficult because of her husband's opposition. She believed it was her duty to obey God rather than men whenever the gospel was condemned and silenced. She quoted Christ's warning in Matthew 10:36–37 not to love family more than Him. Discuss whether you think she was justified in taking this stand, given the difficulties and humiliation it caused to her family.

FOR FURTHER RESEARCH

The best source of information in English on Argula are the books by Peter Matheson. The most affordable is Peter Matheson, *Argula von Grumbach (1492–1554/7): A Woman before Her Time* (Eugene, Ore.: Cascade Books, 2013).

8

How Can I Be Sure I Am Saved?

ELIZABETH ASKE BOWES (ca. 1505–ca. 1572)

In February 1552, Elizabeth Bowes met the Scottish Reformer John Knox in Alnwick, England, a market town about thirty miles south of her place of residence. Her trip might have been motivated by concern for the preacher, who was feeling ill. She also had some burdens to unload and shared them with Knox in a casual setting. But Knox didn't expect such an intimate conversation and backed away, leaving her in a worse condition than before.

She talked about this incident with her brother-in-law, Harrie Wickleif, a friend of Knox, who reported to him her perplexity. Knox apologized. "I remember myself so to have done," he confessed in a letter to her, "and that is my common custom, when anything pierces or touches my heart."

In this case, it touched him deeply, bringing to the surface some thoughts and feelings he had been trying to avoid. "In very deed I thought that no creature had been tempted as I was. And when that I heard proceed from your mouth the very words that [Satan] troubles me with, I did wonder and from my heart lament your sore trouble, knowing in myself the dolour thereof."[1]

---

1. John Knox, Letter 3, in *The Works of John Knox*, ed. David Laing (Edinburgh: Johnstone and Hunter, 1853), 3:350. Quotations from this source have been updated to modern English.

What was the temptation that was common to both Knox and Elizabeth? Some people—especially Knox's Roman Catholic opponents—have been quick to recognize it as a temptation to adultery. After all, Knox was only eight years younger than Elizabeth, and the two had been friends for some time. But the correspondence between them describes a different temptation, one that many Roman Catholics could not perceive because, as John Calvin faulted Cardinal Sadoleto, they "never had experience in serious struggles of conscience."[2]

ELIZABETH AND HER QUESTIONS

As in many other instances in church history, we have only one side of the correspondence between Elizabeth and Knox—twenty-nine of his letters to her, which are mostly transcriptions of the originals. This means we have only his answers and not her actual questions.

To complicate matters, most of the letters originally were not dated. This lack of information has resulted in a distortion of our views of Elizabeth's character and the nature of her relationship with Knox, giving an image of a weak and needy woman, perennially unsure about her salvation and heedless to Knox's explanations.

This is not consistent with the historical accounts that describe a valiant woman determined to know the truth by investigating Scripture and willing to risk everything to uphold it. Only recently has she been given due recognition "as the first Protestant of her sex and class in the whole north-east of England…a region which long remained notoriously attached to the 'old' religion."[3]

Born in 1505 in Richmondshire, England, to a well-to-do family, Elizabeth married the nobleman Richard Bowes when she was sixteen and moved to his castle at Norham, near Berwick. Together, Elizabeth and Richard had five sons and ten daughters.

---

2. John Calvin to Cardinal Sadoleto (1539), Monergism, https://www.monergism.com/john-calvins-letter-cardinal-sadoleto-1539.

3. Patrick Collinson, *The Birthpangs of Protestant England* (London: Palgrave Macmillan, 1988), 77.

John Knox arrived in Berwick in 1549. He was sent there by King Edward's Royal Council in an attempt to place this fiery preacher in a place where he would do the most good without raising uncomfortable controversies with more traditional church leaders. Berwick was only three miles from the Scottish border and was full of refugees from Scotland. After a while, some people came from Scotland just to hear Knox preach.

His name was well known. In 1546–1547, he had taken part in the Protestant rebellion against Cardinal David Beacon, turning Beacon's castle in St. Andrews into a Protestant fortress, and had been called to preach. Eventually, Knox and the other rebels were arrested, and he was sentenced to hard labor in the French galleys—a sentence few men survived. Surprisingly, Knox was freed in 1549, probably in a prisoners' exchange with England, and stayed for some time in London.

By the time Knox met Elizabeth in Berwick, she was already well acquainted with the Protestant doctrine, which King Edward heartily supported. After some time, Knox—a young man in his thirties—expressed his desire to marry the Bowes's fifth daughter, Marjorie. Both Richard Bowes and his brother, Sir Robert, had some reservations. Knox was of a lower social status, without solid financial prospects, and a Scot. Their opposition became final in 1553, when Mary Tudor rose to the English throne, reversing King Edward's religious reforms and bringing the country back to strict Roman Catholicism. Looking out for the family's safety, they could not become related to a stormy Protestant.

Elizabeth stood with Knox and Marjorie. After Knox fled the country, the two women followed him to Scotland where, most likely, Knox and Marjorie married.[4] The implication of their voluntary exile can hardly be overestimated. Later documents show that Richard deprived the two women of their inheritance, probably leaving them to take a hazardous journey on their own with limited finances.

---

4. The place and date of their wedding is unknown.

In July 1556, both the women and Knox left for Geneva, Switzerland, where they stayed until 1559, when Knox was called to help the Scottish Reformation in its militant struggle against the Roman Catholic ruler Mary of Guise, who was ruling for her daughter, Mary Stuart.

Elizabeth returned to England for a while but traveled back to Scotland in 1562 after the sudden death of her daughter. She stayed there to care for her two grandsons, Nathanael and Eleazar, until 1564, when Knox remarried. Four years later, Knox showed his trust in Elizabeth by sending his sons to live with her in England, where they could attend a good university.

GROWING PAINS

Elizabeth's questions to Knox concerned mainly the Christian's assurance of salvation. They were, in some sense, new questions. In the Roman Catholic Church, no one could be sure of their salvation. In fact, asserting such assurance would have been presumptuous. All that Roman Catholics could do was receive the sacraments and try to live a godly life.

Since all those who are honest with themselves know that godly living is never fully attainable in this life, the Roman Catholic Church encouraged believers to offset this lack by offering prayers to Mary and the saints, lighting candles, paying for indulgences, participating in pilgrimages, doing acts of penance and charity, and donating money to the church, among other works. Even then, few people could hope to go straight to heaven but could be thankful for purgatory, the imaginary place where they would be able to pay the penalty for their sins by sacrifice and suffering.

As precarious as this system might seem, it offered Christians the satisfaction of knowing they had done what they could. The pure gospel, as presented by Protestant preachers, seemed too good to be true. The biblical injunction "Believe on the Lord Jesus Christ, and you will be saved" (Acts 16:31 NKJV), was a comforting thought, but difficult to accept when the reality of one's sins came crushing down.

There were times when Elizabeth was tempted to return to the Roman Catholic Mass, just as the early Christians were tempted to return to the Jewish religious system because the idea of Christ's sacrifice being offered "once for all" (Heb. 10:10) seemed insufficient to atone for a seemingly endless proliferation of sins.[5]

THE SURETY OF GOD'S GIFTS

This was Elizabeth's trouble. She often felt too weak and unfaithful to merit God's forgiveness. Knox knew the feeling all too well and constantly reminded her that no one can ever merit God's grace. It's simply His gift to undeserving sinners.

"Remember, dear Sister, what ignorance, what fear, and what appearance of incredulity remained in Christ's disciples after they had heard the plainest doctrine," Knox reminded her, "and after they had seen the power of his works a longer time than you have yet continued in Christ. That is not so diligently and so often rehearsed by the Evangelists without a most special cause but to be a comfort to us, that albeit both fear and doubts remain in our conscience, even of long time, yet is there no danger to such as once have embraced God in his promises, for His majesty is such that he cannot repent of his gifts" (see Rom. 11:29).[6]

It was a comforting thought. But then why do we often read in Scripture that God repented of something He has done? For example, Elizabeth said, "the LORD repented that he had made Saul king over Israel" (1 Sam. 15:35). Couldn't He also repent of granting her salvation?

Knox explained that some parts of Scripture must not be read literally. The Bible often stoops to a language that human beings can grasp. For example, it may attribute bodily parts or human passions to God in order to help our feeble understanding, while we know by the full thrust of Scripture that God is a spirit without parts and is not affected by changeable moods. In Elizabeth's example, God knew from the start that Saul would prove unfaithful, and He knew He

---

5. See the whole Epistle to the Hebrews.
6. Knox, *Works*, 3:349.

would place David on his throne. To a human mind, this might seem like a change of plans, but it's not.

The Bible, Knox continued, "assures us that such as, knowing and lamenting their own corruption and great infirmities, and yet embrace the satisfaction which is by the redemption in Christ's blood, are surely engrafted in Christ's body and therefore shall never be separated nor rent from Him, as witnesses Himself saying, 'Out of my hand can none pluck away.'"[7]

This was the thrust of the gospel, the announcement of the salvation of sinners by grace alone and through faith alone. But this brought up another question.[8] If our salvation is as intimately connected to our faith in Christ as Scripture seems to intimate, what do we do with our frequent lack of faith and the feelings of frustration and impatience that come with it?

Knox explained that even "our impatience (although we should fight against it) is not damnable, seeing we are the members of Christ's body, therein engrafted by faith, which is the free gift of our God, and not proceeding from our works; out of which [body] we cannot be cut by any assaults of our adversary, whom it behooves to rage against us, because he is a spirit confirmed in malice against the Lord and His subjects."[9]

GOD'S STRENGTH IN WEAKNESS

In spite of his occasional frustrations, Knox recognized the value of Elizabeth's questions—both for herself and others. For one thing, they forced him to face his own queries and doubts and investigate Scripture more thoroughly than he would have done without her.

"The exposition of your troubles and acknowledging of your infirmity was first unto me a very mirror and glass wherein I beheld

---

7. Knox, *Works*, 3:363–64, quoting John 10:28.

8. By this expression, I am not establishing a chronological sequence of Elizabeth's letters. These were probably thoughts that circled around in her mind, each linked to the other.

9. Knox, *Works*, 3:359–60.

myself so richly painted forth that nothing could be more evident to my own eyes," he confessed. "And then, the searching of Scriptures for God's sweet promises and for his mercies freely given to miserable offenders (for his nature delights to show mercy where most misery reigns), the collection and applying of God's mercies, I say, were unto me as the breaking and handling with my own hands of the most sweet and delectable ointments, whereof I could not but receive some comfort by their natural sweet odors."[10]

Elizabeth's example of persevering in spite of doubts was also an inspiration to others. "God has wrought great things by you in the sight of other men," Knox wrote.[11] In fact, during a visit to London in March 1553, he read portions of one of Elizabeth's letters to "three honest pure women" who had come to him for advice. At the end of the reading, one of them exclaimed, "Oh, would God that I might speak with that person, for I perceive that there be more tempted than I!"[12]

In spite of her temptations to return to the Roman Catholic Church, when the reality of that choice stared her in the face after Mary Tudor's ascension to the throne, Elizabeth found strength and clarity of thought, leaving England and voluntarily joining the struggling community of English Protestants in exile. After this, Knox's letters to her don't mention any of the issues that had afflicted her before. Of her children, we know with certainty of two who followed their mother's faith, Sir George and Robert Bowes—both highly esteemed in the administration of Queen Elizabeth I.

FOOD FOR THOUGHT

- Have you ever experienced doubts about your salvation similar to those shared by Elizabeth Bowes and John Knox? Why did you doubt, and what helped you to stop doubting?

10. Knox, *Works*, 3:338.
11. Knox, *Works*, 3:386.
12. Knox, *Works*, 3:380.

- Why is it difficult to share doubts with others? How did Elizabeth's confessions help others in different ways?

- Elizabeth's and Marjorie's choice to leave family and country in order to worship as they believed God required was radical but not entirely unusual. Staying in a Roman Catholic country would have required difficult compromises, such as attending Mass. Since Protestants considered Mass a blasphemous and idolatrous ceremony, they saw attendance at Mass as an act of open disobedience to God.[13] The decision to leave family and country, then, became a choice of obeying God rather than men. What do you think about this? Discuss your views.

FOR FURTHER RESEARCH

To read the rest of Knox's correspondence with Elizabeth, see John Knox, *The Works of John Knox*, vol. 3, ed. David Laing (Edinburgh: Johnstone and Hunter, 1853).

For another example of questions raised by a woman on this subject and of the comforting answers she received, see the story of Mary Honywood and John Bradford's letters to her in John Foxe, *Acts and Monuments*, ed. George Townsend and Stephen Reed Cattley (London: Seeley and Burnside, 1838), 7:227–28, https://archive.org/details/actsmonumentsofj07foxe/page/n12. See also Simonetta Carr, "Mary Honywood and Her Flickering, Unquenchable Faith," *Cloud of Witnesses* (blog), Place for Truth: Biblical Doctrine from the Alliance of Confessing Evangelicals, January 14, 2020, https://www.placefortruth.org/blog/mary-honywood-and-her-flickering-unquenchable-faith.

---

13. Protestants considered the Mass idolatrous because Roman Catholics said that the elements turned into the actual blood and body of Christ and encouraged a worship of the elements themselves. It also seemed blasphemous because the priest claimed he had the power to offer up Christ in "a sacrifice of propitiation by which God is appeased," while the Bible tells us that Christ was offered up once and for all. *Catechism of the Council of Trent*, trans. J. Donovan and Fielding Lucas Jr. (Baltimore, 1829), 175.

For other examples of women leaving families and homelands to avoid submitting to Roman Catholic practices, read about the lives of Anne Locke (another friend of Knox) (Simonetta Carr, "Anne Locke—An Influential Woman of the English Reformation," *Cloud of Witnesses* (blog), Place for Truth: Biblical Doctrine from the Alliance of Confessing Evangelicals, July 24, 2019, https://www.placefortruth.org/blog/anne -locke-%E2%80%93-influential-woman-english-reformation) and Anne Hooper (Simonetta Carr, "Anne Hooper—From Rejected Daughter to Single Mother," *Cloud of Witnesses* (blog), Place for Truth: Biblical Doctrine from the Alliance of Confessing Evangelicals, December 7, 2017, https://www.placefortruth.org/blog/anne-hooper-%E2%80%93-rejected -daughter-single-mother).

9

Should We Pray for God's Enemies?

RENÉE OF FRANCE (1510–1575)

In 1528 fourteen-year-old Renée left her home country, France, with much apprehension and hesitation. She returned in 1560, a mature woman with a history of suffering, disappointments, and hard decisions.

A DIFFICULT LIFE

Born a princess (daughter of King Louis XII and Anne of Brittany), she was given in marriage to the heir of the small Italian duchy of Ferrara—Ercole II of Este, a man who didn't find her attractive, who indulged in extramarital affairs, and who was especially annoyed by her support of Protestants.

Their marital problems intensified after 1542, when Pope Paul III allowed the reorganization of the Congregation of the Holy Office of the Inquisition, placing Renée in the dangerous category of Protestant sympathizer. Even then, Ercole turned a blind eye to Renée's religious activities, mostly in an effort to maintain good relations with France, until the pope's insistence became impossible to ignore. Trying to keep a foot in both camps, Ercole asked King Henry II of France to send "a good catholic theologian" to detach Renée from "such an enormous heresy."[1] Henry sent the inquisitor Mathieu Ory,

---

1. Ercole II to Henry II, March 27, 1554, Bibliothèque nationale de France, as quoted in John Calvin and Renée of France, *Lealtà in Tensione*, ed. Leonardo

who, together with the Jesuit Jean Pelleter (already in Ferrara on the same mission), worked hard to bring the duchess back to the Roman Catholic fold. Restrained inside the castle of Ferrara, Renée put up a brief resistance. Perhaps the greatest threat she received as a mother was being prohibited from seeing her daughters until she repented.

The French Reformer John Calvin, who had been Renée's close friend and mentor since his undercover visit at her court in 1526, thought of visiting her in person, but his current circumstances didn't allow him to. Instead, he sent a French pastor, François de Morel, who was a nobleman by birth and could fit well in her court without raising suspicions.

It was too late. Morel arrived in August 1554, when the duke's efforts to "deprogram" Renée had already gained ground. Following an attitude that was common in her day, Renée might have concluded that a fake submission would grant her freedom to resume her practices. Whatever the case, on September 13, 1554, she relented and agreed to attend Mass. Clearly disappointed, Calvin continued to encourage her to look to Christ and hold on to His promises, proving to her jubilant enemies that "those whom God have lifted up are doubly strengthened against any struggle."[2]

In the meantime, Ercole, satisfied by his wife's outward repentance, gave her back her independence, allowing her to slowly return to her former way of life. When he died in 1559, she was free to move to her property at Montargis, France, less than one hundred miles south of Paris. There, she was finally able to benefit from the care and oversight of a pastor and elders in a properly organized church, even though the troubling times didn't allow any of them a sense of permanence and her view of the authority of a temporal ruler over the church didn't always match the view of her pastors.

Once again Calvin intervened, clarifying the distinctive duties of church and state and exhorting her to discharge hers faithfully by

---

De Chirico and Daniel Walker (Caltanissetta, Italy: Alfa and Omega, 2009), 48. Unless specified, all the quotations in this chapter are my translation.

2. John Calvin to the Duchess of Ferrara, February 2, 1555, *Calvini Opera Omnia* (*CO*), vol. 15, letter 2105.

ruling well over her limited territory and by exercising her political influence for the well-being of the church and the spreading of the gospel.

THE HORRORS OF WAR

Calvin was particularly concerned with the role Anna, Renée's oldest daughter, played in the French Wars of Religion. In 1548 Anna had been given in marriage to Francis, Duke of Guise, a Roman Catholic who had become increasingly active in the conflict against the Huguenots (French Protestants). Francis's involvement peaked in March 1562 when he and his men attacked a group of Huguenot worshipers in a barn at Vassy, killing 30 and wounding 150. Because of Francis's personal intervention, this has generally been considered the inciting event leading to the French Wars of Religion. Renée was shaken at the news.

"She has received a most serious blow a month ago from the cruel and repulsive outrage committed by her son-in-law," wrote Morel to Calvin. "She is full of affection for our brothers and sympathizes with their sufferings, but she cannot keep from wishing her son-in-law well on account of her daughter and she wishes he were less guilty. She is in conflict with herself. A desire exists for the ultimate reign of Christ to triumph over the afflictions of the flesh."[3]

This conflict never fully abated. Renée supported the Huguenots but recoiled at the horrors of war. When escalating violence in Montargis forced her to request the assistance of the Huguenots' armed forces, led by Louis, Prince of Condé, the extent of their brutality and destruction left her appalled. She then withdrew her support from Condé, raised a small garrison of soldiers to protect her walls, and made her castle available to refugees from both sides. The number of victims seeking Renée's care soon grew to the point that her castle was described as a hospital. Her decision to break ties with Condé and extend her assistance to everyone in need caused fiery discussions with other Protestants, including Morel, who saw Condé's

---

3. Morel to Calvin, March 1562, *CO*, vol. 19, letter 3761.

military actions as justified in order to protect the threatened and abused Protestant community.

Her political autonomy placed her in a difficult position in February 1563, when Francis, then engaged in a siege of Orléans, decided that the Montargis castle, teeming as it was with Huguenots, represented a threat and had to be taken over. The Royal Council agreed, adding that Renée should be temporarily transferred to another location.

Francis sent a messenger to deliver the unpleasant news, giving as pretext the council's concern for Renée's protection. Renée stalled, claiming her royal rights to maintain a land she had rightfully inherited. As it turns out, she never had to move. On February 24, 1563, Francis died from a wound inflicted by a Huguenot six days earlier, and the Royal Council never pursued her expulsion.

PRAYING FOR OR AGAINST OUR ENEMIES

Renée mourned Francis bitterly. Her grief was compounded because most Huguenots rejoiced over his death, claiming he was in hell; while he was alive, they had criticized her for praying for him. She found these attitudes profoundly contrary to Christian charity.

In answer to her complaints, Calvin exhorted her to be careful not to let her emotions cloud her judgment. He was especially alarmed by Renée's claims that David's imprecatory prayers against his enemies were allowed in his day but were no longer acceptable. Calvin recognized the danger of this line of thought, which creates a dichotomy between the Old Testament and the New. "Madame, this argument would lead to the overthrowing of the whole Scripture, and for that reason we should shun it as we would a deadly plague,"[4] he said.

If there is a dichotomy, he continued, it is not between the Old and New Testaments nor between David's desire to see God's enemies

---

4. Calvin to Renée, January 1564, *CO*, vol. 20, letter 4085, my translation. For a larger treatment of this question, see Simonetta Carr, *Renée of France* (Durham, England: EP Books, 2013), 114–16. See also W. Robert Godfrey, *John Calvin: Pilgrim and Pastor* (Wheaton, Ill.: Crossway, 2009), 148–51.

destroyed and Jesus's command to love our enemies but rather between "an upright, pure, and well-regulated zeal" against those who oppose God's kingdom and a personal hatred for individuals. Only the second is incompatible with the character of a Christian.

Calvin explained that as Christians, we are to love our enemies, "to wish and even procure their good, and to labour, as much as in us lies, to maintain peace and concord."[5] But this love should not supersede our duty to protect our brethren.

To recognize a righteous zeal from an ungodly hatred, Calvin said, "three things are requisite: first, that we should have no regard for ourselves nor our private interests; next, that we should possess prudence and discretion not to judge at random; and finally, that we observe moderation not to exceed the bounds of our calling."[6]

He concluded his letter with an encouragement to persevere. "In any case, Madame, these faults which are giving you pain must not cool your fervor or hinder you in the good path you have undertaken. I know that God has given you enough virtue that you do not need further exhortations. I trust therefore that, in your integrity, you will give an example of charity to those who do not know what charity is, and will confuse those who are false and deceitful toward you."[7]

Renée was too close to the situation to be able to exhibit the poise and composure Calvin advocated. She insisted that her son-in-law had been unjustly demonized through a proliferation of exaggerations and inaccuracies that no one seemed to bother checking and that the Huguenot leaders promoted an extreme and unsightly campaign of retaliation.

In fact, Francis's repeated interventions in protecting her Protestant subjects and interceding for them with the authorities had convinced her that he was showing signs of change. "I know he has persecuted, but I do not believe God reproved him for it, because he gave proof of the contrary before he died," she wrote Calvin. "Yet, no

---

5. Calvin to Renée, January 1564, *CO*, vol. 20, letter 4085.
6. Calvin to Renée, January 1564, *CO*, vol. 20, letter 4085.
7. Calvin to Renée, January 1564, *CO*, vol. 20, letter 4085.

one wishes for this knowledge to spread. In fact, they want to put to silence those who know."[8] In her view, covering up the truth was as bad as lying. "God is the God of truth and His word is sufficiently powerful to defend His own, with no need for them to take up the same weapons used by the devil and his children," she said.[9]

Overall, she felt that Calvin, who lived in Geneva, was not fully aware of the situation in France, especially since the reports he received were mostly from people with identical views about the war and the way it should be handled. She wrote,

> Monsieur Calvin, it saddens me to see that you do not know how half of the people in this kingdom are behaving and how flattery and envy are ruling here, so much that they exhort simple women to express a desire to kill and strangle with their own hands. This is not the rule given us by Jesus Christ and his apostles…. I pray you, Monsieur Calvin, to ask God to show you the truth in all things, as he has showed you before in many respects. I still hope that, through you, God will manifest the hidden malice I see predominant in this world.[10]

Renée did not know, however, that Calvin's health had deteriorated to a point where he was nearing death. Uncharacteristically for a man who rarely talked about himself, Calvin replied by listing in detail his present ailments: "Madame, please forgive me if I dictate this letter to my brother, because of my weakness and the pain caused by several illnesses: breathing impediments, [kidney] stones, gout, and an ulcer of the haemorrhoidal veins, preventing every movement with the potential to give me some relief."[11]

Having received no other recent news on her situation, Calvin was not yet capable of offering a solution to the disagreements. He offered, however, a simple suggestion: "As to the other topics, Madame, if my advice carries any weight for you, I pray you not to

---

8. Renée to Calvin, March 21, 1564, *CO*, vol. 20, letter 4085.
9. Renée to Calvin, March 21, 1564, *CO*, vol. 20, letter 4085.
10. Renée to Calvin, March 21, 1564, *CO*, vol. 20, letter 4085.
11. Calvin to Renée, April 4, 1564, *CO*, vol. 20, letter 4090.

rack your brains over them, as excessive passions always cause much sorrow and close the door to reason and truth."

He left Renée with one last encouraging thought. Even though, as she had complained, some had hated her for being the mother-in-law of a well-known enemy of the Protestant church, "they have all the more loved and honored you as they have realized that this has not swayed you from a right and pure profession of Christianity, not only in words, but most noticeably by actions. On my part, I assure you that this has given me the highest admiration of your virtues."[12]

The letter was dated April 4, 1564. Calvin died twenty-three days later. While we do not have any document describing Renée's feelings at this time, the departure of her faithful friend and mentor must have added a painful blow to her distressed state of mind.

Renée continued to be faithful to her "profession of Christianity," supporting preachers and offering help to those in need while resisting pressure to go against conscience in a war that allowed for too many excesses. This she did until her death on June 12, 1575. According to her wishes, she was buried without pomp and, like Calvin, without a tombstone. Her last will included a beautiful profession of thankfulness to God, who had "kept her and guided her by virtue of the Holy Spirit in this earthly abode, purely by his goodness and liberality, for which she is more obliged and indebted than she may be able to say or appreciate, and for which she must give him continually her most humble thanks."[13]

---

12. Calvin to Renée, April 4, 1564, *CO*, vol. 20, letter 4090.

13. G. Bonet-Maury, "Le testament de Renée de France, Duchesse de Ferrare (1573)," in *Revue historique* (Paris: Félix Alcan, 1891), 46:75, HathiTrust Digital Library, https://babel.hathitrust.org/cgi/pt?id=mdp.39015035907669&view=plaintext&seq=9; my translation.

FOOD FOR THOUGHT

- What do you think of Calvin's explanation of the difference between love for our enemies and righteous zeal against them? Explain why you agree or disagree with him.

- Why do you think Calvin spoke so strongly against a dichotomy between the Old Testament and the New?

- Renée was hurt by the comments of those who were quick to assign Francis, Duke of Guise, to hell and to rejoice over his death without taking into consideration facts that only few people knew. How does this problem of acting without knowledge of all the facts manifest itself today? How can we avoid judging matters without this full knowledge?

- What do you think is a proper reaction for Christians who hear about the death of one of their enemies?

FOR FURTHER RESEARCH

For a fuller description of Renée's life, her many questions, and her correspondence with Calvin, see Simonetta Carr, *Renée of France* (Durham, England: EP Books, 2013). The full text of this correspondence is found in the original French in *Calvini Opera Omnia*, Archive ouverte UNIGE, Université de Genevè, https://archive-ouverte.unige.ch/unige:650.

For a brief review of Renée's life, see Roland Bainton, *Women of the Reformation: In Germany and Italy* (Minneapolis: Fortress Press, 1971), 235–52.

10

How Can I Find Peace of Conscience?

GIULIA GONZAGA (1513–1566)

Giulia Gonzaga's early life sounds like a fairy tale. At age twenty, she was already one of the most envied women in Italy. She owned large properties, and her castle was a favorite meeting place for artists, poets, and musicians. She was considered the most beautiful woman in the country. Yet she was deeply anxious and confused.

In a fairy tale, this introduction would be followed by a quest for the answer—usually a magic talisman brought by a charming prince. Giulia's story was different. Her anxiety came from a painful incapability of obeying God's law, and no talisman could help. Her sinful tendencies, especially her fear of what people would say or her love for material things, got the best of her. Being perfectly aware of the biblical consequences of sin, she felt hopeless.

A DANGEROUS BEAUTY

Giulia was born in 1513 in Gazzuolo, a small city in northern Italy. It was the Italian Renaissance, a time of splendor and beauty as well as political struggle, as noble families fought to maintain their power and territories. It was a struggle for survival, and marital alliances provided the greatest security.

As most noble girls of her day, fourteen-year-old Giulia submitted to her parents' choice of a husband: Vespasiano, Duke of Traetto and Count of Fondi, an esteemed *condottiero* (mercenary captain) from the powerful Colonna family. He was forty-seven. In the summer of 1526, she dutifully left her home and family and moved 370 miles south with a husband old enough to be her father and a stepdaughter, Isabella, who was her age.

Those were troubling times for Italy (the infamous sack of Rome happened less than a year after Giulia's wedding), and Vespasiano was often called to battle. If there were any conflicts between the two coetaneous girls, they worsened when he died in 1528, leaving all his properties to Giulia, as long as she remained unmarried. Isabella considered this decision unfair and spent her life fighting it.

Giulia's life as lady of her castle in Fondi (between Rome and Naples) continued rather peacefully until, in the summer of 1534, a band of Ottoman pirates attacked her properties, apparently with the specific intent of kidnapping her as a present for Sultan Suleiman I. Warned by a servant, she managed to escape.

Realizing she was not safe in her own castle, she moved to Naples, where she rented a small lodging within a nuns' convent. There, she could still conduct her business and receive guests, while visiting her castle from time to time. Eventually, Emperor Charles V, who had been called to resolve the legal dispute between Giulia and Isabella, ended up favoring the latter, allowing her to keep the properties on condition that she give Giulia a high annual salary, a duty Isabella performed irregularly and begrudgingly.

WHAT OTHERS THINK

In Naples, Giulia became better acquainted with Juan de Valdés, a Spanish Reformer who had left Spain to escape the Inquisition. Well-versed in legal matters, Valdés had helped her in her litigation. The two had also obviously discussed personal and religious matters, because in 1536 she felt comfortable enough to reveal to him her innermost feelings.

The occasion was a sermon by Bernardino Ochino, a powerful preacher who had embraced some Lutheran teachings and included them carefully in his addresses. She had heard the friar before, but this time his mention of God's law terrified her, and she asked Valdés for help.

Why did these sermons fill her with torment instead of peace? How could she examine her conscience, as many preachers exhorted her to do, without falling into the deepest despair over her obstinate sins? And why did these feelings continue to plague her, in spite of her devotional practices and long fasts?

She got straight to the point. "Banning all the vain, bombastic speeches and useless ceremonies which are all too common today, I just want to say that I am normally so dissatisfied about myself and everything in this world, and so listless that, if you could see my heart, I am sure you would be moved with compassion, as you would find nothing but confusion, perplexity, and apprehension."[1] This apprehension was due, in part, to Giulia being "strongly conflicted by fear of hell and love of heaven on one side, and fear of people's opinions and love for worldly honors on the other."[2]

Honor and reputation were important for women of her status. From a child, Giulia had been raised to put the honor of her family above personal concerns. That's how she could agree to marry a man more than three times her age. Her feelings didn't matter. If the marriage helped the family to create or strengthen useful alliances, that's what counted.

But God's law taught something different. It taught to put God first above everything, including family ties. It taught to do everything for the glory of God. It taught that sometimes we have to offend our families in order to do what is right. Somehow, Ochino's sermons brought this out in the open, and Giulia felt incapable of taking the necessary stand.

The conversation lasted long, first in front of the church and later at Giulia's residence. Valdés explained that true honor doesn't rest on people's opinions. "By not placing your honor in the hands or at the discretion of other people in the world, you will not rest your hopes in

---

1. Juan de Valdés, *Alfabeto cristiano. Dialogo con Giulia Gonzaga* (Bari: Laterza, 1938), 7–8; my translation.

2. Valdés, *Alfabeto cristiano*, 9.

their honor, nor fear their dishonor. And by doing so, you will speak and deal with them with great freedom and much inner mastery."[3]

LAW AND GOSPEL

But Valdés went further in his advice. To explain Giulia's reaction to Ochino's sermons, he clarified the difference between law and gospel—a difference plainly stated in the Pauline Epistles; reiterated by Augustine, mostly in his explanation of "letter" and "spirit"; and exhaustively exposed by Martin Luther, who defined the ability to distinguish it "the noblest skill in the Christian church."

In a nutshell, the law is whatever God commands us to do. It is, in itself, terrifying for anyone who is aware of our human inability to keep it. The gospel, instead, is the comforting announcement of what Christ has done for sinners.

In Ochino's sermons, Giulia was hearing the law and not the gospel. That's not necessarily because Ochino was not preaching both. It could be that she was focusing only on one part of the message and allowed that to discourage her.

The law is important, Valdés explained: "Without a law there wouldn't be a conscience. Without a conscience, sin wouldn't be known. Without a knowledge of sin, we would not humble ourselves. Without humbling ourselves, we wouldn't know grace. Without grace, we wouldn't be justified, and without justification our souls wouldn't be saved. This is what I believe Saint Paul meant by saying that the law is a pedagogue, or tutor, who leads us to Christ so that we may be justified by faith."[4]

But the law must always be accompanied by the gospel, which will "heal the wounds inflicted by the law, preach grace, peace, and remission of sins, calm and pacify consciences, impart the spirit that allows us to keep what the law shows about God's will and to fight, conquer, and crush the enemies of our souls."[5]

---

3. Valdés, *Alfabeto cristiano*, 12.
4. Valdés, *Alfabeto cristiano*, 22.
5. Valdés, *Alfabeto cristiano*, 22.

If the law terrifies us and seems burdensome, Valdés explained, it's because we don't understand the gospel. "There can't be any fear in the soul that actively and effectively points his eyes on the crucified Christ, considering in full faith Christ's satisfaction and payment in his stead."[6]

OBEDIENCE TO GOD

Valdés's explanation provided some relief. But Giulia still had questions, especially about obedience to God. One of her problems, she said, was her "fear of what people would say and love for worldly honors."[7] She said, "I would like for you to tell me, without flatteries, if you can lead me on a path where I can follow your directions… because I have a strong tendency to follow my own desires, as you must have noticed."

Valdés explained that to follow Christ, she would need to keep her eyes fixed on Him rather than on the things of this world, just as a person who crosses a river must look at the shore and not the waters. He added that obedience to God is a natural fruit of justification:

> We begin to fall in love with God and to obey Him and serve Him, not for fear of hell or love of glory, but merely because we have known that He is worthy to be loved and that He loves us without end. God sets us free, but we don't leave His service in view of this liberty. On the contrary, we are even more subject and obedient to Him, not as slaves but as free, not as mercenaries but as sons. This is the essence of Christian freedom.[8]

This dialogue between Valdés and Giulia, later published as *Christian Alphabet*, includes both Giulia's spirited questions and Valdés's patient but honest answers.

---

6. Valdés, *Alfabeto cristiano*, 48.
7. Valdés, *Alfabeto cristiano*, 48.
8. Valdés, *Alfabeto cristiano*, 123.

GIULIA'S CONTRIBUTIONS TO THE REFORMATION

After Valdés's death in 1541, twenty-eight-year-old Giulia became the main preserver of his teachings, supervising the translation and distribution of his works and other similar books, such as the best seller *The Benefit of Christ*, and keeping a strong network of communication between Italian Reformers and sympathizers of the Reformation.

When the Roman Inquisition was reinstated in 1542 with the specific purpose of eradicating "Lutheran heresies," she assisted some Italians in finding safety north of the Alps. Others, including Giulia and her closest friend Pietro Carnesecchi, a Florentine follower of Valdés, decided to wait, still hoping for a reformation of the church.

These hopes fell low during the Council of Trent, when believers in justification by faith alone were declared accursed, but were raised again in 1555, when Cardinal Reginald Pole, who had until then supported a reformation, came close to being elected pope. Ultimately, Cardinal Gian Pietro Carafa—the brain and strong arm behind the Roman Inquisition—won instead, largely because of his work of propaganda that depicted Pole as an advocate of Lutheran beliefs.

Hope resurrected in 1559 when Carafa died and the people of Rome gave free expression to their rage against the tyrannical pope by rioting in the streets, freeing those who had been imprisoned on heresy charges, and burning the Inquisition buildings.

Soon, Giulia and Pietro realized the Inquisition was there to stay. Pietro was called to a trial but was released for lack of evidence—the fire had destroyed all the papers the authorities had collected on his case. Giulia's name also appeared in the Inquisition's files for her support of the doctrine of *sola fide*, but her powerful cousins were able to intercede and avoid a trial.

In the meantime, her health was getting worse, and she made plans for her death. Pietro could hardly bear the thought of losing his best friend. "To live without you in this malign century is to navigate high seas without oars or sails."

His high seas became particularly turbulent shortly after Giulia's death in 1566. Ironically, she had become the cause of his turbulence by neglecting to destroy the 228 highly incriminating letters she had received from him. He was soon arrested, interrogated under torture, and executed. When the new pope, Pius V, received Giulia's correspondence, he said, "If I had seen it while she was still breathing I would have burned her alive."

Other names were revealed by both Giulia's letters and Pietro's confession. The ensuing persecution, combined with Pietro's highly publicized execution, silenced most dissenting voices in Italy. But it was not the end. The same persecution created a large number of exiles—nourished by the same gospel Giulia had helped to disseminate—who went on to join Protestant churches abroad.

FOOD FOR THOUGHT

- Giulia must have learned much from her talk with Valdés because her later correspondence doesn't mention a struggle of conscience. Rather, she was able to encourage others and devote her life to spreading the gospel. In your view, how can a clear distinction between law and gospel be both comforting and liberating?

- Is it easier to obey God out of gratitude or out of fear? Give some examples in your life.

- Giulia said that her main problem was her fear of what people thought and her desire to achieve honors. Do you agree with Valdés's advice to seek true honor and not worry about what others think? Why or why not? Explain how this attitude can be freeing in our communication with others.

- Why did Giulia have to overcome her fear of others in order to spread the message of the gospel in a dangerous country? List some controversial decisions that show she put God's honor before her own.

- How does our fear of other people's estimation keep us from obeying God today?

FOR FURTHER RESEARCH

For a survey of Giulia's life in English, see Camilla Russell, *Giulia Gonzaga and Religious Controversy in Sixteenth-Century Italy* (Turnhout, Belgium: Brepols, 2006).

For a shorter overview, see Roland Bainton, *Women of the Reformation: In Germany and Italy* (Minneapolis: Fortress Press, 1971), 171–86.

For a children's book on Giulia, see Simonetta Carr, *Giulia Gonzaga* (Grand Rapids: Reformation Heritage Books, 2018).

11

What Can I Do If My Husband Neglects Me?

OLYMPIA MORATA (1526–1555)

Marriage can be challenging. It was probably more so for the noble ladies of times past, when marriages were arranged, men were often at war, and culture expected women to tolerate their husbands' infidelities. In an imaginary dialogue between two women, Theophila (lover of God) and Philotima (lover of honor), the Italian scholar Olympia Morata dealt with some of these issues.

SEEKING HAPPINESS IN MARRIAGE

In her dialogue, Philotima tells Theophila of her husband's "frequent absences." She continues:

> He has left me once again. He doesn't care that I miss him. I feel miserable here alone, but he feels fine. I'm consumed by these and similar worries. When I was a young girl, I just wanted to meet a man who shared my character and inclinations and whose company I could always enjoy. I thought there was no greater happiness in life than to have a husband who loved you dearly and could spend his whole life with you. That's the main reason I got married, to be happy with him. And now that I see that things have turned out differently, my pain is as great as the happiness I so wanted to enjoy.[1]

---

1. Olympia Morata, "Olimpiae Moratae Dialogus Secundus," as quoted in Lanfranco Caretti, "Notizie sugli scritti di Olimpia Morata," *Annali della R.*

After receiving Philotima's permission to speak boldly, Theophila leads her back to Scripture, where we learn that there is no certainty in human affairs. She reminds her of Proverbs 16:9: "A man's heart deviseth his way: but the LORD directeth his steps."

If Philotima had read Scripture more diligently, Theophila says, she would have learned that things often turn out quite differently than we expect. "You wouldn't have thought you would be free of worries just because you got married," Theophila says.[2]

"So, it's no wonder if not everything has turned out well for you, especially since God was not the end you set before yourself."[3] Besides, she continues, all the suffering in this life cannot compare to what we would deserve in view of our sin.

CAN'T WE HAVE IT ALL?

Philotima agreed. Yet, it was difficult for her to see women who lived worse lives and fared better than she. And yes, it's true that, as Theophila reminded her, "they don't have the heavenly goods."[4] But can't we have it all? What about women who were pious and lived happy lives—maybe not at first, but in the long run? Women like Esther and Abigail, who became queens?

"God gives different gifts and different burdens to different people," Theophila explained, "and it's wrong to judge His actions. We know for sure that He does nothing randomly, but does everything for our good. If those things were to our advantage, believe me, He would give them generously and profusely, since He has already given Himself—an unsurpassable gift."[5]

Besides, Esther and Abigail were not pursuing their own happiness. They didn't dream of becoming queens. Esther was willing to risk her life, and Abigail had to share many of the difficulties of David,

Scuola Normale Superiore di Pisa. Lettere, Storia e Filosofia, series 2, vol. 11, no. 1 (Pisa, Italy: Scuola Normale Superiore, 1942), 57; my translation.

2. Morata, "Olimpiae Moratae Dialogus Secundus," 57.

3. Morata, "Olimpiae Moratae Dialogus Secundus," 57.

4. Morata, "Olimpiae Moratae Dialogus Secundus," 58.

5. Morata, "Olimpiae Moratae Dialogus Secundus," 58.

who was still a fugitive when she met him. She encourages Philotima to think of those who suffered more than she ever did, particularly "Christ Himself, the Son of the Almighty God, who suffered greater and more bitter sorrows than any other in the memory of mankind."[6]

She also brings up the more recent example of Sybille of Cleves, Electress of Saxony, who protected the besieged city of Wittenberg during the Schmalkaldic War while her husband, Johann Frederick, was in prison under a life sentence.[7] How difficult that separation must have been, since their letters show they loved each other dearly! Besides, unlike Philotima's husband, Johann Frederick had lost his honor and most of his possessions.

THE SOURCE OF STRENGTH

Once again, Philotima agreed with her friend. She knew she should be content with what God had decided for her, valuing her place as daughter of God above any of the temporary joys this world can provide. But she felt weak and incapable of doing so.

"The best advice I can give you," Theophila replied, "if you can't bear adversities patiently, is to turn to Him who calls to Himself all those who labor and are heavy laden, in order to give them rest. He cannot lie. He will strengthen and give you the promised Holy Spirit, so that you will be able to taste the heavenly goods that will undoubtedly mitigate your grief and quench your thirst for those things—for he who drinks that water will never thirst again."[8]

Theophila reminds Philotima that everyone has battles in this life because the devil does all he can to destroy the lives of Christians, but these battles are temporary because life is short. Any human attempt to avoid all battles and disappointments is ultimately

---

6. Morata, "Olimpiae Moratae Dialogus Secundus," 59.

7. He was imprisoned in 1547, initially under a death sentence, which was converted into life in prison after a political concession. He was eventually freed in 1552 following a turn of events.

8. Morata, "Olimpiae Moratae Dialogus Secundus," 59.

futile. "Even if you could try everything in the world, you will never find rest in anything but in God."[9]

Theophila ends with one more exhortation to trust in God's promises: "Why would there be so many rich and great promises in the sacred books unless God wanted to keep them?" she said. But it is getting late, and Theophila has to go home. "For when the mistress of the house is away, the things left undone become more pressing than what has been done."[10]

A CHILD PRODIGY

Olympia wrote this dialogue in the fall of 1551 to comfort her friend Lavinia della Rovere Orsini, placing herself in the role of Theophila and Lavinia in the role of Philotima. But she also meant it for any woman who was in a similar situation, especially those who lived among nobility, in a world where riches and honors were held in great esteem.

It was a world that Olympia knew well. Daughter of the scholar Fulvio Pellegrini Morato, she entered the Italian court of the duke of Este in Ferrara at age thirteen. By that time, she had mastered a remarkable knowledge of Latin and Greek and extraordinary oratory skills.

Her official title at court was tutor and companion for the duke's oldest daughter, seven-year-old Anna. But her presence was also a sign of prestige. Italian courts competed in obtaining the best artists and scholars. A child scholar was impressive. A female child scholar was a sight to be seen—attracting nobles and intellectuals from other cities.

But child prodigies grow up, and their uniqueness starts to fade. In 1548 twenty-two-year-old Olympia was dismissed from court. The official explanation was that Anna, then seventeen, had moved to France to marry Duke Francis of Guise. There might have been other

---

9. Morata, "Olimpiae Moratae Dialogus Secundus," 59.
10. Morata, "Olimpiae Moratae Dialogus Secundus," 60. A special thanks to David C. Noe for helping me with this translation.

reasons. Her letters suggest that the door was closed to her whole family because of the "hatred and slanders of certain evil people."[11]

In any case, she was faced with a dilemma many child prodigies face today. What should you do if your life, which has been steered in one direction, takes a sudden and radical turn? Olympia had no practical knowledge that could help her widowed mother and four younger siblings or the typical dowry and work skills that were necessary to attract a husband.

Her faith was also at low ebb. Her father had raised her with the Protestant beliefs that had trickled down to Italy and were still spreading at that time, but religion had occupied a small part of her scholarly life. Instead, she was highly influenced by Roman authors such as Lucretius, who questioned God's involvement in human affairs. "I had fallen, you see, into the error of thinking that everything happened by chance and of believing that 'there was no God who cared for mortal things,'" she told her friend Lavinia.[12]

Her dismissal from court jolted her back into reality and helped her to reorder her priorities. "While everyone exalted me to the skies, I realized that I lacked all learning and that I was ignorant."[13] With Lavinia's support, she devoted herself to the study of Scripture and to an urgent cause—a campaign for the freedom of Protestant Fanino Fanini, the first case of death-penalty conviction for religious reasons in the relatively tolerant duchy of Ferrara. Her efforts were eventually frustrated, but Fanini's faith left an indelible mark on her life.

LOVE AND EXILE

Providentially, Olympia found a supportive husband—Andreas Grunthler, a medical doctor from Germany who had come to Ferrara to study. She might have met him earlier at court. In any case, in was a union of hearts and minds, as they both deeply loved each

---

11. Olympia Morata, *The Complete Writings of an Italian Heretic*, ed. Holt N. Parker (Chicago: University of Chicago Press, 2003), 108.

12. Morata, *Complete Writings*, 101.

13. Morata, *Complete Writings*, 101.

other, shared the same Protestant faith, and enjoyed literary studies. They were married in the winter of 1549–1550.

Lavinia, on the other hand, was not happy in her marriage to Paolo Orsini. She was undoubtedly glad to see her friend in a good marriage but couldn't help thinking that Olympia didn't fully understand her pain.

Olympia reminded her that everyone has troubles, and the devil is particularly active in his opposition of Christians. "There is no one who merely wishes to live piously in Christ who does not endure the bitterest griefs and miseries and daily bears his cross," she said.

And Olympia was bearing a different cross. By this time, life in Italy had become dangerous for Protestants, who had been officially declared anathema by the Council of Trent, and Andreas and Olympia decided to leave the country. This meant leaving her family, her friends, and her homeland.

Germany, Andreas's homeland, was the obvious choice, but it was not free of political and religious problems. Soon the two found themselves in the throes of the devastating Margrave War, suffering from famine and pestilence in a besieged city. After a narrow escape, they reached Heidelberg in 1554, where Andreas was offered a professorship in medicine while Olympia tutored students in Greek.

In Heidelberg, Olympia had a chance to enjoy great honors when Elector Frederick II invited her to live at his court and teach at the local university. The nature and extent of this last appointment has been often debated. If it meant an actual chair, she would have been the first woman in history to receive such an honor. It's also possible that she was simply invited to lecture, as a few women had done before. In any case, it was an extraordinary recognition, one that she refused.

Her refusal was mostly due to her illness—probably tuberculosis—which was advancing to its relentless end. But Olympia had also acquired a strong antipathy for court life. In her words, going back to a ruler's court would have represented rather than a promotion, a huge leap backward, "from the finish line back to the starting gate."[14] The finish line—not earthly recognition—had been her overarching aim for most of her adult life, as evident in her last written words: "I long to fade away, so great is my confidence in Christ, and to be with Him in whom my life thrives."[15]

FOOD FOR THOUGHT

- Theophila encouraged Philotima to accept what she couldn't change and stay faithful in the calling that God had given her. Some situations (including marriages) are more challenging than others. How can seeing our situations as vocations that have been especially chosen for us by a loving, all-wise Father help us to face them? Describe a similar experience in your life.

- Theophila's advice was meant for a friend who, in her time and society, had hardly any means at her disposal to stop a husband from spending most of his time away from home and even from philandering. But this doesn't mean that we should not try to improve our situations, if at all possible. The same apostle Paul who said, "Let every man abide in the same calling wherein he was called," also said, "If thou mayest be made free, use it rather" (1 Cor. 7:20–21). What can a woman do today if a husband is neglecting her or being unfaithful?[16]

- According to Theophila, why can't we expect to find full happiness in this life?

---

14. Morata, *Complete Writings*, 197.

15. As quoted in Simonetta Carr, *Weight of a Flame: The Passion of Olympia Morata* (Phillipsburg, N.J.: P&R, 2011), 207. The poem was translated from the original Greek by Chris Stevens.

16. This chapter doesn't deal with actual marital abuses, but it's worth noting that Paul's teachings on marital submission are not a justification for abusive husbands to demand their wives' acquiescence and silence. Even the early Reformers stated that women were fully justified in leaving an abusive husband.

- Philotima learned the hard way not to place her hope for happiness in her husband or in any other creature—what the Puritans called "creature comfort." How can this lesson apply to areas of life besides marriage?

FOR FURTHER RESEARCH

For a biography of Olympia Morata and a collection of her writings, see Olympia Morata, *The Complete Writings of an Italian Heretic*, ed. Holt N. Parker (Chicago: University of Chicago Press, 2003).

12

What Should I Consider in a Marriage Proposal?

CHARLOTTE DE BOURBON (ca. 1546–1582)

In January 1575, the Dutch prince William I of Orange (also known as William the Silent) sent Charlotte de Bourbon—by messenger—a marriage proposal with a long list of warnings. He had been married twice before. A complicated legal dispute over ending his second marriage left him financially obligated to his second wife and children, so he was not able to provide Charlotte with a dower, although he meant to do the best he could in that respect. He had a modest house and was building another—not much, in his opinion, but it could be a start. What's more, he was actively engaged in war against the Spanish rulers and was "beginning to grow old, being about forty-two years of age."[1]

He sent the text of the letter to his brother and to the Elector Palatine, Frederick III, who had taken Charlotte under his care. Charlotte replied with a brief letter, expressing her pleasure at the news. She had been introduced to William by the elector and admired him for his devotion to both God and his country. But she had to wait for a confirmation from the elector and his wife, as this was "the duty of a daughter." "As far as I am concerned, Sir," she wrote, "I hold you in

---

1. Ruth Putnam, *William the Silent: Prince of Orange 1533–1584 and the Revolt of the Netherlands* (New York and London: G. P. Putnam's Sons, 1911), 2:21.

my highest honor and esteem and desire to serve you according to the means God will grant me."[2]

REBELLIOUS NUN

Charlotte's choice to defer the decision to her patrons, whom she viewed as substitute parents, was not just a matter of formality. She was certainly not one to follow authority when it disagreed with God's will.

The only time she was compelled to do just that was when she was twelve and her parents forced her to become a nun at the Abbey of Notre-Dame de Jouarre, France. She had been there since she was a baby, as her parents had placed her in the care of her aunt, the abbess. Her youthful protests were of no avail, but she didn't give up. She began to collect evidence of the coercion and wrote persuasive explanations to be used at a later date. With time, her wisdom and abilities contributed to her promotion to abbess, but her sentiments never changed.

During her stay at the abbey, she adopted the Reformed faith and developed a correspondence with the Protestant queen of Navarre, Jeanne d'Albret, who advised her to take refuge at the palace of Frederick III in Heidelberg, about three hundred miles east of Jouarre. Heidelberg had become a haven for Protestant refugees.

Charlotte left the abbey in February 1572. The circumstances of her flight are uncertain. Some say she jumped over a wall, others that she took advantage of a Huguenot incursion into the abbey. A more plausible explanation is that she left with some excuse, such as visiting another abbey. After all, by that time she had become abbess and enjoyed greater freedom.

PRACTICAL CONSIDERATIONS

Submitting to the elector's advice in the matter of marriage was not merely a simple expression of respect. It was also a wise move.

---

2. Jules Delaborde, *Charlotte de Bourbon, Princesse d'Orange* (Paris: Librairie Fishbacher, 1888), 86; my translation.

Charlotte had been trying to reconcile with her father, Duke Louis of Montpensier, cousin of the king and a leader of the Roman Catholic cause, who had disavowed her after her escape from the abbey. By submitting to the local rulers, she showed her willingness to work through the proper channels, which, in her case, included monarchs as well as relatives. The elector consulted both her father and the king of France.

With the proper approvals, Charlotte and William married on June 24, 1575, in a quiet wedding followed by an intimate supper with friends. She was almost thirty years old.

A LIFE OF SERVICE

Politically speaking, this was not a wise move for William. Charlotte had no dowry and no influential friends, at a time when William desperately needed both in order to advance his cause of Dutch independence against the Spanish rulers.

But money and friends can be acquired, and Charlotte had all the necessary talents and found plenty of opportunities to do so. Her desire to serve William, which she had expressed in her answer to his proposal, was then amply fulfilled.

William's previous marriages had been for financial and political reasons, although the first turned out to be happy. Charlotte was the first woman William had married for love, and she reciprocated. Together, they had six daughters, all about one year apart. Charlotte took care of William's younger children from his previous marriages and established good relationships with his mother and older daughters.

While William went to war, she used the experience she had acquired as an abbess to run the home, negotiate alliances, and raise financial support—displaying, once again, great wisdom and diplomatic skills. These duties required a lot of travel, which gave her firsthand awareness of the horrors of war. Because of this, she often advocated for the suffering communities she met on her way. She then regularly reported to her husband her progress both at home and in her political endeavors. Through her careful and faithful writing, she also managed to reconcile with her father.

At the abbey, she had also acquired an impressive knowledge of medicine, which came in handy in caring for her family. Some of her treatments included chest rubs of chamomile and almond oil for relaxing and a homemade syrup of rose hips and honey for fevers—a recipe William's doctor promptly added to his book of remedies.

CHARLOTTE'S LAST DAYS

Charlotte's medical abilities became particularly essential in March 1582 when William was shot by the Spaniard Juan de Jáuregui, a man hired by an insolvent merchant who hoped to collect the eighty-thousand-ducats reward Prince Philip of Spain had placed on William's head. William barely survived, but he recovered, largely thanks to the constant care of Charlotte and his sister Catherine.

But the shock of the initial news, the constant fear of losing her husband, and the five weeks of relentless nursing took a toll on Charlotte's health—already taxed by frequent pregnancies and a heavy workload. She died on April 28 from a high fever, only eleven days after the thanksgiving service for her husband's recovery.

Her will, which she had prepared at the end of the previous year, provides a clear and detailed explanation of what had truly motivated her life:

> I give, first of all, thanks to God, my Father, who, by His great mercy, has enlightened me in the knowledge of His holy will, and has given me assurance of my salvation and of eternal life, through the infinite merits of Jesus Christ, His son, true God and true man, my only savior and redeemer, advocate and mediator. He has also led me and strengthened me through His Holy Spirit, made me part of His church, where He gave me the grace to call on Him in spirit and in truth with the other believers, hear His Word and partake of His holy Sacraments, and has

confirmed me more and more in the knowledge and assurance of His eternal love toward me.[3]

Strengthened by this assurance, she affirmed her hope in "the blessed day of the resurrection," when, "by the power and grace of Jesus Christ, [God] will resurrect our bodies, glorious, incorruptible, and immortal."[4] She knew death was not the end of her story.

FOOD FOR THOUGHT

- Charlotte faced her proposal of marriage with wisdom, making sure—as much as possible—to show respect to those in authority over her. Undoubtedly, religion was one of her first concerns, which was satisfied by the fact that William shared her faith. What are some practical issues a Christian woman today should take into consideration when answering a marriage proposal?

- A desire to serve, which Charlotte expressed in her answer to William, is rarely included in today's marital vows. It is, however, still part of the formula of the Book of Common Prayer ("Wilt thou obey him and serve him, love, honor, and keep him, in sickness and in health?"), which has been used by the Church of England and many other Protestant churches for centuries. Do you think spouses are called to serve each other? Explain your answer. How does this component of service affect a marital relationship? By extension, are parents called to serve their children? Why or why not? If so, how does this perspective improve our relationship with them?

- Christians are often ready to express their desire to serve God, but serving others has always been difficult. We are often more willing to engage in a formal service (for example, to the underprivileged or to missions), forgetting that our first

---

3. Delaborde, *Charlotte de Bourbon*, 285.
4. Delaborde, *Charlotte de Bourbon*, 285.

responsibility is toward those who are closest to us, those who we can actively serve every day in small but important ways. Can you name some reasons for this tendency?

- At the same time, Charlotte didn't limit her charity to her own home. She also advocated for the suffering communities around her. Have you found a balance in your life between caring for those close to you and others who need help? List some lessons learned along these lines.

- How can neglecting the biblical doctrine of vocation (the teaching that we are called by God to serve wherever we are— 1 Cor. 7:24) lead to underestimating our duty to serve others?

- How is the imitation of Christ in willing servanthood to others a manifestation of a new kind of power rather than of powerlessness?

- How can we preserve our health in our service to others? What ways have you found to do so in your life?

FOR FURTHER RESEARCH

For a short biography of Charlotte's life and an English translation of some of her letters, see Anne R. Larsen and Colette H. Winn, eds., *Writings by Pre-Revolutionary French Women* (New York and London: Garland Publishing, 2000), 107–21.

Does God Care about Hairstyles?

CHARLOTTE ARBALESTE DUPLESSIS-MORNAY
(ca. 1550–1606)

A knock on the door caught Charlotte Arbaleste by surprise. It was a group of elders from the local church with an official request that she take down the thin wires she used to create her elaborate hairstyle. Charlotte pushed back. She had been wearing these wires for fifteen years to keep her hair up and had never received complaints. They were, after all, common among ladies of her rank.

Her discussion with the elders continued for some time. She discovered that before her arrival, the pastor, Michel Bérault, had preached against the type of hair "updos" that we see in some paintings of the time.[1] He had also talked about this with Charlotte's husband, Philippe Duplessis-Mornay, who apparently failed to understand the seriousness of the matter. Far from encouraging further discussion, Charlotte's resistance to the elders' request resulted in the excommunication of her whole family, including Philippe, who was at that time attending an important meeting in another town.

In Philippe's absence, Charlotte sent a letter to the church consistory to explain her position. In a nutshell, she thought the church had usurped its authority by imposing a matter that could be defined as indifferent. She appealed to the French Reformer John Calvin, who, in his commentary on 1 Timothy 2:9, used the word *indifferent* in

---

1. See the painting *Wedding of Duc de Joyeuse with Marguerite de Vaudemont*, by an unknown artist.

reference to hairstyles. In this verse, Paul exhorted women to "adorn themselves in modest apparel, with shamefacedness and sobriety; not with br[a]ided hair, or gold, or pearls, or costly array." But what were the context and reason for this exhortation? And is braided hair an excommunicable offense?

The context, according to Calvin, is prayer. Just as men should pray with pure hands (a "good conscience"), without anger or dissension, "likewise" women should cultivate modesty and sobriety, rejecting the vices that normally accompany an "excessive eagerness and desire to be richly dressed"; namely, pride and a "departure from chastity."[2]

Calvin endorsed "the rule of moderation." "Since dress is an indifferent matter (as all outward matters are)," he said, "it is difficult to assign a fixed limit, how far we ought to go. Magistrates may indeed make laws, by means of which a rage for superfluous expenditure shall be in some measure restrained; but godly teachers, whose business it is to guide the consciences, ought always to keep in view the end of lawful use."[3]

Charlotte believed that the end of the apostle's exhortation was "to reform the conduct rather than fashion, without fiddling with small details."[4] She also questioned whether this was an excommunicable offense. These measures were extreme and reminded Charlotte of the Roman Catholic Church's abuses of power.

Besides, Philippe was still absent, and Charlotte didn't want to make changes without him, she said. Some have questioned her sincerity in this statement since she was managing Philippe's properties on her own, but it's understandable that in a matter that concerned excommunication of their whole family, she would have wanted to talk to him.

---

2. John Calvin, *Commentaries on 1 Timothy, Titus, Philemon*, trans. William Pringle, Christian Classics Ethereal Library, commentary on 1 Timothy 2:9, https://ccel.org/ccel/calvin/calcom43/calcom43.iii.iv.iii.html.

3. Calvin, commentary on 1 Timothy 2:9.

4. Charlotte de Mornay, *Mémoires de Madame de Mornay*, ed. Henriette-Elizabeth de Witt (Paris: Renouard, 1869), 2:289.

Charlotte ended her letter by saying that since her family had not officially become members of the Montauban church, they couldn't technically be excommunicated. She expressed her desire to contact the National Synod.

It's hard to determine with certainty what happened next. Charlotte said she visited a church in another town, where she was allowed to take the Lord's Supper. But in a letter to Charlotte, the pastor of that church stated the contrary, adding that he and all the other local pastors agreed with Bérault.

Charlotte might have also discovered that in 1581, the National Synod had listed among fashions with "notorious marks of immodesty, dissolution," or lavishness items such as "eyeshadows, folds, puffs," and hoops (worn under the skirt to make the hips look bigger)—all things that Charlotte would have considered "indifferent."

In any case, the family continued to move around, traveling to England and eventually settling in Saumur, France, where Philippe became governor and worked in the Protestant academy. Apparently, the issue never came up again.

ST. BARTHOLOMEW'S DAY MASSACRE

There is much more to Charlotte than this brief argument over a hairstyle. She is particularly remembered for her fascinating and well-written memoir, which includes a moving account of one of the most tragic events in Protestant history.

Charlotte was born in Paris on February 1, 1550. Her father adopted the religious convictions of the Huguenots, while her mother remained a Roman Catholic. Charlotte followed her father's faith wholeheartedly. At age eighteen, she married a fervent Huguenot, Jean de Pas, who died of an infection two years later while on military duties. Charlotte was left destitute with a young daughter who was born before Jean could see her.

At that time she lived in Sedan, in the French region of the Ardennes, but returned to Paris in 1570, after her father's death, for the division of properties. Since her father-in-law died around the same time, she remained to discuss any inheritance belonging to her daughter.

She was still there in 1572, when the conflict between Roman Catholics and Huguenots escalated into the infamous St. Bartholomew's Day Massacre—a terrible carnage that claimed the lives of as many as one hundred thousand Huguenots. She hid in a friend's attic. From there, she heard the cries of people being slaughtered or fleeing in terror. "I was overtaken by such perplexity and almost despair," she wrote, "that, if I hadn't feared offending God, I would have preferred to throw myself down than to fall into the hands of this mob and to see my daughter massacred, something I feared more than my own death."[5]

As it turned out, a servant had taken her daughter to Charlotte's grandmother, where she was safe. After the bloodshed was over—quicker than anyone expected—Charlotte moved to another friend's house, but even there she continued to be in grave danger. She finally decided to leave Paris and found a boat going to Sens, about seventy-five miles from Paris.

The trip was adventurous, with a few close calls in which she almost lost her life. From Sens, she continued her travels on donkey-back and by wagon until she arrived in Sedan, penniless but safe.[6]

CHARLOTTE'S LOVE STORY

Charlotte's life changed drastically when a young man came to town. He was Philippe Duplessis-Mornay, just a year older than she. He had just returned from England, where he had fled after the massacre. Along with their common experience of grief and flight, the two discovered they shared many interests, including reading, mathematics, painting, and especially writing.

---

5. *Mémoires de Madame de Mornay*, 2:62.

6. For the full description of these travels, see Charlotte de Mornay, *A Huguenot Family in the XVI Century: The Memoirs of Philippe du Mornay, Written by His Wife*, trans. Lucy Crump (London: Routledge and Sons, 1926), Internet Archive, https://archive.org/stream/huguenotfamilyin00mornuoft /huguenotfamilyin00mornuoft_djvu.txt.

For more than eight months, they spent two or three hours a day together enjoying each other's company. Eventually, Philippe asked Charlotte to marry him.[7] Before answering, she made sure his mother and brother agreed. When they did, she asked for the approval of other relatives and friends whose opinions he valued.

In the meantime, some people thought it was their duty to warn Philippe that Charlotte was not rich. They offered other suggestions, but he was not interested in exploring alternatives or in pursuing better financial options. He replied that worldly "goods were the last thing one should consider in a marriage. The main things are the character of the person with whom one will have to spend a whole life, and especially fear of God and a good reputation."[8]

Being in the service of the Huguenot king Henry of Navarre, who aspired to the French throne, Philippe had to leave on a military campaign soon after his proposal. Mildly wounded, he was captured by the armies of the Roman Catholic Duke of Guise and was released only after Charlotte arranged to pay his ransom. Philippe and Charlotte married in January 1576. As a bridal present, he gave her a book she had urged him to write, *A Discourse of Life and Death*.

A LIFE OF TRAVELS

Philippe continued to earn the trust of King Henry, who sent him on several diplomatic missions, including a trip to England from 1577 to 1578 and a trip to the Netherlands from 1581 to 1582. Charlotte joined him each time, as Philippe thought they should "spend their life together as the misery of the age allowed."[9] Their daughter Elizabeth was born in London, and their son Philippe in Antwerp, Holland.

Wherever they went, Charlotte cultivated her husband's friendships and supported his writing projects, such as his *Treatise of the Church*, an exhortation to right doctrine; and his *Treatise on the*

---

7. For the full account of this moving courtship, see Charlotte de Mornay, *Huguenot Family*.

8. *Mémoires de Madame de Mornay*, 1:89.

9. *Mémoires de Madame de Mornay*, 2:270.

Truth of Christianity, an apologetic work against atheism, Islam, and other beliefs. Philippe's works were appreciated in other countries and readily translated into English.

Over the years, Charlotte and Philippe had eight children together: four boys and four girls. Of these, only two girls and one boy lived past infancy. In spite of his travels, Philippe made a point to be present at the babies' births. Once, when he couldn't make it back on time, he sensed the time when the baby was born.

When Philippe was away, Charlotte kept in touch with him by mail while she managed his estate and entertained people who came to see him. He often committed to her important messages to pass on to others and treasured her opinion on his writings.

Henry's conversion to Catholicism horrified the Mornay family, but Philippe continued to be loyal to him, facilitating the negotiation of the 1598 Edict of Nantes, which granted the Huguenots freedom of worship and greater civil and political rights, and negotiating the 1599 annulment of the king's marriage to Marguerite of Valois—all while maintaining his religious convictions.

A CRUSHING PAIN

Charlotte nourished great hopes for her only surviving son, Philippe. Her memoirs were really meant as a biography of her husband that the boy could use as a model for his life. She gave him a copy when he turned sixteen but continued to record new events as they took place. The young man did follow in his father's footsteps as a brave soldier, faithfully devoted to the Huguenot cause. Charlotte planned to arrange a suitable marriage for him, possibly to the granddaughter of the famed Admiral Gaspar de Coligny. But her hopes were crushed in 1605, when her son died in battle, shot in the chest while rallying his troops to fight.

"Happy end for him," Charlotte wrote in her *Memoirs*, "born in the Church of God, nourished in His fear, noted for his worth while yet so young, lost in a righteous quarrel and in an honourable action. But for us, the beginning of a sorrow which can only end in death, with no other consolation but what the fear and the grace of God can give us while we chew the bitter cud of our grief."[10]

Suddenly, the book on life and death she had encouraged her husband to write came to life as never before, "Diest thou young?" he had written. "Praise God as the mariner that hath had a good winde, soone to bring him to the Porte.... We must rest us in his will, who in the middest of our troubles sets us at rest."[11]

Philippe and Charlotte tried to console each other with similar thoughts. "God now calls upon us to make proof of our faith and obedience," Philippe told her as he gave her the news. "Since it is His doing, we must hold our peace."[12] She immediately "fell into a swoon and convulsions," unable to speak. She tried to look for comfort in thinking of worse scenarios. He could have died in a duel, for example—a less honorable death. Overall, she realized words were insufficient:

> Silence best expresses what followed to all who own a heart. We felt as if our entrails were torn from us, our hopes cut off, and our plans and wishes frustrated; we could not converse with one another for a long while, or think of anything else, for, next to God, he had been our one subject of speech and thought; our daughters, notwithstanding our lack of favour at court, being happily married and settled elsewhere after much trouble so as to leave the house in his sole possession, all our thoughts had thenceforward centred round him; we felt that God, in taking him, had taken everything from us, no doubt to detach us from the world and to save us from all regret at parting, at whatsoever hour he might choose to call us.[13]

---

10. Charlotte de Mornay, *Huguenot Family*, 284.

11. Philippe De Mornay, *A Discourse on Life and Death*, trans. Mary Sydney (London, 1592), Project Gutenberg, https://www.gutenberg.org/files/21789/21789-h/21789-h.htm.

12. Charlotte De Mornay, as quoted in Lucy Hutchinson, *Memoirs of the Life of Colonel Hutchinson* (London: J. M. Dent, 1913), Internet Archive, https://archive.org/stream/memoirsoflifeofc00hutc_1/memoirsoflifeofc00hutc_1_djvu.txt.

13. Charlotte De Mornay, as quoted in Hutchinson, *Memoirs*.

She might have remembered her husband's admonitions to leave the times of one's death in God's hands, just as her desire to leave this life swelled in her heart. "Truly did I not fear M. du Plessis' grief, whose love for me grows as my sorrow grows, I would fain not survive him," she wrote.[14] Those were her last lines in the book she had written for her son "to describe the pilgrimage of [their] lives."[15] Her body, already frail and tried by frequent illnesses, didn't last long under the emotional strain. She died on May 15, 1606.

Her husband, crushed by the double blow of death, found comfort in Christ and in the support of his daughters. He lived long enough to write more apologetic books in response to Roman Catholic attacks and to contribute from afar to the Synod of Dort, to which he had been invited but which King Louis XIII had prevented him from attending.

When the king deprived him of his governorship of Saumur, Philippe became convinced that his responsibilities in this world were over. He died in 1623. Charlotte's book was published soon after his death with the title *Memoires de Messier Philippe de Mornay*.

FOOD FOR THOUGHT

- What do you think of Calvin's interpretation of 1 Timothy 2:9? Do you agree or disagree? Explain why or why not.

- The Reformers emphasized the distinction between scriptural mandates and matters of moral indifference (*adiaphora*). The Heidelberg Catechism explains that good works are those "only which are done from true faith, according to the Law of God, for His glory; and not such as rest on our own opinion, or the commandments of men." They believed it was an important distinction because the Roman Catholic Church had

---

14. Charlotte de Mornay, *Huguenot Family*, 284.
15. Charlotte de Mornay, *Huguenot Family*, 284.

introduced and enforced many new commandments. What do you think about this distinction as a general principle?

- Church history testifies that distinguishing between essential issues and matters of moral indifference has required much wisdom and scriptural discernment. Calvin also warns that Christian liberty should always be subdued to the bond of charity and to peace and order.[16] In view of this, what do you think about Charlotte protesting the consistory's decision to excommunicate her family because of her hair?

FOR FURTHER RESEARCH

For more information about Charlotte, see Charlotte de Mornay, *A Huguenot Family in the XVI Century: The Memoirs of Philippe du Mornay, Written by His Wife*, trans. Lucy Crump (London: Routledge and Sons, 1926), Internet Archive, https://archive.org/stream/huguenot familyin00mornuoft/huguenotfamilyin00mornuoft_djvu.txt; Charlotte de Mornay, *Mémoires de Madame de Mornay*, ed. Henriette-Elizabeth de Witt (Paris: Renouard, 1869); and Lucy Hutchinson, *Memoirs of the Life of Colonel Hutchinson* (London: J. M. Dent, 1913), Internet Archive, https://archive.org/stream/memoirsoflifeofc00hutc_1/memoirsoflifeofc 00hutc_1_djvu.txt.

---

16. For Calvin's views on Christian liberty, see also John Calvin, *Institutes of the Christian Religion*, 2.10.31.

14

What Should a Mother Teach Her Sons?

DOROTHY LEIGH (d. 1616)

One of the best-selling seventeenth-century manuals on parenting was written by a British woman, Dorothy Leigh. What may seem perfectly normal to us was still unusual in an age when women's writings were rarely taken seriously. Most books on marriage, parenting, and even midwifery were written by men.

But Dorothy's distinctly feminine view of marriage and parenting provides an important perspective on the training of her sons. Her reflections on prayer, the Sabbath, the importance of sound preaching, and other aspects of the Christian life are weighty and worthy of notice.

Little is known of Dorothy's life. We know only that her maiden name was Kempe and she married a gentleman from Cheshire County, Ralph Leigh. Together, they had three sons, George, John, and William.

HER BOOK

Dorothy wrote her book, *The Mothers Blessing*, as a letter to her grown children after their father had died. This was an acceptable form of writing for women. What was unexpected was its reception. Printed soon after her death (1616), it became an instant success, so much that twenty-three editions were published before 1674.

While Dorothy might not have anticipated such a response, she clearly hoped that the book would benefit more people than her sons. She dedicated it to Princess Elizabeth of Bohemia, daughter of James I and mother of Elisabeth of the Palatinate, and listed as one of her purposes "to move women to be careful of their children."[1]

As it was common at that time, the book starts with a word of apology for writing, especially since Dorothy is a woman and there are many "godly books in the world that mold in some men's studies."[2] It was her motherly love, she says, that compelled her to write. "Can a Mother forget the child of her womb?"[3]

In a moving paragraph, she recounted the efforts and sacrifices every mother makes for her children, carrying them within her, "so near her heart," bringing them into the world, and praying as she breastfeeds them, "when she feels the blood come from her heart to nourish" them. "Will she not labor now till Christ be formed in them?"[4]

GENERAL ADVICE

Her first advice to her sons was that they might live for Christ and daily "labor for the spiritual food of the soul…as the children of Israel gathered Manna in the wilderness." She stood by her choice of the word *labor*. "It is a labor," she explained, "but what labor? A pleasant labor, a profitable labor, a labor without which the soul cannot live."[5]

She then addressed fear and its unpleasant consequences. Her sons should not fear poverty, she said, for "the fear of poverty makes men run into a thousand sins." It's better to accept that "it is the state of the children of God to be poor in the world."[6]

---

1. Dorothy Leigh, *The Mothers Blessing* (London: Iohn Budge, 1616; Ann Arbor, Mich.: Early English Books Online Text Creation Partnership, chap. 5, p. 17, https://quod.lib.umich.edu/e/eebo/A05259.0001.001?view=toc.

2. Leigh, *Mothers Blessing*, 4. Throughout this chapter, the English of the original text has been updated.

3. Leigh, *Mothers Blessing*, 9, quoting Isa. 49:15.

4. Leigh, *Mothers Blessing*, 10–11.

5. Leigh, *Mothers Blessing*, 5.

6. Leigh, *Mothers Blessing*, 19.

Likewise, they should not fear death, "for the fear of death hath made many to deny the known truth, and so have brought a heavy judgment of God upon themselves."[7] No one can escape death, so instead of fearing it they should be prepared for it by strengthening their faith "with the promises of the Gospel, as 'he that liveth, and believeth, shall not die: and though he were dead, yet shall he live.'" And "whether I live or die, I am the Lord's."[8] This strengthening comes by meditating on God's word—not simply reading it.

A large part of Dorothy's book is devoted to prayer, a duty that is hindered by both the devil and one's nature:

> A man's own nature will never be willing to talk with God; for by nature we run away from him with Adam, and rather hide ourselves with fig leaves, and excuses, than come to God and fall down before him on our faces, confess our sins, acknowledge our unworthiness, crave pardon for Christ's sake of God, for all of our transgressions. Yet Adam had more cause to run away than we have, and we have more cause a great deal to come to God, than he had; for he knew not then that God would call him back again, and give him his pardon in Christ, who should tread down the head of the Serpent, which beguiled him.[9]

HOW TO BE GOOD FATHERS

Dorothy spent much time instructing her sons on the roles of fathers. First, they should make sure their children, "males or females, may in their youth learn to read the Bible in their own mother tongue."[10] Children can start learning to read when they are four. By the age of ten, they should read well. This is their duty during this stage of their life, "to learn how to serve God, their King and Country by reading."[11]

She reminded her sons to bring up their children "with gentleness and patience…for frowardness and curtness harden the heart

---

7. Leigh, *Mothers Blessing*, 21.
8. Leigh, *Mothers Blessing*, 21–22, quoting John 11:25 and Rom. 14:8.
9. Leigh, *Mothers Blessing*, 67–68.
10. Leigh, *Mothers Blessing*, 25. English Bibles were still relatively new.
11. Leigh, *Mothers Blessing*, 47.

of a child, and make him weary of virtue."[12] Also, she included specific instructions for raising girls. After insisting that her sons allow her to name their children, she explained the reason for one of her chosen names: Susan, after Susanna, the heroine of the Jewish book by the same name. In a side note, Dorothy clarified that she didn't consider the book of Susanna to be canonical. But Susanna was a woman who defended her chastity against some old men's indecent proposals, and chastity was, for Dorothy, a cardinal virtue.

She reminded her sons that while traditionally the blame falls on Eve for deceiving Adam, men are often guilty of deceiving women. What's worse, instead of repenting, many men brag about their actions and "laugh and rejoice that they have brought sin and shame to her that trusted them."[13]

The only remedy, she said, is for women to be like Susanna, "chaste, watchful, and wary." In fact, they should behave in a way "that no man may think or deem her to be unchaste."[14] But rape can still happen, carrying with it tough consequences, including the mental anguish of women who, after being raped, "either made away themselves, or at least have separated themselves from company, not thinking themselves worthy of any society."[15] It was a serious problem then as it is now and was equally kept in the dark.

Dorothy also defended the dignity of women against those who saw them only in light of Eve's sin. She reminded her sons that if sin has come into the world by Eve, God chose another woman, Mary, to bring into the world the defeat of sin in fulfillment of Genesis 3:15. If Dorothy's sons had daughters, they needed to consider these ideas.

HOW TO BE GOOD HUSBANDS

Apparently George, John, and William were not yet married because Dorothy instructed them on their choice of a wife. Her first request

---

12. Leigh, *Mothers Blessing*, 47.
13. Leigh, *Mothers Blessing*, 33.
14. Leigh, *Mothers Blessing*, 33–40.
15. Leigh, *Mothers Blessing*, 39.

was that their wives be godly. Second, her sons must see love as a commitment: "Let nothing, after you have made your choice, remove your love from her.... If a man has not enough wit to choose him one whom he can love to the end, yet I think he should have discretion to cover his own folly; but if he lacks discretion, I think he should have policy, which never fails a man to dissemble his own simplicity in this case. If he lacks wit, discretion and policy, he is unfit to marry any woman."[16]

This was an absolute deal breaker for Dorothy. "Do not a woman that wrong, as to take her from her friends that love her, and after a while to begin to hate her."[17] It is so important that Dorothy is willing to disown her sons if they do this. They have no excuse for changing their minds, even if their wives disappoint them. "If thou canst not love her for the goodness that is in her, yet let the grace that is in thyself move thee to do it."[18]

THE PREACHING OF THE GOSPEL

The book concludes with a defense of the gospel and a prayer that God will send more faithful preachers into the harvest, "for the true laborers indeed are not few, but very few," and a sad number of preachers drive many away from Christ "by their idleness and negligence."[19]

Dorothy hoped that at least one of her sons would become a preacher. Her hope seems to have come to fruition since her son William was mentioned by Puritan John Winthrop as "a curate at Denston in Suffolk, a man of very good parts, but of a melancholic constitution, yet as sociable and full of good discourse as I have known."[20]

---

16. Leigh, *Mothers Blessing*, 52, 54.
17. Leigh, *Mothers Blessing*, 54.
18. Leigh, *Mothers Blessing*, 56.
19. Leigh, *Mothers Blessing*, 235, 267.
20. Robert C. Winthrop, *Life and Letters of John Winthrop* (Boston: Ticknor and Fields, 1864), 21n2, Internet Archive, https://archive.org/stream/life andlettersj00wintgoog/lifeandlettersj00wintgoog_djvu.txt.

Dorothy's book continues to be a valuable read. Her voice is honest, direct, humble, and insightful, facing with clarity and discernment many important issues in light of Scripture and for the glory of God.

FOOD FOR THOUGHT

- In reading Dorothy's book, one is left with the impression that she was acquainted with the experiences of women who had been deceived, ridiculed, abused, and abandoned by men and who had been scarred by these experiences. How was her advice helpful to her sons? How can a mother influence her sons in a unique way?

- The saying "If we don't catechize our children, the world will" finds many applications in this case, as Dorothy strove to steer her sons away from behaviors her society seemed to tolerate, such as unsuitable attitudes of men toward women. What are some messages our society is giving in this area, and how are they contrary to the Bible?

- Some subjects, such as sexual and emotional abuse, may be difficult to face in our children's education. How can a parent emphasize respect for all human beings as fellow creatures made in the image of God?

- While not justifying men's violence to women, Dorothy believed that women should be "chaste, watchful, and wary," behaving in a way "that no man may think or deem her to be unchaste." Throughout history there has been a tendency to go to extremes, either blaming women for inciting men to violence or demanding that men respect women's choices of clothes or behavior even if they may not be appropriate in certain settings. What are your views? Do you think Dorothy's advice to her sons was well balanced in this respect? Why or why not?

• Dorothy's image of a mother laboring again to bring her children to spiritual birth in Christ is quite moving. List some ways in which a mother's work is never done.

FOR FURTHER RESEARCH

For the full text of *The Mothers Blessing*, see Dorothy Leigh, *The Mothers Blessing* (London: Iohn Budge, 1616; Ann Arbor, Mich.: Early English Books Online Text Creation Partnership, https://quod.lib.umich.edu/e/eebo/A05259.0001.001?view=toc).

15

Should Women Be Educated?

BATHSUA MAKIN (ca. 1600–1675)

As media and culture challenge us to think biblically about the place of women in today's world, it might be useful to remember that there was a time when women were discouraged from reading, studying, and thinking independently. In fact, the Roman Catholic Church's opposition to the translation of the Scriptures in the vernacular was often reinforced by an apparently appalling thought: Even women will read them!

The logic was simple. Women are generally ignorant, so if we give them Scripture, they will end up misinterpreting it. The answer: they should be content with what their priests, fathers, and husbands share with them. Some women recognized the fallacy of this reasoning. If the problem is ignorance, shouldn't we correct that instead?

BATHSUA'S LIFE

One of these women was Bathsua Makin (born Reginald), born around the year 1600 in a district of London. Her father was a schoolmaster who gave Bathsua and her younger sister Ithamaria a good education, including knowledge of Greek, Latin, French, and some Hebrew and Syriac.

At sixteeen, Bathsua collaborated with her father on two publications. The first one, *Ad Annam…Reginam*, was an instructional booklet on how to use an original shorthand system called radiography. The second one, *Musa Virginea*, was a collection of Bathsua's poems in six languages, written in praise of King James I and members of his family. Apparently, this ambitious undertaking was not fully appreciated. When the volume was presented to the king as a rare sample from a woman who could read and write in several languages, he replied, "But can she spin?"[1] This was typical of King James, who was also quoted as saying, "It hath like operation to make women learned as to make foxes tame, which only teaches them to steal more cunningly."[2]

Other people at court held Bathsua in great esteem, including the king's physician George Eglisham, who praised her abilities both in the medical and literary field. From ancient times, women had traditionally been family healers, passing on remedies from mother to daughter. Bathsua, however, went beyond this conventional role and studied the works of contemporary physicians. Some records show that she cured one of King Charles I's chaplains "of the palpitation of the heart."[3]

In 1622, Bathsua married Richard Makin, who was about her age and was in the service of the king. Together, they had eight children: Anna (1623), Richard (1626), Anna (1628), Bathsua (1629), Mary (1629), Richard (1630), John (1633), and Henry (1642). The first two died in infancy.

In spite of her busy life as a mother, in 1640 Bathsua accepted Charles I's invitation to tutor his daughter Elizabeth in Greek, Latin, Hebrew, French, Italian, Spanish, and mathematics. Later, she tutored other women, including Lucy Hastings, Countess of Huntingdon, and her children. According to some scholars, her teaching was dictated by financial struggles.

Bathsua was a follower of Czech educator John Amos Comenius, who promoted a natural and pleasant method of teaching from

---

1. William J. Thoms, ed., *Anecdotes and Traditions: Illustrative of Early English History and Literature* (London: Nichols and Sons, 1839), 125.

2. Miles Sandis, *Prudence, The First of the Foure Cardinall Virtues* ([London], 1634), 128.

3. As quoted in Frances N. Teague, *Bathsua Makin, Woman of Learning* (London: Associated University Presses, 1998), 55.

an early age (one of Comenius's books, *The School of Infancy*, was a manual for mothers on early education), with an emphasis on learning Latin.

Her educational pursuits culminated in the 1670s when she opened a school for girls at Tottenham, a district of London. It was there that she wrote *An Essay to Revive the Antient Education of Gentlewomen* (1673), which includes a lively defense of women's education, beginning with a list of educated women both in the Bible and in history. Her letters show that her mind stayed lucid until her death in 1675.

BATHSUA'S ARGUMENTS

Bathsua was not famous for her patience, and her arguments were fiery. But she made some good points that—interestingly—are not completely outdated, especially when it comes to the education of women in biblical and theological studies. In 1673 Bathsua outlined her thoughts on the education of women in *An Essay to Revive the Antient Education of Gentlewomen, in Religion, Manners, Arts and Tongues*. After giving a long list of well-educated women in the Bible and in history, she answered some common objections, such as "No man wants to marry a learned woman," or "Educating women is against our customs."

A frequent objection was that education would distract women from their main task of running a home. Bathsua's reply was simple: the same could be said for men. Anything can become a distraction. No one, however, denies the value of education for men. To the contrary, "men are judged to be more capable of country business by liberal education. Most ingenious contrivances, even in husbandry trades, have been invented by scholars."[4]

---

4. Bathsua Makin, *An Essay to Revive the Antient Education of Gentlewomen, in Religion, Manners, Arts and Tongues* (London: J. D. and Tho. Parkhurst, 1673), A Celebration of Women Writers, https://digital.library.upenn.edu/women/makin/education/education/html. The online version doesn't include page numbers.

Likewise, married women, "by virtue of this education, may be very useful to their husbands in their trades…and to their children, by timely instructing them, before they are fit to be sent to school,"[5] just as Eunice and her mother, Lois, instructed Timothy (2 Tim. 1:5).

To those who pointed out that the wise woman's list of tasks in Proverbs 31 doesn't include reading, Bathsua suggested a more careful exegesis: "To buy wool and flax, to die scarlet and purple, requires skill in natural philosophy. To consider a field, the quantity and quality, requires knowledge in geometry. To plant a vineyard, requires understanding in husbandry: She could not merchandize, without knowledge in arithmetic: She could not govern so great a family well, without knowledge in politics and economics."[6]

And if it's true that, as some people claimed, many women, beginning with Eve, have misused their knowledge and brought trouble into the world, what is the logical solution? Deprive women of all knowledge, or give them greater knowledge so they can discern truth from error? "I think the greater care ought to be taken of them,"[7] Bathsua said. "[Learning] will be a hedge against heresies," she wrote. "Women ought to be learned, that they may stop their ears against seducers."[8]

She clarified her goals: "I do not intend to hinder good housewifery, neither have I called any from their necessary labour to their book," she wrote. Likewise, she was not trying "to equalize women to men, much less to make them superior."[9] She only wanted to equip women to nurture their God-given intellectual faculties and then use them for God's glory and the good of their families, the church, and others.

---

5. Makin, *Essay to Revive.*
6. Makin, *Essay to Revive.*
7. Makin, *Essay to Revive.*
8. Makin, *Essay to Revive.*
9. Makin, *Essay to Revive.*

FOOD FOR THOUGHT

- Today, the education of women is taken for granted. Still, women are often discouraged from getting into theological studies. It might be partially due to peer pressure. If we are in a circle of women who shun theological studies, we tend to conform. Overall, Christian women seem to prefer books on homemaking, marriage, or parenting, which they consider more practical. But are they? What are a few ways theology is a practical study?

- Think of the women described in this book. How did knowledge of theology inform the answers to their questions?

- Some objections given by today's women to the study of theology are "I will leave it to the men"; "I am too busy with home and children"; "I am not smart enough." How do you think Bathsua would have answered?

FOR FURTHER RESEARCH

For a biography of Bathsua Makin and the full printed text of her essay, see Frances Teague, *Bathsua Makin, Woman of Learning* (London: Associated University Presses, 1998).

16

How Do I Know the True God Is the One Described in Scripture?

ANNE BRADSTREET (1612–1672)

Late in her life, Anne Bradstreet wrote a letter to her children, retelling her story for their "spiritual advantage" and for "the glory of God."[1] She started with her childhood in England, where her parents, Thomas and Dorothy Dudley, gave her an excellent education. Pious as a child, Anne was shaken out of teenage indifference when she contracted smallpox at age sixteen. Her recovery from the dreadful illness moved her to devote her life to God.

Around 1625, the Dudleys moved to Boston, England, to be under the preaching of the renowned John Cotton. It was there that Anne met Simon Bradstreet, eight years her senior, who was a friend of the family. The two married in 1628.

It was a difficult time for Puritans like the Bradstreets and the Dudleys, who chafed under the religious compromises imposed by Archbishop Laud. In March 1630, Anne, Simon, Thomas, and Dorothy sailed to New England on board John Winthrop's flagship, the *Arbella*.

According to Cotton Mather, it was Anne who persuaded her husband to emigrate. When she arrived in Salem in June 1630, however, she was baffled by what she saw. "I found a new world and new manners, at which my heart rose. But after I was convinced it was the

---

1. Anne Bradstreet, *The Poems of Mrs. Anne Bradstreet (1612–1672): Together with Her Prose Remains* (n.p.: The Duodecimos, 1897), 313.

way of God, I submitted to it and joined to the church at Boston."[2] Much ink has been spilled over the meaning of this statement. One thing is sure. Things were drastically different in the New World.

For one thing, the settlers still lived in poor conditions. About eighty had died the year before, and many of the survivors were weak and sickly, with supplies barely sufficient for two weeks. Rather than receiving help, the new arrivals found themselves compelled to share what little they had until they moved away.

The Dudleys and the Bradstreets continued to change residence, finally settling in Andover (Merrimack). Both Anne's husband and her father held important public offices, each serving several terms as governor of Massachusetts.

ANNE'S POEMS

Anne's poems were collected into a booklet with a typically long name: *The Tenth Muse Lately Sprung Up in America, or, Severall Poems, Compiled with Great Variety of Wit and Learning… by a Gentlewoman in Those Parts.* This work, now known as The Tenth Muse, was published in London in 1650, apparently at the initiative of Anne's brother-in-law John Woodbridge. Anne expressed surprise at the news but went to work to revise some texts and add new poems in view of a second edition, which was published in Boston after her death.

As the first English woman and the first New Englander to publish a collection of original poems, Anne was often criticized by those who thought that women should stick to sewing and housekeeping. "I am obnoxious to each carping tongue who says my hand a needle better fits," she said in her prologue.[a] Some even accused her of plagiarism.

In spite of these few detractors, Anne's works received immediate and abundant praise by men and women alike. Today, her works continue to delight both those who identify with her trust in God's sovereignty and those who are puzzled by it.

---

a. Bradstreet, *Poems*, 101.

---

2. Bradstreet, *Poems*, xxv.

ANNE'S DOMESTIC LIFE

Anne found joy in her marriage and family life. In a poem, she expressed her love for her husband, whose love she prized "more than whole mines of gold":

> If ever two were one, then surely we.
> If ever man were loved by wife, then thee;
> If ever wife was happy in a man,
> Compare with me ye women if you can.[3]

The only initial mar to the couple's happiness was a delay in having children, something Anne described as "a great grief" and occasion of "many prayers and tears."[4] But the first child finally came. They called him Samuel, a fitting name for a long-awaited son. Seven more children followed: Dorothy, Sarah, Simon, Hannah, Mercy, Dudley, and John.

Anne continued to write poems about her life at home—many addressed to her husband, children, and grandchildren. Of all her works, these domestic poems are particularly appreciated for their honesty and immediacy. They bring the reader close to the author's heart through a variety of feelings and emotions: her excitement at the arrival of a letter from her husband, her fear of death before childbirth, her struggle with repeated bouts of illness ("like a consumption"[5]), and her painful bereavements.

In 1657 she expressed her anxiety over the trip her son Samuel took to England and resolved to remember that he was God's before he was hers. Samuel was

> the son of prayers, of vows, of tears,
> The child I stayed for many years.

But now it was time to leave him in the hands of the "mighty God of sea and land."[6]

---

3. Bradstreet, *Poems*, xxviii.
4. Bradstreet, *Poems*, 315.
5. Bradstreet, *Poems*, 315.
6. Bradstreet, *Poems*, 332.

"No friend I have like Thee to trust," she told God, "for mortal helps are brittle dust." And if, in God's sovereignty, He chose not to bring Samuel back to her, her only request was that God would grant her full assurance of her son's salvation:

> Persuade my heart I shall him see
> Forever happified with Thee.[7]

Particularly disastrous was the burning of Anne's home in 1666, which destroyed all the family's goods, including a collection of over eight hundred books—an impressive number at that time, especially in New England. The fire started suddenly, barely giving Anne time to run outside and watch helplessly the flames that consumed her "dwelling place." Her pain reached a point when she could "no longer look." But as she turned away her eyes, she "blessed his name that gave and took." Her submission to God is summed up in a simple phrase: "Yea, so it was, and so 'twas just."[8] Ultimately, Anne found her consolation in remembering the much more glorious house Christ was preparing for her in heaven. "There's wealth enough," she said. "I need no more."[9]

ANNE'S TRIALS, DOUBTS, AND REASONING

But Anne's faith was not always unshakable. It had to mature with time, largely through a diligent study of Scripture. In the end, she revealed some of her questions, doubts, and answers in her letter to her children.

Her first question was whether God even existed: "I never saw any miracles to confirm me," she said, "and those which I read of, how did I know but they were feigned?"[10] Soon, however, she found an answer to her question because the testimony God has given of Himself in creation is too loud to be ignored.

---

7. Bradstreet, *Poems*, 332.
8. Bradstreet, *Poems*, 344.
9. Bradstreet, *Poems*, 345.
10. Bradstreet, *Poems*, 318.

"That there is a God my reason would soon tell me by the wondrous works that I see," she wrote, "the vast frame of the heaven and the earth, the order of all things, night and day, summer and winter, spring and autumn, the day providing for this great household upon the earth, the preserving and directing of all to its proper end. The consideration of these things would with amazement certainly resolve me that there is an Eternal Being."[11]

The next question was more specific: "How should I know he is such a God as I worship in Trinity, and such a Saviour as I rely upon?"[12] Eventually, these doubts about the reliability of Scripture were dispelled by her consideration of the effect it had on her own life, "that no human invention can work upon the soul"; the preservation of Scripture throughout history; the convincing biblical story of creation; and the fulfilled biblical prophecies, "which could not have been so long foretold by any but God himself."[13]

Other doubts included the possible legitimacy of the Roman Catholic Church. If God exists and He is truly the God revealed in Scripture, how do we know the Protestant interpretation of Scripture is correct? She came to a conclusion only after examining the Roman Catholic claims on one hand, and their "lying miracles" and what she deemed "vain fooleries" on the other hand.

But if the Protestant interpretation of the Bible is correct, why are there so many divisions and even gross errors among Christians? This thought was so discouraging that she ended up asking, "Is there faith upon the earth?" She continued, "But then I remembered the words of Christ that so it must be and that, if it were possible, the very elect would be deceived."[14] This last thought settled the matter. "That hath stayed my heart, and I can now say, 'Return, O my Soul, to thy rest, upon this rock Christ Jesus will I build my faith, and if I perish, I perish'; but I know all the powers of hell shall never prevail

---

11. Bradstreet, *Poems*, 318.
12. Bradstreet, *Poems*, 318.
13. Bradstreet, *Poems*, 318–19.
14. Bradstreet, *Poems*, 319–20, quoting Matt. 24:24.

against it. I know whom I have trusted, and whom I have believed, and that he is able to keep that I have committed to his charge."[15]

This section on questions and doubts takes up about half of Anne's letter to her children, showing that her mental process occupied a large portion of her life. By writing all this down, she probably hoped that this process and the answers she eventually found could help her children if they ever faced similar doubts.

She wrote her last poem, "As Weary Pilgrim," in 1669, when her health was already failing. In it, she listed many of the pains and hurdles of this world that will soon be over and expressed her desire

> to be at rest
> And soar on high among the blest.

She then described some of the joys of heaven and the bodily resurrection, concluding with a prayer:

> Such lasting joys shall there behold
> As ear ne'er heard nor tongue e'er told.
> Lord make me ready for that day,
> Then come, dear Bridegroom, come away.

She died on September 16, 1672, in North Andover, Massachussetts, probably of tuberculosis, an illness she had endured for some time. She was sixty years old.

FOOD FOR THOUGHT

- Have you ever had, like Anne, doubts and questions about the existence of God, the reliability of Scripture, the interpretation of Scripture, and the reality of a true church? If so, what was the nature of your doubts, and how did you resolve them?

- What is the value of facing religious doubts and being honest about them? What are some obstacles to doing so?

15. Bradstreet, *Poems*, 320; with allusions to Ps. 116:7; Est. 4:16; Matt. 16:18; and 2 Tim. 1:12.

• Some parents hesitate to share any account of their religious struggles with their children. In what ways do you think Anne's honest account might have helped her children?

• Anne mentions four main questions that plagued her: Is there a God? If so, is He the God revealed in Scripture? And if so, is the Protestant interpretation of Scripture correct? Given the widespread discord among Christians, is there still faith on earth? She then gives a few answers. Explain why you think her answers are sufficient—or not. Would you add any more? (For example, she doesn't mention Christ's resurrection, which today is considered one of the greatest proofs for both the existence of God and the validity of Scripture.)

• The "vain fooleries" of the Roman Catholic Church (among other things) convinced Anne that their interpretation of Scripture was not valid. What do you think she meant by this phrase?

FOR FURTHER RESEARCH

For a more recent collection of Anne's works, see Anne Bradstreet, *The Works of Anne Bradstreet*, ed. Jeannine Hensley (Cambridge, Mass.: Harvard Press, 1967).

17

Are Mind and Body Separate?

ELISABETH OF THE PALATINATE (1618–1680)

"I ask you please to tell me how the soul of a human being (it being only a thinking substance) can determine the bodily spirits, in order to bring about voluntary actions?"[1] This is how Princess Elisabeth Simmern van Pallandt of Bohemia, also known as Elisabeth of the Palatinate, addressed the French philosopher René Descartes in 1643.

Elisabeth, who had come to The Hague, Netherlands, as a refugee with her family, had met Descartes during one of his visits. They discussed mathematics and philosophy and kept corresponding by letters. Her first existing letter to Descartes was in 1643, when she was twenty-five and he was forty-seven. In the course of their correspondence, she expressed her interest in his metaphysical theories and surprised him by providing an answer to an intriguing geometrical problem.

A TROUBLED FAMILY

Elisabeth was born on December 26, 1618, in Heidelberg in today's Germany. It was the first year of the devastating Thirty Years War, and her life was marked by troubles from the start.

---

1. Elisabeth of Bohemia and René Descartes, *The Correspondence between Princess Elisabeth of Bohemia and René Descartes*, ed. and trans. Lisa Shapiro, The Other Voice in Early Modern Europe series (Chicago: University of Chicago Press, 2007), 62.

Her parents, Frederick V, Elector Palatine, and Elisabeth Stuart, daughter of James I of England, were at that time struggling as rulers of Bohemia. In 1620, after a crucial loss at the Battle of White Mountain, they were forced to exile to the Netherlands, leaving young Elisabeth and her older brothers, Henry Frederick and Charles, with their paternal grandmother, Louise Juliana of Nassau, daughter of the legendary William of Orange.

Louise raised the children according to her Reformed convictions and gave them a solid early education. When at age nine Elisabeth joined her parents, she found that her family had increased by eight more children. Two more followed later, for a total of thirteen.

If The Hague provided a more peaceful environment, Elisabeth's family still faced many troubles. In 1629 her brother Henry Frederick died in a drowning accident. Three years later, her father died unexpectedly of infected wounds he had contracted in battle, leaving the family in dire poverty. In 1638 her brother Rupert was captured by agents of Emperor Ferdinand III and held in captivity for three years due to the inability of Rupert's family to pay the required ransom. Through all this, Elisabeth's mother held the helm of the family while refusing to dismantle from her rooms the black drapes of mourning for her husband.

Elisabeth and her siblings received a thorough education, both religious and secular. They rose at dawn to pray, read the Bible, memorized the Heidelberg Catechism, then spent the rest of the day learning a great variety of school subjects. Young Elisabeth was exceptional in her passion for learning. Her sisters nicknamed her "La Grecque" because of her love for ancient Greek.

Religion continued to be of utmost importance to her and determined her refusal of a marriage proposal by the Roman Catholic King Ladislas IV of Poland in 1633. Ultimately, she remained unmarried.

MIND AND BODY

By the time he met Elisabeth, Descartes had already made news with his *Cogito ergo sum* argument ("I think, therefore I am"). Instead of starting with a revealed or presumed knowledge, he had started from the supposition that everything could be an illusion and had tried to find one thing that was definitely real. He finally concluded that we can doubt everything except the fact that we are thinking. We can doubt the existence of our body (physical senses could be an illusion) but not the existence of a thinking mind. He then made the mind the starting point for the confirmation of all knowledge.

His idea of a complete distinction between mind and body came as a natural consequence of his argument: "There is a great difference between mind and body in this respect," he wrote in his *Meditations*, "that body is by its nature always divisible, but mind clearly indivisible: for certainly when I consider the mind, or myself so far as I am only a thing that thinks, I am able to distinguish no part in me, but I understand to be a thing plainly one and entire: and although my whole mind seems to be united to my whole body, I recognize that if a foot or arm or any other part of my body is cut off, nothing is thereupon withdrawn from my mind."[2]

While a dualism between body and soul is expressed in the Bible and has been affirmed by theologians and philosophers alike, Descartes's definition of the mind as a completely different substance that is united to the body in an unspecified way raised new questions for Elisabeth and others. If the mind is a separate, immaterial substance, she wondered, how can it affect a material body? It was a difficult question. The interaction of mind and body in daily tasks is hard to deny, but it's difficult to determine how it occurs.

After apologizing for her "stupidity in being unable to comprehend," Elisabeth confessed she had never "been able to conceive of such an immaterial thing as anything other than a negation of matter which cannot have any communication with it. It would be easier for me to concede matter and extension to the soul, than the capacity of moving a body and of being moved, to an immaterial body."[3]

---

2. Richard Lowndes, *René Descartes: His Life and Meditations* (London: Frederick Norgate, 1878), 200–201.

3. Elisabeth of Bohemia and Descartes, *Correspondence*, 68.

Elisabeth never found Descartes's answers satisfactory. He had tentatively suggested the pineal gland, in the center of the brain, as the site of connection between the mind and the body. But he didn't specifically explain how this would function and how this gland, being material, could communicate with and affect an immaterial substance. Most likely, he didn't see this net distinction of substances as an impediment to interaction.

In the end, he told Elisabeth to adhere to what she found easiest to believe. If she found it "easier to attribute matter and extension to the soul than to attribute to it the capacity to move a body and to be moved by one without having matter," she could do so. Eventually, he said, she would arrive at the right conclusion. But maybe she should ease up on her quest for the principles of metaphysics, as "it would be very harmful to occupy one's understanding often in meditating on them."[4]

THE EMOTIONS

In spite of philosophical disagreements, Elisabeth and Descartes remained good friends, and he was often concerned for her poor health. Once when she was plagued by a persistent low-grade fever and dry cough, he suggested melancholy as a possible cause and the persuasions or at least distractions of a reasonable mind as a remedy. When she resisted this idea, he recommended that she read Seneca's *De Vita Beata*, a Stoic classic on mastering emotions.

Elisabeth was not impressed by what she read. First, she didn't think that sadness could be overcome by willpower, as Seneca suggested, or by virtue acquired through "the right use of reason," as Descartes had suggested.[5] While it's true that the mind can restrain emotions, some bodily ailments can impair the mind—something that Seneca had not taken into account. Besides, an emotion disturbing a person's serenity isn't antithetical to virtue. For example, regret, as upsetting as it is, is good and useful because it moves the one

4. Elisabeth of Bohemia and Descartes, *Correspondence*, 71.
5. Elisabeth of Bohemia and Descartes, *Correspondence*, 99.

experiencing it to repentance, and empathy for others is a positive feeling, even though it involves personal pain.

She encouraged Descartes to write more about this subject to remedy the deficiencies in Seneca's writings. The result was his treatise *On the Passions of the Soul*, published in 1649, two years after his last-known letter to Elisabeth. In it, he conceded that the body can affect the emotions but reiterated the power of the rational mind to overcome them.

RETIREMENT

In 1660, at forty-two years of age, Elisabeth entered the Lutheran convent at Herford, even though she maintained her Reformed convictions. Seven years later she became its abbess, presiding over the surrounding community.

By this time, the Thirty Years War had ended, leaving in its wake unprecedented devastation. Since the war had largely been motivated by religious conflicts, many people, including Elisabeth, became advocates for religious toleration. Her convent became a refuge from religious persecution, even for sects such as the Labadists (a group emphasizing communal life and inner illumination) and the Quakers.

She died on February 12, 1680, after a long and painful illness, most likely a form of internal cancer. Today she is mostly remembered as the woman who caused Descartes to reconsider and elaborate some of his theories.

FOOD FOR THOUGHT

- The Bible teaches that God created human beings as units of body and soul. While the soul lives on without the body after death, it will reunite with the body in the final resurrection. The separation of body and soul is unnatural and is due to sin. In this context, Christians have given different answers to the question of how body and soul interact. The simplest and most biblical of these seems to be that body and soul function as a harmonious unit, and not as two different substances

joined together, like bread and cheese in a sandwich.[6] Do you
hold to a different view? Explain your thoughts.

- Given the difficulties in a discussion of the interaction
  between mind and body, some people have come to the conclusion that there is no soul and the mind is simply a function
  of the brain. In appearance, this seems to be a scientific explanation. In reality, many scientists have admitted that there are
  many aspects of the human mind that science cannot explain.
  Why is it important for Christians to read about these issues?

- Equating the mind with an immaterial soul, separate from the
  body, has caused some people to deny the existence of mental
  illness, or at least to question its definition. On the contrary,
  those who view the mind as affected both by brain functions
  and by the soul are more willing to accept the idea of brain
  disorders that influence different areas of human thought,
  responses, and emotions. What is your position on this issue?

- How did Elisabeth understand the relation between mind and
  body when it comes to emotions, and what do you think of
  her view? Have there been times when an illness made you
  feel depressed or anxious?

- Do you think there is a danger in giving as much importance
  to the mind as Descartes did? How could this end up reducing human beings to their thinking selves and discounting
  those whose mental abilities have been impaired? Besides
  being uncharitable, do you find it contrary to biblical teachings? If so, how?

---

6. See John W. Cooper, "The Current Body-Soul Debate: A Case for Dualistic Holism," *Southern Baptist Journal of Theology* 13, no. 2 (2009): 36, https://
sbts-wordpress-uploads.s3.amazonaws.com/equip/uploads/2015/10/SBJT-V
13-N.2_Cooper.pdf.

• Seneca, the Stoic who failed to impress Elisabeth, believed that the mind can master the emotions through willpower. Descartes thought his positive frame of mind and the fact that he had been "accustomed for a long time to having no sad thoughts"[7] might even account for his not having unpleasant dreams. What do you think of this in light of biblical teachings? The Stoics argued that a good man being tortured is still a happy man because it is only his body—not his soul—that is being harmed. Elisabeth, instead, took into account that suffering can affect human beings in ways that are unpredictable, no matter how strong their willpower. While Christians can certainly rely on God's strength during persecution, if they withstand torture it's only by God's grace and not because of inner virtue or willpower. Do you think the Stoics' teaching can be difficult and even harmful, underestimating some forms of pain and suffering—for example, those that come from abuse? If so, give some examples of how this can happen.

• By pointing out that the body can have some effects on the emotions that the mind cannot control, Elisabeth was reminding Descartes that humans don't have as much control over themselves and their lives as they would like to have. Why is this a helpful reminder?

• Descartes suggested melancholy as the cause of her illness without investigating her case. What dangers do you see in the tendency to give advice based on personal or common notions or in oversimplifying someone's situation?

• For Elisabeth, the relationship between the mind and the body was not simply an intellectual challenge. It was a practical matter, played out in her everyday life. How does the way we view these issues affect the way we lead our lives?

---

7. Elisabeth of Bohemia and Descartes, *Correspondence*, 107.

• Elisabeth expressed her disagreements with Descartes with humility, courtesy, and respect. What can we learn from this? Do you think our society places enough emphasis on the ability to listen carefully to other people's opinions? If not, what can be done about it?

FOR FURTHER RESEARCH

For more information about Elisabeth and the texts of her correspondence with Descartes, see Princess Elisabeth of Bohemia and René Descartes, *The Correspondence between Princess Elisabeth of Bohemia and René Descartes*, ed. and trans. Lisa Shapiro, The Other Voice in Early Modern Europe series (Chicago: University of Chicago Press, 2007).

For more information about Descartes, with a mention of his discussion with Elisabeth, see Justin Skirry, *Descartes: A Guide for the Perplexed* (New York: Continuum, 2008).

For a comprehensive exposition of various views on the interaction of body and soul, see John W. Cooper, *Body, Soul, and Life Everlasting* (Grand Rapids: Eerdmans, 1989); or a summary of the volume in John W. Cooper, "The Current Body-Soul Debate: A Case for Dualistic Holism," *Southern Baptist Journal of Theology* 13, no. 2 (2009): 32–50.

See a shorter treatise of the same subject in Simonetta Carr, "Elisabeth of the Palatinate and the Mind-Body Problem," *Modern Reformation*, September 9, 2020, https://modernreformation.org/resource-library /web-exclusive-articles/the-mod-elisabeth-of-the-palatinate-and-the -mind-body-problem/.

18

What Could We Fear?

LUCY HUTCHINSON (1620–1681)

In 1660 Lucy's worst fears came true. After ascending to the throne of England, Charles II began a campaign to cleanse his ranks of potential traitors. Many of the people who had signed his father's death warrant were arrested and tried. These included John Hutchinson, Lucy's husband of twenty-two years.

Some of the prisoners recanted their views and were freed. John's speech was more ambiguous. "If he had erred," he said of himself, "it was the inexperience of his age, and the defect of his judgment, and not the malice of his heart, which had ever prompted him to pursue the general advantage of his country more than his own." He added that "if the sacrifice of him might conduce to the public peace and settlement, he should freely submit his life and fortunes to their disposal."[1]

But if John was willing to sacrifice his life, Lucy was not willing to let him do it. Until then, she had kept quiet at his request, but she couldn't restrain herself any longer. She took paper and pen and wrote a letter in his name. Initially, she just meant to show it to him, but when two men told her that the judges were leaning in his favor, she delivered it to them. It was the first time she had disobeyed her husband, she said. We don't know what helped to move the heart of

---

1. Lucy Hutchinson, *Memoirs of the Life of Colonel Hutchinson* (London: Henry G. Bohn, 1863), 404.

the judges in John's favor: his speech, her letter, or both. But John and Lucy recognized it was ultimately the Lord's hand, and this realization quieted his heart when he discovered her intervention.

What little peace the Hutchinsons enjoyed, however, ended abruptly three years later with a second arrest—this time completely unjustified. In spite of John's protests of innocence and Lucy's pleadings with the House of Lords, the government kept him locked up in Sandown Castle, Kent, where he died from complications of an illness.

He left behind Lucy and seven of their children: four sons (Thomas, Edward, Lucius, and John) and three daughters (Barbara, Lucy, and Margaret). Two other children, another John and Adeliza, had died in infancy. Like her mother before her, Lucy was left with debts to pay, which she resolved by selling John's properties.

She was also left with the difficult task of consoling her children and clearing John's reputation. To do so, she wrote a long account of the events of their lives during the disastrous English Civil War. This account is greatly appreciated by modern historians not only for the abundance of details but also for the description of how the war affected and disrupted families—hurting the most vulnerable, such as mothers and children.

Lucy decided to start the narrative with an account of her life, as "a means," she said, "to stir up my thankfulness for things past and to encourage my faith for the future." In fact, her entire work can be considered a song of thankfulness, as she ascribed every event to the providence of God—"the Almighty Author of all beings," who "conducts the lives of men from the cradle to the tomb [and in so doing] exercises no less wisdom and goodness than he manifests power and greatness in their creation."[2] It's this constant remembrance of God's wisdom and goodness alongside His power and greatness that allowed Lucy to trust herself to God's providence, which, without this constant realization, could at times seem puzzling or even cruel.

---

2. Hutchinson, *Memoirs*, 1.

GOD'S PROVIDENCE IN LUCY'S LIFE

Lucy saw God's providential work throughout her life. She was born on January 29, 1620, in the Tower of London—the second of ten children. Her father, Allen Apsley, lieutenant of the Tower, had a limited education but provided his children with excellent tutoring. He particularly insisted on giving Lucy a strong foundation in Latin, which was still the gate to higher education.

Lucy's love for learning was impressive. Her mother found it troubling—a little inappropriate for a young girl. She encouraged Lucy to memorize sermons. Lucy complied but continued to read other stories and poems and wrote some of her own.

Apsley died in 1630, leaving the family in debt. Lucy's mother remarried, but the new union was unhappy and ended in separation. Lucy's experience was very similar to what some children of divorced parents have to endure today. She was shifted between different members of her family. Because of financial need, she was pressured to marry soon and well.

But she was not interested in marrying—not until she met her future husband, John. And here is where her education came into play. Before he even met her, John visited her home and became intrigued by her excellent choice of Latin books. Later, when he heard one of her poems being recited in the household of a mutual friend, he became absolutely obsessed with the desire to meet her. This obsession surprised him. He had never felt a pull toward romantic relations. How strange that now he "should have such strong impulses towards a stranger he never saw," Lucy said.[3]

To her, this was an obvious manifestation of God's providential work. "Certainly, it was of the Lord (though he perceived it not), who had ordained him, through so many various providences, to be yoked with her in whom he found so much satisfaction."[4]

The actual meeting didn't disappoint. Love and admiration were mutual, and the couple married on July 3, 1638. The next year, they

---

3. Hutchinson, *Memoirs*, 57.
4. Hutchinson, *Memoirs*, 57.

had twin children, Thomas and Edward, who kept Lucy busy. The others soon followed.

LUCY'S WRITINGS

After her memoirs, Lucy found time to write other works, including a translation of John Owen's Latin work *Theologoumena panto-doupa*, which was meant as an introduction to an explanation of true theology. Most likely Lucy listened to Owen's sermons at the home of a common friend (the 1662 enforcement of the Act of Uniformity had outlawed Puritan preaching) and showed a great admiration for his teachings.

Her beliefs were clearly expressed in a warm letter to her daughter Barbara—an admonition to increase her knowledge of Scripture and stand firm against the proliferation of heretical sects. The letter, posthumously published as *On the Principles of the Christian Religion*, is filled with a mother's concern for her daughter and indicative of Lucy's theological clarity. This letter stresses the gospel as the foundation for our complete trust in God's providence. For example, after a detailed explanation to her daughter of the loving and sacrificial role of each person of the Trinity "in this most admirable and wise design of bringing lost men to glory and communion with God by Jesus Christ," Lucy exclaimed, "This knowledge of God's love to us begets a love of Him in us, and an inexpressible joy in considering Him as our Redeemer, where we behold infinite and eternal wisdom designing our good and our glory, infinite power and goodness executing those councils, and all the glorious attributes of God working for our happiness. Were but our faith herein confirmed, what could we fear? This is the great mystery of God, the true knowledge of which leads to eternal life."[5]

Her most creative work, however, is a biblical poem by a customary lengthy title, *Order and Disorder, or, The World Made and*

---

5. Lucy Hutchinson, *On the Principles of Christian Religion, Addressed to Her Daughter, and on Theology* (London: Longman, Hurst, Rees, Orme, and Brown, 1817), 41.

Undone. Being Meditations upon the Creation and the Fall; as It Is Recorded in the Beginning of Genesis. Published anonymously, this work has been consistently recognized as hers.

The contents of the poem, in five divisions, are apparent in the title, but Lucy's communication of the biblical events is remarkable. This is, for example, how she expressed the astounding revelation of the gospel in Genesis 3:15:

> Thou [Satan] in this war His heel shalt bruise, but He
> Thy head shall break. More various Mystery
> Ne're did within so short a sentence lie.
> Here is irrevocable vengeance, here
> Love as immutable. Here doth appear
> Infinite Wisdom plotting with free grace.[6]

With the gospel came also a prediction of a long-standing war between the Seed of the Woman and the seed of the devil, a war Lucy had experienced in more ways than one, as she clung to the firm promise that, as strong as the forces of evil might seem, "their war must end in final overthrow."[7]

Once again, it's the gospel that gives Lucy faith to trust God's providence, which

> distributes every lot,
> In which th' obedient and the meek rejoyce,
> Above their own preferring Gods wise choice.[8]

According to Lucy, this willingness to prefer God's choice is a product of God's grace, freeing His children

> from Hell's mists which benight the natural mind,
> And lust's strong fetters which the free will bind.

---

6. Lucy Hutchinson, *Order and Disorder* (London: Margaret White for Henry Mortlock, 1679; New York: Bartleby.com, 2009), 5.66–71, https://www.bartleby.com/239/5.html.

7. Hutchinson, *Order and Disorder*, 5.96.

8. Hutchinson, *Order and Disorder*, 5.676–78.

Instead, they are "by soft impulses led."[9] She mentioned this in reference to the animals that God brought to the ark (Gen. 7:1–9). The animals came willingly even though God had planned it all from the beginning.

For Lucy, God is the only "most true substantial good," and the only true ill mankind suffers is "divorce from him by our repugnant will." And yet this divorce doesn't have to continue because God welcomes His children again. That's why Lucy could say,

> Return, return, my soul to thy true rest,
> As young benighted birds unto their nest,
> There hide thy self under the wings of love
> Till the bright morning all thy clouds remove.[10]

For Lucy, that "bright morning" came in October 1681, when she joined the Lord she loved.

FOOD FOR THOUGHT

- In her letter to her daughter, Lucy explained that "nothing is left to hazard, or contingency, or accident, but all is conducted by the providence of God to those just and holy ends He hath appointed, with an unsearchable wisdom and goodness, which we are to believe and rely on in all things, though our narrow understandings cannot penetrate into his mysterious paths till the day of the revelation of the righteous judgment of God, when we shall see a most beautiful order in all those things which now appear so confused to our dim sight."[11] How does knowledge of God and confidence in the perfection of His attributes, especially His wisdom and goodness, help Christians face their various circumstances?

---

9. Lucy Hutchinson, *Order and Disorder*, ed. David Norbrook (Oxford: Blackwell, 2001), 7.353–55.

10. Hutchinson, *Order and Disorder*, 5.697–700.

11. Hutchinson, *On the Principles of Christian Religion*, 28.

• Do you agree with Lucy's rhetorical question, "Were but our faith herein [in the gospel] confirmed, what could we fear?" Explain why.

• Lucy disobeyed her husband in order to save his life. She said it was the first time, and she didn't dare do it again during his second arrest. Although John was clearly displeased, the couple eventually concluded that God had used Lucy's actions for His good purposes. How can a clear understanding of God's providence be a deterrent to the harmful habit of spouses blaming each other for what happens?

• Although Lucy was not excusing her disobedience to her husband, in her poem *Order and Disorder*, she called Rebecca's deceiving Isaac "pious fraud" since Isaac was about to bless Esau, while God had already chosen Jacob as the next patriarch in the messianic line (Gen. 27:5–13). This is a controversial view. What do you think? Should Rebecca have trusted the Lord, even when it looked as if her husband was about to defeat God's purposes?[12] Why or why not?

• Lucy's belief that her memoirs were "a means to stir up [her] thankfulness for things past and to encourage [her] faith for the future" was well founded. The Bible is full of exhortations to remember God's works—especially when one's faith is at low ebb. Tell of some occasions when you found this to be true in your life.

• To Lucy, even human virtues such as courage are gifts of God's providence. In the course of the war, she learned "that the best and highest courages are but the beams of the Almighty; and when He withholds His influence, the brave turn cowards, fear unnerves the most mighty, makes the most generous base, and great men to do those things they blush to think

---

12. See "Jacob Deceives Isaac," Ligonier Ministries, https://www.ligonier.org/learn/devotionals/jacob-deceives-isaac/.

on; when God again inspires, the fearful and the feeble see no dangers, believe no difficulties, and carry on attempts whose very thoughts would, at another time, shiver their joints like agues."[13] What are the benefits of remembering this in our daily lives? Do you find it easy to do so?

FOR FURTHER RESEARCH

The following is a list of Lucy Hutchinson's writings (also available online):

Lucy Hutchinson, *Memoirs of the Life of Colonel Hutchinson* (London: Henry G. Bohn, 1863).

See also Lucy Hutchinson, *The Principles of the Christian Religion* (London: Longman, Hurst, Rees, Orme and Brown, 1817).

There is now also a complete collection of all her works: *The Works of Lucy Hutchinson*, ed. Elizabeth Clarke, David Norbrook, and Jane Stevenson (Oxford: Oxford University Press, 2018).

---

13. Hutchinson, *Memoirs*, 207.

19

Why Am I Troubled?

MARY WHITE ROWLANDSON (ca. 1637–1711)

Mary Rowlandson's account of her experience as a prisoner of war became an immediate best seller. In fact, it was the first best seller in America and the first of what became a popular genre: accounts of captivity among Native American tribes.

Her book—initially written for the benefit of her children—was first published in 1682 with the title *The Soveraignty and Goodness of God, Together with the Faithfulness of His Promises Displayed*. It included a preface—probably written by the well-known pastor Increase Mather—and ended with the last sermon by Mary's first husband on the sovereignty of God. It continued to be a popular book well into the nineteenth century.

Today, her account is often discounted as partial and biased since she calls her captors "ravenous beasts" and "cruel heathens."[1] Her harrowing experience and her candor in describing her actions, feelings, and questions, however, cause most readers to sympathize with her rather than criticize her. Besides, some modern scholars recognize that her description of Algonquian life is fairly accurate, and her account introduces us to both compassionate and cruel captors. In any case, the Algonquians are not the main characters in this tale and

---

1. Mary Rowlandson, *Narrative of the Captivity and Restoration of Mrs. Mary Rowlandson*, Project Gutenberg, 2009, introduction and "The First Remove," http://www.gutenberg.org/files/851/851-h/851-h.htm.

are not mentioned in her conclusion. The protagonist is God. Every event is a part of His purpose in a much larger story, and what mattered to Mary was her response to God's providence in her life.

CAPTIVE

Born around 1637 in Somerset, England, Mary immigrated to America with her family two years later. In Lancaster, Massachusetts, her father, John White, became a successful landowner. Around 1656 Mary married Joseph Rowlandson, the town's pastor, about thirty years older than she. The couple had four children. The oldest, Mary, died just five days past her third birthday. The others were Joseph, another Mary, and Sarah. In spite of common hardships, the Rowlandsons lived a fairly calm and ordinary life.

In 1675 the devastating conflict between New England colonists and several Native American nations (the so-called King Philip's War, after the English name of the Wampanoag chief, Metacom) put an end to the family's peace. The apprehensions that filled the first year of war came to a head on February 10, 1676, at dawn, when Lancaster was attacked by King Philip's confederation.

At first Mary witnessed the raid from her window. She saw homes on fire and people trying to flee. She heard gunshots and cries. Then the Native American warriors came to her house, set it on fire, and shot their guns in all directions. In the end, representatives of the Algonquian tribe captured Mary and her children and led them away to join another group of captives. She and her youngest child, six-year-old Sarah, were wounded.

The trip through the "vast and desolate wilderness" was difficult.[2] Even though the Algonquians tried to accommodate Sarah by having her ride a horse, Mary had to helplessly listen to her persistent cries of pain, "I shall die, I shall die."[3] At the end of the first

---

2. Rowlandson, *Narrative of the Captivity and Restoration*, "The Second Remove."

3. Rowlandson, *Narrative of the Captivity and Restoration*, "The Second Remove."

seemingly interminable day, Mary sat on the snow-covered ground with her feverish child in her arms.

The journey continued northward for over three hundred miles to the Algonquian village of Wenimesset, in today's Worcester County, Massachusetts. By the time they arrived, it was obvious that Sarah would not live much longer. The captors' repeated suggestions to "knock your child on the head"[4] in order to put an end to her pain provided no acceptable option and no comfort to Mary. Finally, Sarah died in her mother's arms, nine days after contracting her wounds.

Mary kept note of everything she experienced and observed. At that time, many Native American nations were suffering deprivations (one of the reasons for the war), which Mary experienced firsthand. She traveled with them from place to place in cold weather, eating foods she would have previously considered unimaginable, such as half-cooked horse liver, horse's feet, and bear meat, and working as a slave for an Indian squaw. Her ability with needle and thread increased her value, and she was often able to make clothes in exchange for food.

The Algonquians allowed her to keep a Bible they had taken, among other things, from the village, and she read it avidly. Some portions, such as Deuteronomy 28, persuaded her that the calamity that had fallen on their village was a result of their sins. Deuteronomy 30, however, provided assurance of God's mercy and unbreakable promises. "I do not desire to live to forget this Scripture, and what comfort it was to me," she wrote.[5]

SURVIVOR

Mary's captivity lasted about eleven weeks. On May 2, 1676, she was ransomed and reunited with her husband. Her two surviving

---

4. Rowlandson, *Narrative of the Captivity and Restoration*, "The Third Remove."

5. Rowlandson, *Narrative of the Captivity and Restoration*, "The Third Remove."

children, who had been separated from their mother for most of their captivity, were released a few months later.

After a brief period in Boston, Mary spent the rest of her life in Wethersfield, Connecticut, where her husband was called as pastor. He died in 1678 at sixty-eight years of age. The following year she married Captain Samuel Talcott, one of the administrators of Joseph Rowlandson's estate. Talcott was a widower with six sons and two daughters. No children were born from Mary's marriage to Talcott, who died in 1691. She survived him by twenty years.

While some things returned to normal, much of Mary's life was no longer the same. For at least some time, she couldn't sleep peacefully at night. "When all are fast about me," she wrote, "and no eye open, but His who ever waketh, my thoughts are upon things past, upon the awful dispensation of the Lord towards us, upon His wonderful power and might, in carrying of us through so many difficulties, in returning us in safety, and suffering none to hurt us."[6]

She concluded her book with reflections that are reminiscent of Ecclesiastes:

> I have seen the extreme vanity of this world: One hour I have been in health, and wealthy, wanting nothing. But the next hour in sickness and wounds, and death, having nothing but sorrow and affliction.... The Lord hath showed me the vanity of these outward things. That they are the vanity of vanities, and vexation of spirit, that they are but a shadow, a blast, a bubble, and things of no continuance. That we must rely on God Himself, and our whole dependence must be upon Him.[7]

She pondered the nature of suffering:

> The portion of some is to have their afflictions by drops, now one drop and then another; but the dregs of the cup, the wine of astonishment, like a sweeping rain that leaveth no food, did

---

6. Rowlandson, *Narrative of the Captivity and Restoration*, "The Twentieth Remove."

7. Rowlandson, *Narrative of the Captivity and Restoration*, "The Twentieth Remove."

the Lord prepare to be my portion.... Yet I see, when God calls a person to anything, and through never so many difficulties, yet He is fully able to carry them through and make them see, and say they have been gainers thereby.[8]

These reflections changed her view of daily obstacles: "If trouble from smaller matters begin to arise in me, I have something at hand to check myself with, and say, why am I troubled? It was but the other day that if I had had the world, I would have given it for my freedom, or to have been a servant to a Christian. I have learned to look beyond present and smaller troubles, and to be quieted under them. As Moses said, 'Stand still and see the salvation of the Lord' (Exodus 14.13)."[9]

FOOD FOR THOUGHT

- Mary's abduction and captivity changed her life. After she returned home, her daily troubles looked small in comparison to what she had experienced. If the Lord kept and delivered her from a seemingly inescapable situation, she believed that He would continue to sustain her and deliver her throughout life. Discuss a time when you came to a similar realization after a difficult trial.

- Mary's understanding of all temporal things as vanity led her to place all her dependence on God. When the things around us grow in importance in our lives, we tend to lose sight of God. When has this happened in your life?

- During her captivity, Mary was puzzled by the way God provided for the needs of the Algonquians, in spite of their recent violence. Think of some Bible passages in which the biblical

---

8. Rowlandson, *Narrative of the Captivity and Restoration*, "The Twentieth Remove."

9. Rowlandson, *Narrative of the Captivity and Restoration*, "The Twentieth Remove."

authors express the same puzzlement at God's preservation of those who appear most wicked. How did these authors resolve this perplexity? In hindsight, can you see some good reasons why God preserved the Algonquians and provided for their needs?

• During her captivity, Mary read her Bible and tried to make sense of what had happened to her and her family. She was convicted of her sins while reading Deuteronomy 28 but rejoiced in the gospel promises of Deuteronomy 30—so much that she intended to remember them forever. In what other Bible passages have you noticed this frequent pattern of law and gospel?

• After her deliverance, Mary stopped talking about the Algonquians and focused on the lessons she learned from her experience. Was this a wise thing to do, or would there have been a better way to deal with this?

FOR FURTHER RESEARCH

For the full text of Mary Rowlandson's book, see Mary Rowlandson, *Narrative of the Captivity and Restoration of Mrs. Mary Rowlandson*, Project Gutenberg, 2009, introduction and "The First Remove," http://www.gutenberg.org/files/851/851-h/851-h.htm.

20

Can Women Write about Theology?

ANNE DUTTON (ca. 1692–1765)

From the time of her youth in seventeenth-century Northampton, England, Anne was described as a lively and outspoken girl. Over the course of her life, she combined this zeal and candor with her natural clarity of thought and expression in order to provide scriptural encouragement and advice.

Her endeavors raised quite a few eyebrows. Was it proper for a woman to provide counsel to others—men included—especially when this counsel was published for all to read? Anne offered a well-considered and coherent reply.

A LIFE MOVED WITH PASSION FOR THE GOSPEL

Anne Dutton was born into the Williams family in Northampton, England. According to her gravestone, her birth occurred in 1691/1692, but her memoirs point to 1695. Raised in a Baptist family, she blossomed under the ministry of John Moore, in which she found "fat, green pastures. The doctrines of the Gospel were clearly stated," she said, "and much insisted on in his ministry."[1]

In 1715 Anne married Thomas Cattell, a congregant at her church. Soon after that, apparently for business reasons, the couple moved to London and joined the Baptist church in Cripplegate. The

---

1. J. A. Jones, "Memoir of Mrs. Anne Dutton," in Anne Dutton, *A Narration of the Wonders of Grace* (London: John Bennett, 1833), xiii.

minister there, John Skepp, preached "with abundance of glory, life, and power," the same "free grace" that had given Anne so much encouragement and hope.[2]

Sadly, Thomas died unexpectedly in 1720, causing Anne to return to her family in Northampton. It was a difficult time for Anne, who found comfort in remembering that God is not only all powerful but all merciful and does all things for the good of His children.

Soon after her arrival in Northampton, Benjamin Dutton, a clothier who had studied to become a minister of the gospel, asked for her hand in marriage. He explained his choice by saying that she would make "a brave minister's wife."[3] Her beauty might have played a part, as it was later praised even by some of her critics. She accepted the proposal, and the two married the following year. Soon after their marriage, Benjamin was licensed to preach and started to bring the gospel in different places.

Anne moved around with her husband. It was a difficult time, mostly due to her poor health. She also didn't see her husband much because of his travels. To make ends meet, once he had to serve two different churches at the same time. His struggle with alcoholism was an additional challenge. Overall, it was also a time of reflection, when Anne started to write some meditations in order to remember what God was teaching her.

In 1728 the couple moved to Wellingborough, a town where they had earlier spent a couple of months and where Anne had been spiritually thriving under the ministry of William Grant. Benjamin began to assist Benjamin Winckles, pastor of a church in nearby Armsby, in bringing the gospel to the area between Armsby and Wellingborough. Winckles was a kind man who encouraged Dutton in his battle against addiction and defended him against the censure of unforgiving Christians. He eventually recovered, but not without a fierce fight.

---

2. Jones, "Memoir," in Dutton, *Narration of the Wonders of Grace*, xiii.

3. Benjamin Dutton, *The Superaboundings of the Exceeding Riches of God's Free-grace, Towards the Chief of the Chief of Sinners Shewn Forth in the Lord's Gracious Dealings with…Benjamin Dutton* (London: J. Hart, 1743), 129.

Around 1731 Benjamin was called to be the pastor of the Baptist chapel in Great Gransden, Huntingdonshire, where the couple stayed for the rest of their lives. Anne, who continued to be childless, devoted much time to writing letters and essays with the encouragement of her husband, her "dear Yokefellow," as she called him.[4]

It was Benjamin who, in 1740, urged her to publish these writings. She agreed, seeing her writing as a ministry to others and a way to use her God-given talents for His glory. In the meantime, the church in Great Gransden was growing, so much that in 1743 they built a new meetinghouse and minister's house.

The same year, Benjamin traveled to America to raise funds for the building and took Anne's books with him as tools for the encouragement of others. He stayed there until 1747. Anne was encouraged by his success but missed him terribly and was concerned for their pastorless church. They expected him back every year, but each time there was some impediment.

In 1747 she heard that a ship carrying her husband had finally returned, but she didn't hear from him for six months. "This try'd me exceedingly," she said.[5] Finally, a letter came, but it didn't bring good news. "Instead of my husband's safe return, I heard of his Death, and that he was cast away on his Passage home, by the foundering of the Ship! How grieving was this to Nature! How trying to my Faith and Hope! The real loss of my dear Yokefellow; the seeming Denial of my earnest Prayers; and the Failure of my Expectation, as to his Return."[6]

Anne stayed in Great Gransden, where she was comforted by the arrival of another good minister, and continued to write. In 1764 she began suffering from a throat condition that prevented her from swallowing food, which might have been cancer. In any case, she knew her life was not going to last much longer. With this thought in mind, she worked sixteen to eighteen hours per day in order to

---

4. Anne Dutton, *The Autobiography*, vol. 3 of *Selected Spiritual Writings of Anne Dutton*, ed. Joann Ford Watson (Macon, Ga.: Mercer University Press, 2006), xliv, for example.

5. Dutton, *Autobiography*, 242.

6. Dutton, *Autobiography*, 243.

prepare eight volumes of her unpublished letters for publication. She died the following year.

ANNE'S PURPOSE FOR WRITING

Anne's published work, over fifty volumes of poetry, letters, hymns, treatises, and an autobiography, attracted the censure of some who thought writing for publication was improper for a woman. This concern was compounded by the fact that many of her letters contained advice to men, including ministers such as John Wesley, George Whitefield, and Philip Doddridge.

Her reply, attached to the autobiography, includes four arguments of defense. First, she wrote only to the glory of God and for the benefit of others. Second, she believed that the publication of her writings was "not against any of the Laws of Christ in the sacred Records."[7] The biblical references to women being silent in the church in 1 Timothy 2:12 and 1 Corinthians 14:34–35, she said, speak specifically of "Publick Authoritative Teaching in the Church" and do not include personal writings.[8]

Her third argument rested on the biblical exhortation to edify one another (Rom. 14:19). She believed this command was given to all, male and female. "And unless women were excluded from being members of Christ's mystical body," she said, "their usefulness, in all due means, ought not to be hindered."[9]

Finally, her writings were meant to be read privately by people at home. She brought up the biblical example of Priscilla teaching Apollos in a private setting (Acts 18:26).

Thankfully, Anne also had many supporters, including her husband and other ministers. Whitefield, for example, was convinced that her lucid, warm, and scripturally grounded way of writing provided invaluable counsel and strength to many people.

---

7. Dutton, *Autobiography*, xlvi.
8. Dutton, *Autobiography*, xlvi.
9. Dutton, *Autobiography*, xlvii.

THE VALUE OF HER WRITINGS

Anne's theological writings and letters of advice were greatly esteemed in her day, even though she often had to publish them anonymously or under the initials A. D. because few printers were willing to publish works by a woman.

Some of her most vibrant theological works are the ones addressed to those who, in her view, had fallen prey to false doctrines. In these, she showed not only a clear understanding of Scripture and of the gospel, but also the vigor that springs from it—which stood in opposition to some people's suggestions that a belief in God's unconditional grace made people lazy.

Anne deeply cherished this belief in God's unconditional grace. She understood that, due to original sin, men and women are born spiritually dead with no ability to choose God, let alone to save themselves. She was convinced this is what the Bible taught, and that the whole work of salvation, from the initial election to the final glorification, rests completely on God.

On this issue she disagreed with Wesley, who rejected the idea of God's predestinating grace and believed that human beings are responsible for choosing God by an act of their own will and guarding their faith throughout their lives. She particularly disagreed with his teaching that Christians can reach perfection in this life and must strive to do so.

Wesley interpreted her opposition as an indication that she had not yet "crucified the flesh with its affections and lusts."[10] Her reply is a testimony to the extent to which her assurance of God's grace had permeated her life.

If she had not yet crucified the flesh, Anne said, it meant she didn't yet belong to Christ. "But oh! for ever adored be Free-Grace," she said, "the boundless Grace and Faithfulness of my God, my Interest in Christ, is not so soon destroy'd in itself, as it is by your Affection. No, blessed be God, that stands firmer than Heaven and

---

10. John Wesley, *The Works of John Wesley: Letters II, 1740–1755* (Oxford: Clarendon Press, 1982), 15.

Earth, upon the solid Basis of the eternal Will, immutable Covenant, Word, and Oath of a God that cannot lie!"[11]

In other words, she believed that her flesh *had been* crucified because of Christ and not through any effort of her own. This doesn't mean that she didn't believe in fighting sin. She devoted many letters to this subject. But she saw this struggle to fight sin and to obey God as a natural, grateful response to God's grace that will continue throughout our earthly lives, finding perfection only in the next.

One of the most prevalent themes in her writings is her Trinitarian understanding of the Christian life and faith. Her work in this respect is both similar and complementary to John Owen's *On Communion with the Triune God*, which she knew and quoted. Her strength lies in her ability to communicate in practical and vibrant terms the ways in which each person of the Trinity operates in the great work of redemption and the ways in which this understanding enriches a Christian's daily life.

Her writings also show great wisdom and compassion. For example, when Howell Harris, a leader of the Methodist revival in Wales, asked her to write a tract to reprove backsliding Christians, she didn't write as sharply as he would have liked, explaining that—after all—both wise and foolish virgins were sleeping. "There needs a great deal of spiritual wisdom," she said, "to cry aloud against sin without wounding the faith of God's dear children, as to their interest in Christ and his Salvation."[12]

And her ministry to others was not limited to her correspondence. "Visiting the Saints is one of the Duties of Love we owe them," she wrote in a "Letter to All the Saints." "They that fear the Lord, should speak often to one another.... And let us not make Excuses,

---

11. Anne Dutton, *Letters*, vol. 1 of *Selected Spiritual Writings of Anne Dutton*, ed. JoAnn Ford Watson (Macon, Ga.: Mercer University Press, 2003), 7.

12. Anne Dutton to Howell Harris (letter 921), July 13, 1743, The National Library of Wales, Aberystwyth, UK, as quoted in Michael Sciretti, "Anne Dutton as a Spiritual Director," *Christian Reflection: A Series in Faith and Ethics*, Center for Christian Ethics at Baylor University, 2009.

that we han't Time, etc. Short visits well improv'd, are far preferable to long ones misimprov'd."[13]

Besides her service as an apologist, adviser, and comforter, Anne provided great inspiration to other women of her time, including Selina Hastings and Ann Steele, the famous hymn writer who inherited Anne's Bible and continued much of her work of encouragement to others.

FOOD FOR THOUGHT

- Anne believed that the biblical references to women being silent in the church (1 Tim. 2:12 and 1 Cor. 14:34–35) speak about "Publick Authoritative Teaching in the Church,"[14] and not about personal writings. Most Christians today hold to this belief. What is your opinion?

- Anne also believed that the exhortation to edify one another (Rom. 14:19) was given to all, male and female.[15] What do you think? List some other commandments that are given to all Christians, both men and women. What commandments make a distinction between men and women?

- Wesley explained his belief in earthly perfection by defining *perfection* as "completion" rather than lack of error. Even so, Anne stood by her conviction that all of salvation, including the progressive work of sanctification—whether it leads to completion or actual perfection—rests entirely on the faithfulness of God in Christ and not on a person's individual

13. Anne Dutton, *Miscellaneous Correspondence*, vol. 5 of *Selected Spiritual Writings of Anne Dutton*, ed. JoAnn Ford Watson (Macon, Ga.: Mercer University Press, 2007), 90.

14. Dutton, *Autobiography*, xlvi.

15. Anne was not the first one to hold this conviction. We still have letters from many Christian women who exhorted, admonished, and instructed Christian men. For example, Olympia Morata wrote a fervent letter of admonition to a pastor who had become an alcoholic.

efforts. Explain how these different views of salvation can generate different views of the Christian life.

FOR FURTHER RESEARCH

For a full study of Anne Dutton and her thought, see Anne Dutton, *Selected Spiritual Writings*, 6 vols., ed. JoAnn Ford Watson (Macon, Ga.: Mercer University Press, 2003–2007).

For a short survey of her life and thought, see Michael Haykin, "Anne Dutton and Her Theological Work," in *Eight Women of Faith* (Wheaton, Ill.: Crossway, 2016), 53–66.

For a short article on Benjamin Dutton, see Simonetta Carr, "The Familiar Case of Benjamin Dutton," *Cloud of Witnesses* (blog), Place for Truth: Biblical Doctrine from the Alliance of Confessing Evangelicals, July 28, 2020, https://www.placefortruth.org/blog/the-familiar-case-of -benjamin-dutton.

21

Can I Marry a Nonbeliever?

KATA BETHLEN (1700–1759)

Kata Bethlen started her autobiography with her most painful memory: her forced marriage, at age seventeen, to her Roman Catholic half brother.

Her family—one of the wealthiest and most influential in Transylvania—had firmly adhered for generations to the tenets of the Protestant Reformation. In fact, her ancestors had contributed to the creation of the independent Transylvanian state, a small but staunch Reformed region surrounded by powerful Roman Catholic and Muslim nations.

In 1711, the Roman Catholic Hapsburgs imposed their rule over Transylvania. Kata's uncle, Miklós Bethlen (1642–1716), one of the last "freedom fighters," spent his last years in prison and exile.

A PAINFUL MARRIAGE

Kata inherited the religious zeal of her forefathers, and the idea of marrying a Roman Catholic was distressing and frightening. Her protests proved futile, as did her brothers'. Her mother, Borbála Nagy, had made up her mind.

Kata's prospective husband was Count László Haller, a son of Borbála's second husband—also a Roman Catholic. László was a nice young man with a happy disposition and a healthy sense of humor. What's more, he was sincerely in love with Kata.

He would have made a great husband if it hadn't been for his religion. Kata knew the biblical warnings against marrying outside of one's faith but couldn't see a way out, especially when Borbála reinforced her parental authority with a threat: if Kata refused the engagement ring, she would no longer be her daughter.

Kata found the pressure overwhelming. She didn't want to displease her mother. Besides, the idea of being sent out without any form of support was frightening. Most of all, she felt completely unprepared to make such a serious decision.

"What then could I do?" she wondered. "I dared not so much as reply and accepted the ring. Oh, hapless hour, which for others obtains such joy, but to me brought unspeakable bitterness and sorrow." That night she couldn't sleep, tormented by the prospect of a union so deeply divided and of the "poisonous fruits of this type of marriage."[1] Her worst fears materialized. Immediately after the wedding, the local father superior came to pressure her to convert. Kata held her own.

Her husband's family was a tougher foe. She was in bed, feeling ill after delivering twin boys, when the family staged what we would call an intervention to persuade László to act quickly—before she could negatively influence her children. "They asked him in the course of conversation if there might be any hope in my regard," Kata recalled, "that he might be able to make me leave my religion. He replied that he had observed no inclination in me. At that, one and another instructed him what he should do with me, the more speedily to change my mind."[2]

Her sister-in-law gave specific instructions. László had to be forceful, even cruel. Since Kata's mother had died and her brothers were away, she had no one to run to. He should use sleep deprivation, knocking at her door when she was tired, then give her the silent treatment. If she inquired about his bad mood, he should answer, "I

---

1. Kata Bethlen, *A Short Description of the Life of the Countess Kata Bethlen by Herself: Written in Transylvania in the 1740s*, trans. Bernard Adams (Lincolnshire, UK: Shaun Tyas, 2004), 18.

2. Bethlen, *Short Description*, 24.

have cause enough to be ill humoured, and shall never be otherwise until you leave your religion!"[3]

HOPE FOR AN ANTAGONISTIC HUSBAND

László's conscience must have told him this was not a good idea. Even a local priest confirmed that it would only alienate Kata. In spite of this, László tried it out. When Kata threatened to leave him, he relented and asked for her forgiveness.

He never again tried to convert her, although the twins—Sámuel and Pál—were baptized as Roman Catholics. László warned the religious authorities to leave Kata alone. After this, she began to nurture strong hopes for her husband's salvation. Soon, he began to read her Bible daily—a Magyar translation by the Reformer Gáspar Károli.

Their marital bliss didn't last long. In 1719 László fell prey to an outbreak of pestilence. Kata stayed by his bed, keeping him in prayer and reminding him that eternal life could be obtained only "through the perfect satisfaction and intercession of Jesus Christ alone, putting away all confidence in his own merit and the prayers of saints."[4] After some time, he became delirious and couldn't recognize anyone. His last words were the Apostles' Creed in song. He died without any Roman Catholic ceremony and left Kata with the twins and pregnant with a baby girl, Borbála. Sámuel died a year later when he was only two.

For a while László's family left Kata alone, thanks to the intervention of two brothers-in-law, who defended her interests in spite of their religious differences. "I bless my good God," she wrote, "who exercised His mercy upon me, ordaining that I should live a life free of affliction among kinsfolk of foreign religion, and not permitting that the poison of evil tongues should harm me."[5]

---

3. Bethlen, *Short Description*, 25.
4. Bethlen, *Short Description*, 28.
5. Bethlen, *Short Description*, 32.

NEW CONFLICTS

When Kata remarried in 1722, however, some members of László's family claimed the customary right to keep her two remaining children. She fought back, supported by her second husband, Count József Teleki, and by most of the people in her village. As it often happened with complaints leveled by the nobility, her case reached the imperial court, which concurred with László's family.

"In this way were my children taken from me," Kata wrote, "that I might not bring them up under the care of a mother in accordance with my religion. I had so many grievous thoughts and severe afflictions on account of that affair that my heart all but melted within me, but the merciful God extended consolation to me even in such a condition."[6]

József Teleki was a widower, twenty-six years older than Kata, and shared her religious beliefs. The couple had three children, Zsigmond, Gábor, and Klára, who died in the summer of 1731 from a widespread epidemic. Zsigmond, who was already eight years old, was able to console his parents before he died, reminding them of God's promises, which he had memorized.

But their sorrows were not over. József's health was very poor, and he died the next year, leaving Kata alone. "My God left me alone as a cottage in the plucked vineyard," she said.[7] From then on, she affixed the word *arva* (orphan) to her name.

She later moved to a property she had inherited from her family. Even there troubles persisted, as she had to battle with ill health and defend her properties against both the unfair legal claims of her in-laws and sudden disasters, such as a fire that burned down her house, leaving her temporarily homeless and destitute. "I have been like Moses' thorn-bush," she said later at the beginning of her autobiography, "which, although it burned with a fierce fire, nevertheless was not consumed."[8]

---

6. Bethlen, *Short Description*, 40.
7. Bethlen, *Short Description*, 44. A reference to Isa. 1:8.
8. Bethlen, *Short Description*, 14.

One of the most painful events of this time was the opposition of her daughter Borbála, who called her a heretic and a persecutor of Roman Catholics, all while pretending to be her friend. In her defense, Kata explained that she was not a heretic but followed the religion of the apostles. As for persecuting Catholics, no Protestant in Transylvania had the power to do so. But even if they did, "it would not accord with the faith and religion of true Protestants to persecute anyone for their religion, for God grants lordship over souls to no power but Himself."[9] Thankfully, Kata's son Pál, in spite of being faithful to the Roman Catholic religion in which he was raised, stood up for Kata.

KATA'S WORK FOR THE HUNGARIAN REFORMATION

In spite of all these problems, she devoted time and resources to projects that were dear to her heart: founding and maintaining Reformed churches and schools (including a school for girls), publishing Reformed writings in Hungarian, building a library (one of the largest of her time), and supporting Reformed preachers. Among the books she led to publication are two of her own religious works: *Memories of Exile* (1733) and *Strong, Protecting Shield* (1759).

She also worked to improve the region where she lived, creating gardens and shops for the production of paper, embroideries, and glassworks. She studied medicine and science in order to help the community with their medical and farming needs.

Two of her protégés were the Reformed pastors Mihály Aitai and Péter Bod, who studied at Leiden with her support. In 1743, Bod became Kata's personal chaplain. In the end, her daughter reconciled with her, and Kata was able to enjoy some peace, surrounded by the love of her close relatives, including her brothers. After her death in 1759, Bod published her autobiography, which included some letters and prayers.

Kata's writings are pregnant with a sense of God's sovereign wisdom and care for His own, in both comfortable and trying

---

9. Bethlen, *Short Description*, 83.

circumstances. Her style is both elegant and colloquial, marked by a refreshing honesty about her feelings and shortcomings.

The account is vivid and moving, interspersed with prayers and expressions of praise, which are as frequent and natural as her thoughts. Fully persuaded that her sins merited far worse than her misfortunes, she asked God for the strength to persevere: "Don't let me retreat from the hope that is placed on you," she wrote in a poem in 1743. "Rather, relight my heart, that I may keep knocking at the door of grace."[10] It is a prayer that God fully answered.

FOOD FOR THOUGHT

- Kata succumbed to her mother's insistence and married a nonbeliever. Although he eventually became a Christian, she had to suffer much in the process. Normally, Christians have taken 2 Corinthians 6:14 ("Be ye not unequally yoked together with unbelievers") as an injunction not to marry a spouse who doesn't share the same faith, just like the ancient Jews were not supposed to marry people from other nations. What is the wisdom of this commandment?

- During her difficult life, Kata asked God to keep her hope alive and to allow her to "keep knocking at the door of grace." How does the realization that even our recourse to God's grace is a gift of God, who keeps our faith and hope alive, a comfort in life's hard times?

FOR FURTHER RESEARCH

For the full version of Kata's memoirs, see Countess Kata Bethlen, *A Short Description of the Life of the Countess Kata Bethlen by Herself*, trans. Bernard Adams (Lincolnshire, UK: Shaun Tyas, 2004).

---

10. Jean de Saint Blanquat, "Kata Bethlen l'orpheline," *Foi & Vie* (2010/2): 75, Academia, https://www.academia.edu/10354416/Kata_Bethlen_lorpheline?auto=download.

For another story on the difficult decision to disobey a parent who orders something that is contrary to God's will, see Agnes Beaumont, *The Narrative of the Persecutions of Agnes Beaumont*, ed. Vera J. Camden (East Lansing, Mich.: Colleagues Press, 1992); summarized in Simonetta Carr, "Agnes Beaumont and Her Fateful Ride," July 30, 2019, *Cloud of Witnesses* (blog), Place for Truth, https://www.placefortruth.org/blog/agnes-beaumont-and-her-fateful-ride.

22

Can I Be a Secret Christian?

MARIE DURAND (1711–1776)

Marie Durand was born on July 15, 1711, in the French village of Bouschet de Pranles. Largely unknown outside France, she is remembered for her steadfastness to her faith while imprisoned for thirty-eight years in the Tower of Constance. In fact, she has become a symbol of resistance and was held up as an example during the Nazi occupation of France.

POLITICAL RESISTANCE

There is more to her story. She was born at a difficult time in the history of the French Protestants, who were also known as Huguenots. Just a year before her birth, a Protestant armed rebellion against an abusive government had come to a definite end.

The rebellion was in many ways justified. In 1685 King Louis XIV revoked Henry IV's Edict of Nantes, which granted some freedom of worship and civil and political rights to French Protestants. Louis ordered all Protestant churches to be destroyed, pastors to be banned from the country, their properties confiscated, and their children left in the care of Roman Catholic families. Their congregations were forbidden to leave the country. They had to stay and become Roman Catholics. It was then that some Protestants started their rebellion. The actual war lasted only two years (1702–1704), but individual battles continued until 1710.

THE ENLIGHTENMENT
AND THE FRENCH REVOLUTION

The persecuted Huguenots received much support from French philoso-phers of the Enlightenment, such as Voltaire and Jean-Jacques Rousseau. While disagreeing with the main tenets of Christianity (Voltaire ques-tioned the goodness of God while Rousseau defended the innate goodness of man), they defended Protestants from a human rights perspective.

Naturally, the Huguenots were grateful to these men. With time, how-ever, the church felt compelled to meet the philosophers' standards and to formulate a more rational and practical religious creed focusing on love for humankind and minimizing the mysteries of the faith. It didn't help that Swiss churches already had been abandoning many tenets of the historical creeds and confessions, favoring a new catechism by Jean-Frédérick Ostervald that compromised many important doctrines, such as justification by faith alone and the Trinity.

As time went on, Paul Rabaut firmly opposed these changes. "I will not reject a mystery for the only reason that it cannot be understood," he wrote. Regrettably, some of the most fervent promoters of the new direction of the church were the sons of Antoine Court and Paul Rabaut—Antoine Court de Gébelin and Jean-Paul Rabaut Saint-Étienne. Deeply concerned, Paul Rabaut wrote in 1776, "This freedom for which so many of our people yearn, I fear it as much as I desire it." Still, he concluded, "I have no trouble putting my fate in the hands of Wise Providence."

His fears were justified, as the French Revolution turned fiercely against the Christians who had fully subscribed to the ideals of the Enlightenment at the expense of their historical creeds and confes-sions. On December 5, 1793, Jean-Paul Rabaut Saint-Étienne, who had become a member of the French convention, was arrested, prosecuted, and executed by the new revolutionary government. After erecting in the Cathedral of Notre Dame, Paris, a statue to Reason, the new regime proceeded to close down churches and monasteries, destroy religious monuments, and persecute all religions.

Marie's parents were Protestants but rejected violent methods of resistance. In order to stay alive, they made some concessions, allowing a Roman Catholic baptism of their children and sending their son, Pierre, to the local school, which was under Roman Catholic instruction. At home, however, they read from the Bible, a Protestant (most likely Genevan) catechism, a psalter, and a few other Christian books.

In spite of constant danger, they even attended clandestine worship meetings until a meeting was raided in 1719 and Marie's mother, Claudine, was arrested. She never came back, and no one knows what happened to her. Pierre also disappeared.

RELIGIOUS ORTHODOXY

A few months later, Marie and her father, Étienne, received news from Pierre. He had escaped to Switzerland, where he wanted to study for the pastorate. It was not a sudden decision. He had been talking to Huguenot pastors for a while. The time just seemed ripe.

In Switzerland, Pierre met other young men who were concerned about the lack of ordained pastors and the disorganization of the French church. Many French preachers had no training, and extemporary "prophecies" had taken prominence over a thoughtful study of God's Word. The French Reformers in Switzerland found this situation more dangerous than persecution.

Antoine Court, the most prominent of these reformers, organized a synod to discuss these and other problems, such as the convening of regular worship meetings, the restoration of church discipline, and the establishment of consistories and synods. Pierre adhered to this agenda wholeheartedly, becoming an ordained minister in 1726 and devoting his life to the faithful preaching of the gospel in France. It was an extremely dangerous task, especially after 1724, when the new king of France, Louis XV, ordered the execution of all Protestant preachers.

In 1729 a troop of soldiers raided Étienne's house, searching for any evidence of Pierre's presence. Étienne was arrested and was asked to write a letter to his son to persuade him to resign and recant his faith. Étienne obliged, putting Pierre in a difficult situation. In the end, Pierre chose to continue to preach.

MARIE'S ROLE

What about Marie? She was alone for a few months, until she accepted a marriage proposal from a family friend. It is not known if the marriage took place or if the couple was just engaged. In any case, their joy didn't last long. On July 14, 1730, one day short of Marie's nineteenth birthday, the couple was arrested, simply because of their ties to Pierre. Marie was imprisoned in the Tower of Constance, an ancient fortress in the southern town of Aigues-Mortes.

This is where we first hear her voice, in her letters to friends and especially to her niece Anne, Pierre's daughter, who became an orphan after her father's execution in 1732 and her mother's death in 1747. Many of Marie's letters were also addressed to prominent politicians and to Protestant churches in request for help or in gratefulness for their assistance. She was probably the most literate of the women in prison, and she used her skills to lead devotions, teach the young children who were born in the Tower, and write letters to raise awareness of the women's condition and ask for provisions and relief.

"We are surrounded by darkness, smoke choking us," she wrote to a prominent lady at the royal court, most likely Madame de Pompadour, a favorite of Louis XV. "It is the horror of horrors, we could say early hell...in order to follow the divine principles of a religion which commands us to render unto Caesar what belongs to Caesar and to God what is God's."[1]

---

1. Étienne Gamonnet, *Lettres de Marie Durand (1711–1776): Prisonière à la Tour de Constance de 1730 à 1768* (Montpellier, France: Nouvelles Presses du Languedoc, 1998), 161.

THE TOWER OF CONSTANCE

The Tower of Constance is located in a swamp full of disease-carrying mosquitoes in southern France near the town of Aigues-Mortes (French for "dead waters"). Initially built as a fortress, from 1686 onward it was used as a prison for Huguenots who refused to convert to Roman Catholicism.

The building consisted of two main levels, with a tower on top. The prisoners' hall was a large room on the middle level. Light came from a large grated hole in the ceiling and some narrow openings in the walls. The same openings also let in snow in the winter and rain and malaria-carrying mosquitoes in the summer. The place was so humid that the firewood was often wet and filled the room with thick smoke. On some occasions, the prisoners were allowed to go on the terrace, a flat, open space at the top of the tower, to get some fresh air.

Each prisoner had a bench covered with straw, a sheet, and a blanket. The prison provided water and a pound and a half of bread per person. Through her letters, Marie was able to solicit other provisions from friends, such as rice, beans, lard, and chestnuts (a main product of the region). Gifts of cloth and yarn allowed the women to repair their clothes.

As it was for most prisoners, Marie's health suffered greatly from the unhealthy environment. She suffered from rheumatism, sinus infections, and possibly malaria. Marie's best friend Isabeau had a mental health crisis when her son was taken from her. Young girls who were imprisoned with their mothers usually stayed in the Tower, while young boys were taken away after weaning and sent to live with relatives or other families. Isabeau's separation from her son came right after news that her husband had died in another prison. By the time Isabeau left the prison, her mind was unable to function well.

Her correspondence allowed her to stay in touch with pastors who sent letters of encouragement and guidance to the women. For example, Antoine Court reminded the female prisoners who had been "prophetesses" in the rebellion: "Occupy yourselves with things that are good and holy. Nourish your souls with sound things, with the Word of God, and stop running after the fantasies which you have so often proven to be vanity and nothing. Only the Word of

God can make you wise, teach you, and make you succeed in every good work."[2]

The most constant pastoral counsel came from Paul Rabaut, a French pastor who had been trained in Court's seminary and remained faithful to Protestant orthodoxy against attempts to dilute the message and edit the catechisms. While forced into hiding, Rabaut was also able to meet influential political leaders who in 1768, after a long battle, ensured the freedom of the imprisoned women.

Marie spent her last days in her family home, where she died in 1776. She was supported until the end by a French church in Amsterdam.

Today, she is rightly remembered for her persistence in her religious convictions, which was truly admirable, given that she was surrounded not only by disease, death, and despair but also by frequent pressure to recant. But it's also important to remember her and her family as protagonists of a courageous time of French revival that, unlike some modern forms of revival, aimed at recovering the Reformed tradition and protecting the church from private and arbitrary biblical interpretations.

FOOD FOR THOUGHT

- Marie could have easily recanted her faith, only to resume it later. Other Christians did it. In fact, the women had many opportunities to leave. At one point, the Tower's supervisor, moved by the women's pleas, gave them a way out: They didn't have to renounce their faith. They just had to say they were sorry and ask for the king's forgiveness. Most of the women refused even this offer. What do you think kept them from resorting to these ways of escape?

In a letter to her niece, Marie said,

---

2. *Bulletin historique et littéraire* (Société de l'Histoire du Protestantisme Français) (Paris: Librairie Sandoz et Fischbacher, 1881), 30:511.

The times seem long and, in fact, they are. Our flesh complains because we are naturally impatient but, my dear girl, let's put to death our evil desires (Col. 3:5). Let's be the violent to take heaven by force (Matt. 11:12). Let's seek the kingdom of God and His righteousness, and all these things will be added unto us (Matt. 6:33). Let's forsake our ways and return to the Lord who, in His greatest wrath, remembers mercy (Hab. 3:2).[3]

How did these verses comfort Marie during her thirty-eight years in prison?

FOR FURTHER RESEARCH

There are currently no full biographies of Marie Durand in English, although at least two are under way. French speakers can read Étienne Gamonnet, *Lettres de Marie Durand (1711–1776): Prisonière à la Tour de Constance de 1730 à 1768* (Montpellier, France: Nouvelles Presses du Languedoc, 1998), which includes accurate biographical notes; and Frédéric Mayor, *La famille Durand du Bouschet de Pranles* (Lyons, France: Réveil, 1984).

For an excellent overview of Marie's time, see Geoffrey Adams, *The Huguenots and French Opinion 1685–1787* (Waterloo, Ont.: Wilfrid Laurier University Press, 1991).

To have a better understanding of the church in Marie's time, see Martin Klauber, *The Theology of the French Reformed Churches: From Henry IV to the Revocation of the Edict of Nantes* (Grand Rapids: Reformation Heritage Books, 2014).

For a children's book on Marie Durand, see Simonetta Carr, *Marie Durand* (Grand Rapids: Reformation Heritage Books, 2015).

---

3. Gamonnet, *Lettres*, 129.

23

Must I Forever Mourn?

ANNE STEELE (1717–1778)

Anne Steele is remembered as one of the first British woman hymn writers and one of the best appreciated during her time and in the following century. The introspective, searching notes of her hymns, uttered with uncommon honesty, made them particularly cherished by many Christians, who found in them a way to express their own feelings.

ANNE'S LIFE

Anne was born in 1717 at Broughton, Hampshire. Her father, William Steele, was both a pastor and a successful merchant who offered his family a comfortable life. Her mother died in 1720, probably from giving birth to her second son, Thomas, who lived less than two months. Three years later, William remarried, and in 1724 a daughter, Mary, was born. The three Steele children, William Jr. (Anne's older brother), Anne, and Mary, formed a close bond of friendship.

Anne's stepmother, Anne Cator Steele, was a sensitive woman who cared for her children's religious and academic education. Her decision to send her daughters to school was much contested within the family—one uncle called it a sin. But Anne Cator believed it was possible for women to gain a secular education without being affected by the "vanitys with which the world aboundeth."[1]

---

1. Anne Cator Steele, *Diary*, March 29, 1731, as quoted in Cynthia Y.

A popular story claims that Anne's fiancé drowned shortly before their intended wedding, but it is not confirmed; her father simply referred to the young man as a dear friend of the family. Staying unmarried was her choice, and she refused at least two proposals, including a passionate plea from Baptist pastor and hymn writer Benjamin Beddome. She preferred tranquility, solitude, and an ordinary life at home.

Some descriptions of Anne as an invalid have also been exaggerated. Records show that her 1735 fall from a horse, which is often suggested to be the cause of her health troubles, didn't stop her from continuing to ride (and fall), and she was confined to her room for only the last eight years of her life due to a chronic illness that led to her death on November 11, 1778.

This is not to say she didn't suffer. Her health was frail from a young age, and she was plagued by a variety of painful conditions. She often complained of headaches, general weakness, and stomach troubles. Like most people suffering from chronic illnesses, Anne found that her ailments were a frequent cause of discouragement and "faintness and dejection of spirit."[2]

HYMNS OF SORROW

In Anne's time, hymns had begun to take a predominant place in worship, often replacing the biblical psalms that had been used for centuries. Much of this change can be traced back to Isaac Watts, who doubted that the Old Testament Psalms could adequately express the Christian experience. Over time, this view ended up exacerbating the wrong perception of a divergence between the Old and the New Testaments and deprived worshipers of the wide range of emotions the Psalms powerfully convey.

Aalders, *To Express the Ineffable: The Hymns and Spirituality of Anne Steele* (Eugene, Ore.: Wipf & Stock, 2008), 18.

2. Anne Steele to her sister, Mary Bullock Steele, March 16, 1762, as quoted in Aalders, *To Express the Ineffable*, 138.

While most hymns by Watts and his contemporaries are well written, moving, and scripturally sound, few of them delve into the depths of pain and questioning that characterize some of the psalms. Anne Steele's hymns were among these few, as were hymns and poems by William Cowper, who suffered from some form of mental illness.

Anne's writings are studded with questions: How can my words express the majesty of God? Why am I suffering? Will this suffering last forever? Is God hearing my prayers? Do I really belong to Christ? Does He really belong to me? Can His "Spirit rest in such a wretched heart as mine?"[3] And if so, why do I still look for happiness in earthly things?

SUFFERING IN THE LIGHT OF GOD'S SOVEREIGNTY

From an early age, Anne had learned that everything in this life—including disappointing and painful circumstances—is ordained by God, who works all things for His glory and for the good of those who love Him. This thought is not in itself of much comfort to sufferers unless they know that this sovereign God is truly "just, and wise, and kind"[4]—something that Anne brought up repeatedly in her poems.

But sometimes God may not seem just, wise, and kind. How do we know He really is? Anne reminds us that while our human minds can't discern God's thoughts and plans in everything He does, we can know His faithfulness in what He has done in the past and how He has preserved His people in the biblical narrative, in the history of the church, and in their individual lives.

In fact, the culmination of God's wisdom and love is seen in the life, death, and resurrection of His Son for our sins. Of all her hymns, Anne's thirty-nine-verse "Redeeming Love" is a moving retelling of the gospel story, from the original sin of Adam and Eve, in whose

---

3. Anne Steele, *The Works of Mrs. Anne Steele* (Boston: Munroe, Francis, and Parker, 1808), 74. See Internet Archive, https://archive.org/details/worksofmrsannest00stee/page/n3/mode/2up.

4. *Works of Mrs. Anne Steele*, 146.

"crime we fell"; to Christ's "stupendous" and "mysterious" sacrifice in order "to expiate mortal guilt."

> "'Tis finish'd," now aloud he cries,
> "No more the law requires":
> And now (amazing sacrifice!)
> The Lord of life expires.[5]

And the story continues, as Christ rises from the dead and ascends to heaven, while "sin, death, and hell low vanquish'd lie beneath his awful feet." On His glorious throne, His love remains unchanged.

> The names he purchas'd for his own,
> Still on his heart he bears.
> Still with prevailing pow'r he pleads
> Their cause for whom he died;
> His spirit's sacred influence sheds,
> Their comforter and guide.
> For them, reserves a radiant crown,
> Bought with his dying blood;
> And worlds of light, and joys unknown,
> Forever near their God.

In response to this unfathomable story, Anne can only fall beneath Christ's cross, as "my Lord, my life, my sacrifice, my Saviour, and my all."[6]

ASSURANCE OF GOD'S LOVE AND PRESENCE

Even though the gospel story is told with no uncertain terms, Anne's confidence in God's love for her was still wavering, much to her puzzlement and frustration. If "faith leads to joys beyond the sky," she wondered, "why then is this weak mind afraid to raise a cheerful eye to more than sense can find?"[7]

---

5. *Works of Mrs. Anne Steele*, 34.
6. *Works of Mrs. Anne Steele*, 35–36.
7. *Works of Mrs. Anne Steele*, 32.

Anne realized that feelings have a strong pull downward: "Sense can but furnish scenes of woe in this low vale of tears."[8] They cloud our view of heaven and constrain us in a vicious cycle of unsound hopes and despair. But this realization does not always come swiftly, and like many other sufferers, Anne had to wade through muddy waters, wondering,

> Why sinks my weak desponding mind?
> Why heaves my heart the anxious sigh?
> Can sov'reign goodness be unkind?
> Am I not safe, if God is nigh?[9]

Unafraid to express her doubts, Anne worked through them, struggling with her "weak, inconstant mind,"[10] which she found frail and ready to stray.

Anne's struggles were concerning to at least one of her friends. After visiting her in 1763, Congregationalist minister Caleb Ashworth wondered about "some expressions [she] dropt of doubt."[11] Her reply was not reassuring: "The thoughts which occasioned those expressions of doubt which you observed, frequently occur."[12] But if Ashworth was familiar with Anne's writings, he knew that these doubts were necessary for her process of inquiry and refinement of her faith.

While feelings are fleeting and unreliable, Anne knew that some of them, such as the calming of her inner tempest before God's word and her undying desire to be His, are so counterintuitive that they can be inspired and sustained only by God:

> Whene'er to call the Saviour mine,
> With ardent wish my heart aspires,

---

8. *Works of Mrs. Anne Steele*, 32.

9. *Works of Mrs. Anne Steele*, 93.

10. *Works of Mrs. Anne Steele*, 94.

11. Caleb Ashworth to Anne Steele, August 31, 1763, as quoted in Aalders, *To Express the Ineffable*, 113.

12. Anne Steele to Caleb Ashworth, September 9, 1763, as quoted in Aalders, *To Express the Ineffable*, 114.

> Can it be less than pow'r divine,
> Which animates these strong desires?…
>
> And when my cheerful hope can say
> I love my God, and taste his grace,
> Lord, is it not thy blissful ray,
> Which brings this dawn of sacred peace?[13]

Ultimately, Anne knew that the only reliable source of comfort is the gospel and its promises as they are revealed in God's Word. She asked,

> And can my hope, my comfort die,
> Fix'd on thy everlasting word,
> That word which built the earth and sky?

Her answer, in this case, was an unchangeable no.

> If my immortal Saviour lives,
> Then my immortal life is sure;
> His word a firm foundation gives,
> Here, let me build, and rest secure.
> Here, let my faith unshaken dwell,
> Immoveable the promise stands;
> Nor all the pow'rs of earth or hell,
> Can e'er dissolve the sacred bands.
> Here, O my soul, thy trust repose;
> If Jesus is forever mine,
> Not death itself, that last of foes,
> Shall break a union so divine.[14]

Anne lived with her father and stepmother until her father's death in 1769, then she moved to the home of her brother William. She died nine years later, on November 11, 1778, at the age of sixty-two. Her hymns continued to be popular into the nineteenth century. Obscured for some time, they are being newly appreciated and set to new tunes.

---

13. *Works of Mrs. Anne Steele*, 75.
14. *Works of Mrs. Anne Steele*, 39.

FOOD FOR THOUGHT

- In her letters, Anne associated the pain of chronic illness with "faintness and dejection of spirit," as well as "inquietudes and gloomy apprehensions." Have you experienced similar feelings during an illness? What has helped you at those times?

- Much of Anne's struggle was motivated by the apparent contradiction between God's promises and our present life. He promises strength, and yet we feel weak. He tells us He's near, and yet He seems distant. Anne learned not to rely on her feelings and to trust God's Word even when it seemed contrary to what she could perceive in this world. What has helped you come to this realization? Why is it important that we not rely on our feelings? Is this a lesson that Christians learn once, or do we need to learn it over and over? Why do feelings and perceptions have such a strong pull on us?

- Some theologians have referred to this contrast between what we see and feel and what God's Word tells us as a contrast between the already and the not yet. Christ's kingdom has been inaugurated, but it's not fully here. We are new creatures in Christ, but our renewal is not yet complete. Martin Luther said we are simultaneously sinful and righteous. Explain why you do or don't agree with this assessment. How can understanding this contrast be helpful in overcoming discouragement in our present situation?

- The story of Anne's fiancé drowning might have been constructed or embellished to justify her choice of a single life, which was normally discouraged. In reality, Anne told her half sister Mary that, in considering a marriage proposal, she "saw no flowers, but observ'd a great many thorns, and I suppose there are more hid under the leaves…; besides I think the path is much smoother on this side of the Hedge than the other, and I am too stay'd [staid] to ramble for the sake of novelty."[15] Mary replied that everyone else puts up with the thorns. Do you tend to agree with Anne or with Mary? Are the "thorns" of marriage a good reason to avoid it?

- The monastic movement was based on the idea that a single life gave Christians more time to spend in religious practices. Some women also found in monasteries a good environment where they could devote their lives to studies and writing. Most Protestant Reformers, instead, believed that marriage helps Christians to grow and mature, provides support and companionship, and allows parents to raise their children in the Lord. That said, there is a difference between encouraging marriage and making it a requirement. How should Christians behave toward those who want to stay single? Do you find that this choice is still tacitly disapproved in Christian churches? Explain your answer.

FOR FURTHER RESEARCH

For a full biography of Anne Steele, see J. R. Broome, *A Bruised Reed: The Life and Times of Anne Steele* (Harpender, UK: Gospel Standard Trust Publications, 2007).

See also Cynthia Y. Aalders, *To Express the Ineffable: The Hymns and Spirituality of Anne Steele* (Eugene, Ore.: Wipf & Stock, 2008); and Priscilla Wong, *Anne Steele and Her Spiritual Vision* (Grand Rapids: Reformation Heritage Books, 2012).

For a shorter survey of Anne Steele's life, see Michael G. Haykin, "Anne Steele and Her Hymns," in *Eight Women of Faith* (Wheaton, Ill.: Crossway, 2016), 81–92.

---

15. Anne Steele, in *Nonconformist Women Writers, 1720–1840*, ed. Timothy Whelan and Julia B. Griffin (London: Pickering & Chatto, 2011), 2:307.

24

How Can I Help the Needy?

ISABELLA MARSHALL GRAHAM (1742–1814)

"Who are these children, that idly ramble through the streets, a prey to growing depravity and vicious example?" Isabella Graham asked in 1804. By that time, she had created a vast program of assistance to the needy, which included the very children she mentioned. So why were they now in the streets, "running about in the most imminent danger, apparently without protection"?[1]

"They are fed, they are clothed, their mothers' fireside is made warm for them," Isabella continued, "but no culture is provided for their minds, nor protection from baneful example. These will, in time, follow that of the older ones, and grow up the slaves of idleness and vice, in the certain road to ruin."[2] They needed more than food and clothes. They needed to learn to read, particularly the Bible.

EARLY JOYS AND PAINS

Isabella Marshall Graham was born in Lanarkshire, Scotland, on July 29, 1742, to a family of landowners who were devout Presbyterians. An inheritance allowed her to attend boarding school for seven years. At seventeen, she made profession of faith in the

---

1. Isabella Graham, Joanna Bethune, Divie Bethune, *The Power of Faith Exemplified in the Life and Writings of the Late Mrs. Isabella Graham* (New York: American Tract Society, 1843), 232.

2. Graham et al., *Power of Faith Exemplified*, 232.

A MOTHER'S PRAYER

Like Monica of Tagaste, Isabella prayed frequently for her only son. On one occasion, as he left her to travel by sea, she wrote down her prayer:

He has been with me but for a short time, and ill I have improved it; he is gone from my sight and my heart burst with tumultuous grief. Lord, have mercy on the widow's son—"the only son of his mother."

I ask for nothing in all this world for him; I repeat my petition: Save his soul alive, give him salvation from sin. It is not the danger of the sea that distresses me; it is not the hardships he must undergo; it is not the dread of never seeing him more in this world; it is because I cannot discern the fulfilment of the promise in him. I cannot discern the new birth nor its fruits, but every symptom of captivity to Satan, the world, and self-will. This, this is what distresses me; and, in connection with this, his being shut out from ordinances, at a distance with Christians; shut up with those who forget God, profane his name, and break his Sabbaths, men who often live and die like beasts; yet are accountable creatures, who must answer for every moment of time, and every word, thought, and action. O Lord, many wonders hast thou shown me; thy ways of dealing with me and mine have not been common ones—add this wonder to the rest. Call, convert, regenerate, and establish a sailor in the faith. Lord, all things are possible with thee: glorify thy Son and extend his kingdom by sea and land; take the prey from the strong. I roll him over upon thee. Many friends try to comfort me; miserable comforters are they all. Thou art the God of consolation; only confirm to me thy gracious word, on which thou causedst me to hope, in the day when thou saidst to me, "Leave thy fatherless children, I will preserve them alive." Only let this life be a spiritual life, and I put a blank in thy hands as to all temporal things.[a]

_____

a. Graham et al., *Power of Faith Exemplified*, 76.

Church of Scotland under the ministry of John Witherspoon, who would later become president of the College of New Jersey (now Princeton University). At twenty-three she married John Graham, an army surgeon in a British army regiment.

When her husband was stationed in Canada (first Quebec, then Montreal), twenty-five-year-old Isabella accompanied him there, leaving with her family in Scotland an infant son who was too young for the journey. The baby died within the year.

After Canada, John was assigned to Fort Niagara in western New York, a place Isabella particularly enjoyed. There, she raised three daughters: Jessie, Joanna, and Isabella. In 1773, just as the family was making plans to retire from the army and move to New England, Isabella's husband was ordered to Antigua, in the Caribbean. As usual, she followed him with their children. The next year John was overtaken by a fever and died just before the birth of their fifth child, also named John.

Overwhelmed with grief, thirty-one-year-old Isabella returned to Scotland with her children, struggling to provide for them and for her elderly father, who had recently become a widower. To do so, she opened a small school in their town and later a girls' boarding school in Edinburgh. She also became active in charitable works.

FOUNDER OF SOCIETIES

In 1785 Isabella met again with John Witherspoon, who was back in Scotland for a visit. Impressed by her work, he encouraged her to return to the United States, something she had been thinking of doing. By that time, her father had died, and her son was boarding with friends. Taking her daughters with her, she left for New York in July 1789.

Soon after her arrival, she established a boarding school for girls, which immediately earned a good reputation and attracted many affluent young ladies, including future first lady Anna Harrison. What made her school unique was the personal care she took of the students, making them part of her life.

At the same time, Isabella grew increasingly distressed over the condition of widows and other women who could not meet their basic needs, let alone pursue education. New York was a city of sharp contrasts, with a great disparity between rich and poor. Life was particularly difficult for widows, who grew numerically after the yellow fever epidemics of 1795, 1799, and 1803.

Isabella knew what it was like to be a widow and single mother, but at least her education had allowed her to open a school and earn a living as an instructor. Women with no education were instead forced to compete with each other for basic work. Some resorted to begging or prostitution. She discussed this problem with other ladies who, in 1797, joined her in founding the Society for the Relief of Poor Widows with Small Children (SRPW).

Until then, women had performed charitable acts individually or within a church. This was one of the first women's societies to be fully organized and legally registered for a charitable pursuit with active and successful fund-raising efforts. As the society progressed, Isabella left her job at the school to devote her time to charity.

The society helped 98 widows with 223 children during the first winter, and the numbers continued to grow. But Isabella was not satisfied with providing material help. She offered the women education, friendship, encouragement, and assistance in finding jobs. During the particularly trying winter of 1807–1808, she bought flax and spinning wheels and found commissions on the women's behalf.

EDUCATING THE CHILDREN

Soon, Isabella realized that even this was not enough. While the women were busy, their children were roaming the streets with many opportunities to get into trouble. "They quarrel, they swear; and such, no doubt, will lie and steal,"[3] she said. To remedy this problem, she recruited volunteers from among her former students and the daughters of SRPW workers and opened a school for these

---

3. Graham et al., *Power of Faith Exemplified*, 232.

children. Instruction included the three *R*'s, vocational training, and Scripture memorization.

"Snatch their little innocents from the whirling vortex," Isabella told the volunteers; "bring them to a place of safety; teach them to know their Father, God; tell them of their Saviour's love; lead them through the history of his life: mark to them the example he set, the precepts he recorded for their observance, and the promises for their comfort: and by teaching them to read, enable them to retrace all your instructions, when their eyes see you no more."[4]

In 1806 the challenge of finding a place for six children who had recently lost their widowed mother prompted her to found the Orphan Asylum Society with the help of other ladies, including her daughter Joanna and her friends Sarah Ogden Hoffman and Elizabeth Hamilton, widow of Alexander Hamilton.

These efforts were not unhindered at a time when women could not vote and were not expected to act outside the sphere of their home. "An association of ladies for the relief of destitute workers and orphans was a new thing in this country," Isabella told her group of volunteers. "It was feeble in its origins; the jest of most, the ridicule of many, and it met the opposition of not a few. The men could not allow our sex the steadiness and perseverance necessary to establish such an undertaking. But God put his seal upon it; and under his fostering care, it has prospered beyond the most sanguine expectations of its propagators."[5]

LAST YEARS AND LEGACY

In 1807 Isabella retired as first director of SRPW but continued to visit women in their homes—especially widows and wives of men who were confined to institutions. She and Sarah Hoffman also accompanied the city missionary, John Stafford, to the almshouse, city hospital, asylum, and prison. She died of cholera on July 27, 1814—two days before her seventy-second birthday.

---

4. Graham et al., *Power of Faith Exemplified*, 232.
5. Graham et al., *Power of Faith Exemplified*, 232.

Today, Isabella's name is remembered in the history of charitable societies as one of the first and most active pioneers. Few people read her writings, which include letters of encouragement to friends in need and new converts, devotional writings, and poems. In these, Isabella wrote with great wisdom and honesty, revealing a deep-rooted faith and an impressive theological foundation, both tried in the furnace of personal heartaches, frustrations, and disappointments.

Isabella gave a glimpse of this furnace in her poem "The Inward Warfare"—a candid portrayal of the struggle most Christians know all too well. Here, she revealed an aspect of her life that is usually ignored in hagiographies and commendatory memorials of her accomplishments—an aspect that brings her closer to us and gives greater weight to her words of encouragement.

> Strange and mysterious is my life!
> What opposites I feel within:
> A stable peace, a constant strife,
> The rule of grace, the power of sin!
> Too often I am captive led,
> Yet daily triumph in my head.
>
> I prize the privilege of prayer,
> But oh! what backwardness to pray!
> Though on the Lord I cast my care,
> I feel its burden every day.
> I seek his will in all I do,
> Yet find my own is working too....
>
> Thus diff'rent powers within me strive,
> And death, and sin, by turns, prevail.
> I grieve, rejoice, decline, revive,
> And vict'ry hangs in doubtful scale.
> But Jesus has his promise passed
> That grace shall overcome at last.[6]

---

6. Graham et al., *Power of Faith Exemplified*, 407–8.

FOOD FOR THOUGHT

- As a widow with limited means, Isabella would have been justified in focusing on her own needs. Instead, she was touched by the needs of those around her and found ways to help them. Explain why focusing on our own needs is a frequent justification for not helping others. What can a person with limited means do for others?

- Search Scripture for references to the poor. What does this study tell you about God's attitude toward the disadvantaged and needy?

- Isabella encountered much opposition, both from men in general who thought that founding societies was not a work fit for women and from some Christians who believed that her Sunday schools were an infraction of God's commandment to keep the Sabbath holy. In answer to this last objection, Isabella could have easily quoted Matthew 12:11–12 or the Reformed catechisms, which allow for "works of necessity and mercy"[7] on the Sabbath and go as far as saying that "God wills that the ministry of the Gospel and *schools* be maintained."[8] Do you think she was right—and why? What would you have done differently?

- The word *schools* in the Heidelberg Catechism refers to Sunday schools, where Scripture and the catechisms were taught to both children and adults. Today, some Sunday schools have become a substitute for the worship service, with the idea that children are not old enough to sit in the regular worship service. Is this a good idea or bad idea? Why?

- Isabella's poem "The Inward Warfare" shows that far from being a superwoman, she battled with religious indifference, unbelief, doubts, and fears. Where did she draw her comfort?

---

7. Westminster Shorter Catechism 60.
8. Heidelberg Catechism 103, emphasis added.

Read her biography, *The Power of Faith*, to find out more about her reliance on Christ, which is especially evident in her letters and prayers.

FOR FURTHER RESEARCH

For a biography of Isabella Graham, complete with some of her letters, poems, and prayers, see Isabella Graham, Joanna Bethune, and Divie Bethune, *The Power of Faith Exemplified in the Life and Writings of the Late Mrs. Isabella Graham* (New York: American Tract Society, 1843).

25

How Can I Not Oppose Tyranny?

PHILLIS WHEATLEY (ca. 1753–1784)

Whatever moved the Wheatleys to buy the little slave girl who had just arrived from Africa, it was not her physical strength. Small, frightened, and skinny, she looked too frail to do much work. The Wheatleys' choice might have been because, with her missing front teeth, the girl looked like she was seven years old, almost the same age as the youngest of their children, Sarah, at the time of her death. They called the African girl Phillis, the name of the ship that had brought her to America.

AN IMPRESSIVE MIND

John Wheatley was a prosperous merchant in Boston. He and his wife, Susanna, had lost two other children along with Sarah. Their oldest children, twins Nathaniel and Mary, were eighteen at that time and lived at home.

It didn't take long for the Wheatleys to be impressed by Phillis's quick mind. Susanna was particularly interested in her education, although the task of instructing her was given to Mary. According to John Wheatley, within sixteen months Phillis learned to understand English well enough to read even the most difficult portions of the Bible. She later studied literature, history, and geography and even learned some Latin. Her favorite poets were John Milton and Alexander Pope.

It is not known how early Phillis began writing. Her first-known letter was written in 1765, just four years after her arrival in America. It was addressed to Samuel Occom, a friend of the Wheatleys who was involved in missionary work to his fellow Native Americans. A poet himself, he probably encouraged Phillis in her first attempts.

Phillis's first published poem, "On Messrs. Hussey and Coffin," appeared in 1767 in the *Newport Mercury*. It was inspired by an adventurous story Phillis heard from these two men, Hussey and Coffin. She gave God the credit for saving their lives during a storm at sea.

But the poem that earned for her transatlantic fame was one she wrote on the sudden death of the famous preacher George Whitefield. She addressed it to Selina Hastings, Countess of Huntingdon, who was a correspondent of Susanna Wheatley. In this poem, fourteen-year-old Phillis affirmed that the gospel was for all human beings, Africans included:

> Take Him, ye Africans, He longs for you,
> Impartial Savior is His title due:
> Washed in the fountain of redeeming blood,
> You shall be sons, and kings, and priests to God.[1]

FIRST PUBLISHED AFRICAN AMERICAN AUTHOR

By 1772 Phillis had written enough poems to be able to collect them in a book. But acquiring a publisher was not an easy task. A publisher told her she had to find three hundred people who would be willing to preorder her book by paying in advance. She also needed to have recommendations by some reputable Bostonians.

The reason such a recommendation was necessary was that many people found it difficult to believe that Africans could write poetry—or make any relevant contribution to the fine arts or human knowledge. For example, in 1776 the philosopher David Hume wrote, "I am apt to suspect the negroes, and in general all the

---

1. Phillis Wheatley, *Memoir and Poems of Phillis Wheatley: A Native African and a Slave*, ed. Margaretta Matilda Odell (Boston: Geo. W. Light, 1834), 47.

other species…to be naturally inferior to the whites."[2] His colleague Immanuel Kant added, "The Negroes of Africa have by nature no feeling that rises above the trifling."[3] They based these convictions on their unawareness of any African who could achieve "anything great in art or science or any other praiseworthy quality."[4] If Phillis were, in fact, the author of these poems, she would have shattered this notion.

And she did. The letter of recommendation, titled "Attestation," was written by some of the brightest minds in the city, including Thomas Hutchinson, governor of Massachusetts; James Bowdoin; John Hancock; Rev. Samuel Cotton; Rev. Mather Byles; and Rev. Samuel Cooper. Many of these men were Harvard graduates, and many were poets. All of them were convinced, by meeting Phillis and seeing her write in their presence or by talking with people who witnessed her writing, that she was truly the author of her poems.

In one of her poems, Phillis put into words what she had shown by her example:

> Some view our sable race with scornful eye,
> "Their colour is a diabolic die."
> Remember, Christians, Negros, black as Cain,
> May be refin'd, and join th' angelic train.[5]

Even with the attestation, Phillis had a hard time finding three hundred subscribers. Many people were leery of these proposals, having paid for books that were never published. Through Susanna's connections in England, one English publisher, Archibald Bell, agreed to take on the project. He was also a friend of the Countess of Huntingdon, who undoubtedly had a great influence on the decision. She recommended that Phillis sit for an engraving to place on

---

2. David Hume, "Of National Characters," in *Essays, Moral, Political, and Literary*, by David Hume (Indianapolis: Liberty Classics, 1985), 208n10.

3. Immanuel Kant, *Observations on the Feeling of the Beautiful and Sublime*, trans. John T. Goldthwait (Berkeley: University of California Press, 1960), 110.

4. Kant, *Observations*, 111.

5. Wheatley, *Memoir and Poems*, 42.

the frontispiece of the book—a great honor for any author that was rarely granted to women, especially in their first publishing venture.

Taking advantage of a transatlantic trip Nathaniel Wheatley had planned for both business and personal reasons, Phillis accompanied him to London, where she was given the royal treatment by many members of high society. She was, after all, a curiosity—a poetess born in the unfamiliar regions of Africa and educated while in slavery. Her hosts took her on a large tour of the city, showing her impressive sights, and showered her with gifts (mostly books) at her departure. She returned to Boston in September. Three months later, the collection *Poems on Various Subjects, Religious and Moral*, came off the press.

SUCCESS AND FREEDOM

John Thornton, a friend of the Wheatleys who hosted Nathaniel and Phillis during their stay in London, expressed some concerns that the sudden fame might go to the young woman's head. But Phillis was prepared. She had foreseen this temptation and prayed against it. In her reply to Thornton, she explained that knowing her gifts were given by God, who wanted her to use them for "His glory and the good of mankind,"[6] was sufficient to keep her humble and to impress her with a deep sense of responsibility.

Phillis kept Thornton abreast of the sad news in the Wheatleys' household. Phillis had returned to find Susanna in a poor state of health. In spite of a few glimmers of hope, Susanna died on March 1, 1774. Her last days on earth left a strong impression on Phillis.

"I saw with grief and wonder the effects of sin on the human race," she wrote to John Thornton. "Had not Christ taken away the evenom'd sting, where had been our hopes? What might have not we fear'd, what might have not we expect'd from the dreadful King of Terrors? But *this* is matter of endless praise, to the King eternal,

---

6. As quoted in Vincent Carretta, *The Writings of Phillis Wheatley* (Oxford: Oxford University Press, 2019), 125.

immortal, invincible, that *it is finished*."[7] Phillis was comforted to see Susanna leaving this life in peace, knowing that Christ had defeated death for her.

Phillis told her friend Obour Tanner, an enslaved African young woman in Newport, Rhode Island, that losing Susanna was like losing "a Parent, Sister, or Brother."[8] Susanna had been the closest person to her on an emotional level since she had arrived in America.

Now more than ever, Phillis missed Susanna's advice. Partially at the insistence of their friends in England, the Wheatleys had freed Phillis three months before Susanna's death. She was still allowed to live with them but had to take care of her own expenses. They probably expected her to make some money from the sales of her book.

But this was not as easy as it sounded. Phillis learned that she had to budget her income, plan for the future, and find new marketing ideas. In one of her letters, she told a friend to watch for pirated copies of her book. As she had done in the past, she continued to raise some money by writing poems on commission.

Thornton warned Phillis about a possible loss of supporters whose patronage depended on their connection with Susanna. Her response seems to indicate that she had already experienced this reaction. But she had learned there was an even greater threat. "The world is a severe schoolmaster," she said, "for its frowns are less dangerous than its smiles and flatteries, and it is a difficult task to keep in the path of wisdom."[9]

LIBERTY AND JUSTICE FOR ALL

A major obstacle in what seemed a promising future was the start of the American Revolution. Rebellion against British rule had been brewing in Boston for some time, but by 1775 the hostilities escalated to a point that Phillis followed Nathaniel and Mary, with their

---

7. As quoted in Carretta, *Writings of Phillis Wheatley*, 122.

8. Phillis Wheatley, *The Poems of Phillis Wheatley*, ed. Julian D. Mason Jr. (Chapel Hill: University of North Carolina Press, 1989), 204.

9. As quoted in Carretta, *Writings of Phillis Wheatley*, 125.

respective spouses, to Providence, Rhode Island. She stayed there at least until the following year, when General Washington and his army expelled the British from Boston.

Like many Americans, Phillis had mixed feelings about the war. "Even I a mere spectator am in anxious suspense concerning the fortune of this unnatural civil contest," she wrote to Obour. "Possibly the ambition & thirst of Dominion in some is design'd as the punishment of the national views of others, tho' it bears the appearance of greater Barbarity than that of the uncivilz'd part of mankind."[10] Her faith, however, prevented her from despairing. "But Let us leave the Event to him whose wisdom alone can bring good out of Evil & he is infinitely superior to all the Craftiness of the enemies of this seemingly devoted Country,"[11] she continued.

It was her strong belief in God's wisdom and power and His ability to "bring good out of evil" that allowed Phillis to accept with thankfulness what God had done and continued to do in her life. In one of her first poems, written when she was still in her teens, she recognized God's hand in bringing her to America, where she had come to know Christ:

> 'Twas mercy brought me from my *Pagan* land,
> Taught my benighted soul to understand
> That there's a God, that there's a *Saviour* too:
> Once I redemption neither sought nor knew.[12]

During the last century, some critics used this poem to blame Phillis of approving of slavery as a means to bring Africans to Christ. This was far from the poem's meaning, as they would have discovered if they had read the entirety of her writings. In fact, her poem merely reflected the attitude expressed by other Africans, including the abolitionist Ottobah Cugoano, who wrote, "In some manner, I may say with Joseph, as he did with respect to the evil intention of his

---

10. As quoted in Carretta, *Writings of Phillis Wheatley*, 131.
11. As quoted in Carretta, *Writings of Phillis Wheatley*, 131.
12. Phillis Wheatley, *Poems on Various Subjects, Religious and Moral*, ed. W. A. Jackson (Denver: W. H. Lawrence, 1887), 17.

brethren, when they sold him into Egypt, that whatever evil intentions and bad motives those insidious robbers had in carrying me away from my native country and friends, I trust, was what the Lord intended for my good."[13]

In a letter to Thornton, Phillis demonstrated a keen understanding of Paul's exhortation in 1 Corinthians 7:21: "Art thou called being a servant? care not for it: but if thou mayest be made free, use it rather." Phillis understood that accepting the calling God has for each of us doesn't mean we shouldn't seek to improve our condition. The key for a Christian is to remember the big picture: "For he that is called in the Lord, being a servant, is the Lord's freeman: likewise also he that is called, being free, is Christ's servant" (1 Cor. 7:22).

This is what Phillis wrote to Thornton. After announcing that she had just gained her freedom, she added, "If this had not been the Case, yet I hope I should willingly submit to servitude to be free in Christ. But, since it is thus, Let me be *a servant of Christ*, and that is the most perfect freedom."[14]

In another letter, this time to William Legge, Earl of Dartmouth, who had just been appointed secretary of state for the colonies, Phillis explained how her experience as a slave, forcibly taken from her parents and her land, informed her love for freedom of every kind:

> Should you, my lord, while you peruse my song,
> Wonder from whence my love of Freedom sprung,
> Whence flow these wishes for the common good,
> By feeling hearts alone best understood,
> I, young in life, by seeming cruel fate
> Was snatch'd from Afric's fancy'd happy seat:
> What pangs excruciating must molest,
> What sorrows labour in my parent's breast?

---

13. Ottobah Cugoano, *Thoughts and Sentiments on the Evil and Wicked Traffic of the Slavery: And Commerce of the Human Species, Humbly Submitted to the Inhabitants of Great-Britain* (Ann Arbor: University of Michigan Library, 2005), 13.

14. As quoted in Carretta, *Writings of Phillis Wheatley*, 125.

> Steel'd was that soul and by no misery mov'd
> That from a father seiz'd his babe belov'd:
> Such, such my case. And can I then but pray
> Others may never feel tyrannic sway?[15]

She was even more explicit in a letter to Samuel Occum:

> God grant Deliverance in his own Way and Time, and get
> him honour upon all those whose Avarice impels them to
> countenance and help forward the Calamities of their fellow
> Creatures. This I desire not for their Hurt, but to convince them
> of the strange Absurdity of their Conduct whose Words and
> Actions are so diametrically, opposite. How well the Cry for
> Liberty, and the reverse Disposition for the exercise of oppres-
> sive Power over others agree, I humbly think it does not require
> the Penetration of a Philosopher to determine.[16]

LATER YEARS

Phillis was still well known and influential during the American
Revolution. She even wrote a letter to George Washington to con-
gratulate him on his appointment as general of the Continental
Army, and he invited her to visit him at his headquarters in Cambridge, Massachusetts. But fame doesn't always translate to financial
security, especially during and after a major war.

Soon after John Wheatley's death in March 1778, Phillis
announced her upcoming marriage to John Peters, a free Black man
who dealt in different trades. They married on November 26 of the
same year. Peters kept a fruitful business for a while, until he ran into
debts he could not pay due to his insolvent debtors. In the meantime,
Phillis's plans to publish a second volume of poems failed, mostly for
the same reasons she couldn't publish her first volume in America.
This time she didn't have the option to seek a publisher in England

---

15. Wheatley, *Poems on Various Subjects*, 67.
16. Wheatley, *Poems of Phillis Wheatley*, 204.

because, due to the war, British publishers were not printing books by American authors.

Little is known about Phillis's last years. A popular account that depicts her husband as a scoundrel and her later life as a heartbreaking tragedy has recently been disproved, due to several inaccuracies and a seeming motive to demonstrate that Phillis was happier when enslaved. We know only that Phillis died on December 5, 1784, most likely of an asthmatic condition that had plagued her for most of her life. Her husband was probably still in prison. As a Black person, she was buried in an unmarked grave. But her fame lived on, and her writings continued to be an inspiration to others. To Blacks and abolitionists, they stood as obvious evidence that no race is more intelligent than another. To Christians, they are a reminder that submission to God and a concern for justice are not mutually exclusive.

FOOD FOR THOUGHT

- How can a Christian cultivate thankfulness to God and submission to His will in whatever condition she is found while working, at the same time, to improve this condition? How can we apply 1 Corinthians 7:20–24 to our situations?

- Do you see a dichotomy between submission to God and a concern for justice? Why or why not? Can you explain how keeping a balance between these requires wisdom?

- Phillis Wheatley saw a contradiction between the patriots' fight for freedom and their acceptance or promotion of slavery. What contradictions can you see in today's society?

- Phillis spoke clearly against slavery, as did her pastors and other Christians in her circle. Do you think Christians have the duty to speak out against injustices done to other people? Why or why not?

- During Phillis's life, many pastors thought it was their duty to speak about political issues such as the American Revolution. Today, many people believe that pastors should simply preach the gospel and pray for their rulers, leaving their congregants free to make their own political choices. Where do you stand on this issue? What might be the dangers of the political involvement of pastors? What is most profitable for Christian unity?

- While many pastors in Phillis's time and later have attacked racism as sin, Phillis insisted on its incongruity for a people who claimed to love freedom. Her approach was probably more effective when speaking to a general public that included nonbelievers. What do you think? Can this approach be more beneficial when speaking about some of the evils of our generation, such as abortion? How would you argue against racism or abortion with a nonbeliever?

- Kant's and Hume's misconceptions stemmed from the Enlightenment's ideas of reason as the highest faculty of a human being and, consequently, a standard of humanity. Explain why this view is or is not supported by Scripture. In what other ways has this view influenced our modern thought? If we maintain this view, where do we place people with mental disabilities or illnesses such as Alzheimer's?

- The ideas of the Enlightenment's philosophers on what constitutes a true human being is as old as the garden of Eden. The temptation to seek an "enlightened" status that makes one human being better than another has continued throughout history. That's how the term *barbarian* came into use, when the Greeks wanted to distinguish themselves as an enlightened nation against the other "barbaric" populations around them. The idea has reached an all-time low with eugenics, the teachings that the human species should be improved by giving preference to people with desirable hereditary traits and discouraging others from procreating or even succeeding. Where do you notice this temptation to prefer one race or group of people today? Can this temptation affect even those who intellectually believe that all human beings are equal? Give some examples.

- In the 1960s, some people said that Phillis's voice was "too white." What are your thoughts about "White" or "Black" voices? How do biblical exhortations to be of one mind in Christ (Phil. 2:2) apply to our differences in race, culture, and political views? What unites us, and where can differences be allowed and appreciated?

FOR FURTHER RESEARCH

For an excellent and thorough biography of Phillis Wheatley, see Vincent Carretta, *Phillis Wheatley: Biography of a Genius in Bondage* (Athens: University of Georgia Press, 2011).

For a collection of her writings, see Phillis Wheatley, *Complete Writings*, ed. Vincent Carretta (New York: Penguin Books, 2001).

For a complete collection of Phillis Wheatley's writings arranged in chronological order with helpful comments, see Vincent Carretta, *The Writings of Phillis Wheatley* (Oxford: Oxford University Press, 2019).

26

What Have I to Do with Idols?

"What have I to do henceforward with vain idols of this earth?" wrote Ann Griffiths at the end of the eighteenth century.[1] They are all "masks and fetishes," as Rowan Williams wrote in a liberal translation of Ann's poem.[2] And yet even Christians feel their pull.

Ann understood that knowing Christ and reveling in His beauty and love are the only ways to detach oneself from idols and recognize their vanity. "Nothing can I find among them to compete with his high worth. Be my dwelling in his love through all my days."[3] This was her wish. "O to spend my life in a sea of wonders!" she said in another poem.[4] And she did. Her life, spent almost entirely within the narrow confines of her Welsh farm, was lived in a constant and exciting discovery of the wonders of God's scriptural revelation.

ANN'S LIFE

Dolwar-Fach, the farm where Ann was born in 1776, was located in the parish of Llanfihangel-yng-Ngwynfa, in the northeastern county

---

1. E. Wyn James, ed., *Flame in the Mountains: Williams Pantycelyn, Ann Griffiths and the Welsh Hymn*, trans. H. A. Hodges (Tal-y-bont, Ceredigion, Wales: Y Lolfa, 2017), hymn XIII.3. The question is taken from Hosea 14:8.

2. Rowan Williams, *The Poems of Rowan Williams* (Grand Rapids: Eerdmans, 2002), 100.

3. James, *Flame in the Mountains*, hymn XIII.3.

4. James, *Flame in the Mountains*, hymn XV.

of Montgomeryshire, Wales. She was the fourth of five children. Her parents, John and Jane Thomas, were well respected in the area and reasonably well off. Being Anglican, they made sure the Bible and portions of the Book of Common Prayer were read daily in their home.

Ann received a basic formal education. She could read and write Welsh and learned some English, although she never became fluent in it. Her days were spent on the farm, taking care of the daily upkeep of the home and spinning wool—the most important product of her region.

Although the Welsh Methodists were still formally members of the established Anglican Church in Ann's day, they held their own independent meetings, which met with the disapproval of many, including Ann. In 1796, however, she experienced a religious crisis after hearing a sermon in an open-air evangelistic meeting in Llanfyllin, a market town some five miles northeast of her home. She felt strongly convicted of her sins, so much that she doubted God could ever love her. Unable to find relief in her local parish church, she decided to listen to a preacher in one of the Methodist meetings she had so despised. There, she found concrete answers to her doubts.

As often as possible, she would travel over the Berwyn Mountains to attend the large Methodist meetings in Bala, over twenty-five miles northwest of Dolwar-Fach, in the company of other Methodists from her area, including her elder brothers, John and Edward, and a family servant, Ruth Evans, who was one of Ann's dearest friends.

Bala was the home of Thomas Charles, the main leader of the Methodists in north Wales. He was one of the pioneers of the Sunday school movement[5] in Wales and one of the founders of the Bible Society. The story of Mary Jones, the young girl who walked over twenty-five miles to purchase a Bible from Charles, is well known in

---

5. At that time, Sunday schools were different from what we today call by the same name. In Ann's day they were meant to give basic reading instruction, based on the Scriptures, to both adults and children, enabling them to read the Scriptures on their own (see "Food for Thought" in chapter 24 of this book). Under the leadership of Thomas Charles, Sunday schools spread widely throughout Wales.

the Christian church. Few people remember that Ann Griffiths took a similar journey as often as possible, although from the opposite direction, in order to hear Charles preach.

In 1794 Ann's mother died. Since Ann's older sisters had married, Ann became the mistress of the house. When ten years later her father died too, twenty-eight-year-old Ann and her brother John, who had never married, ran the farm together.

Later that year, Ann married a local farmer and fellow Methodist, Thomas Griffiths, who then moved to Dolwar-Fach. Their happiness was short-lived. The next year, their first daughter, Elizabeth, survived only two weeks after her birth, and Ann, ill and frail, died about two weeks after the baby. The cause of Ann's death is not clear, but the stress of childbirth might have aggravated an existing condition—probably tuberculosis, the same disease that later killed both her brother and her husband.

Ann was buried at Llanfihangel on August 12, 1805. The funeral sermon, given by Ruth Evans's husband, John Hughes, centered on a text Ann had quoted in her letters: "For to me to live is Christ, and to die is gain" (Phil. 1:21).

ANN'S SONGS

The death of this young Welsh farmer's wife would have gone unnoticed to the world if Ruth had not memorized some of Ann's poems. Ruth could not write, so the poems were later written down by her husband, John, a young Methodist leader who had been Ann's mentor and confidant for some years. Published by Thomas Charles within a few months of Ann's death, the poems were also included around the same time in a hymnbook published by Robert Jones of Rhos-lan, another Welsh Methodist preacher.

These early editions, however, contained some strong editing. The edition that was closer to Ann's original words was published in 1905, straight from John Hughes's notebooks. That edition also included Ann's surviving letters: seven to Hughes and one to Elizabeth Evans, Ruth's sister.

Most of Ann's poems were set to music and became immediately popular. Even literary critics consider them unique for their ability to weave together biblical verses in a natural expression of the soul's gratitude to God. In fact, the major dramatist, poet, and literary critic Saunders Lewis called her longest hymn, "Rhyfedd, rhyfedd gan angylion" (Wondrous sight for men and angels), "one of the majestic songs in the religious poetry of Europe."[6]

Two elements contribute to making Ann's poems exceptional. The first is Ann's passion. Her discovery of God's free grace in Christ had come as a liberating force out of her anguish of feeling incapable of finding favor with God—an anguish so intense that she had rolled on the floor in pain. To Ann, this discovery was just the beginning of a life lived basking in God's "sea of wonders." And these wonders permeate her works with a force and immediacy that few poets can express.

The word *rhyfedd* ("wonder" or "wondrous") in its variations appears prominently in Ann's works. Much of the wonder comes from what she, echoing 1 Timothy 3:16, called a "mystery of godliness,"[7] the paradox of the God of gods appearing "in my nature, tempted, like the lowest of mankind, a babe, weak, powerless, the infinite true and living God"; of "the creation moving in him, and he dead in the tomb";[8] and of "the law [of God] held in honour" while "transgressors walk forth free."[9]

This last paradox is especially close to Ann's heart because her conviction of sin was still strong:

> Sinner is my name and nature,
> Fouler none on earth can be;
> In the Presence here—O wonder!—
> God receives me tranquilly;
> See him there, his law fulfilling,
> For his foes a banquet laid,

---

6. James, *Flame in the Mountains*, hymn XXII.1.
7. James, *Flame in the Mountains*, hymn III.3.
8. James, *Flame in the Mountains*, hymn XXII.4.
9. James, *Flame in the Mountains*, hymn I.2.

God and man 'Enough!' proclaiming
Through the offering he has made.[10]

This is the wonder that permeated Ann's life. And the God who could go to such lengths to love His foes—and Ann perceived clearly that she belonged by nature in that group—was worthy of much love and contemplation:

There he stands among the myrtles,
Worthiest object of my love;
Yet in part I know his glory
Towers all earthly things above;
One glad morning
I shall see him as he is.[11]

But for Ann, contemplation was not an end in itself. Meditations on the beauty of Christ as He is revealed in Scripture moved her to deep gratitude and made the idols of this world look like rubble and her trials like vapor.

The second element that makes Ann's poetry powerful is firmly connected to the first: her careful exploration of God's word. Her poems are so pregnant with Scripture that some critics have accused her of simply stringing Bible verses together. But that is far from the truth. Ann spoke the language of Scripture because she read it, memorized it, and meditated on it constantly. She often held her Bible open while she was spinning and amazed her companions when, on the long trips back from Bala, she could recite almost verbatim much of the sermon she had heard there.

Ann was careful to limit her contemplation to God's word, keeping her subjective feelings subordinate to the objective biblical truth "in its invincible authority."[12] Even her imagery comes strictly from the Bible. This has caused some interpretative problems for literary

---

10. James, *Flame in the Mountains*, hymn II.2.

11. James, *Flame in the Mountains*, hymn XIII.1.

12. Ann Thomas to John Hughes, April 1802 (letter VI), in James, *Flame in the Mountains*.

critics who are unfamiliar with Scripture. For example, some have seen an "erotic element" in the closing line of one of her hymns—"I shall kiss the Son for ever, turning from him nevermore,"[13]—when in reality this is a reference to Psalm 2:12, where kissing the Son is an expression of homage.

Likewise, another poem starts with Ann's contemplation of Christ "standing among the myrtles,"[14] an image that might sound purely poetic if not related to the imagery in Zechariah 1:8, where Christ "stood among the myrtle trees," announcing His plans of redemption of His people.

ANN'S LEGACY

Ann and her poems are popular in Wales. Much has been written about her. There are stained-glass windows in her memory. Her hymns are often sung at Welsh services, particularly "Wele'n sefyll rhwng y myrt-wydd" ("There He Stands among the Myrtles"), set to the tune Cwm Rhondda. In 2003 a new translation of this hymn by Rowan Williams was sung at his enthronement as archbishop of Canterbury.

Outside Wales, Ann is still rather unknown. This is to our loss. Her poems can enrich us by leading us to Scripture and uncovering treasures we often leave buried through familiarity or neglect. Especially, they will lead us to Christ, remind us why He is truly the "worthiest object of [our] love," and train our souls to engage in constant contemplation of His beauty. This is what Ann would have wanted most.

FOOD FOR THOUGHT

- When have you felt that the "vain idols of this earth" have exercised a pull on you? An idol is everything we place before God, everything that has priority in our hearts when we fail

---

13. James, *Flame in the Mountains*, hymn XII.7.
14. James, *Flame in the Mountains*, hymn XIII.1.

to run to God in prayer or that prevents us from obeying God. What idols are particularly tempting for you?

• Ann discovered what many Christians still ignore. We often try to fight sin in our own strength. Or even if we acknowledge that we should fight in God's strength, we often struggle to understand what that means in practical terms. Ann knew that many of our temptations and sinful desires lose their power when we realize who God is for us in Christ and who we are in Him. Can you give some practical examples of how this realization can make a difference in our daily lives?

• Familiarity with the Bible can be a debilitating problem for Christians, causing us to rest on our set interpretations and to miss the ever-fresh wonders God continues to communicate. Ann could say with confidence, "O to spend my life in a sea of wonders!" because she kept finding in God's treasure "things new and old" (Matt. 13:52). Her cry echoes Paul's doxology: "O the depth of the riches both of the wisdom and knowledge of God!" (Rom. 11:33). Which of these have become problems in your life: familiarity with God's Word, trying to read too much, trying to read too fast? Programs for reading through the Bible in one year can be helpful, but if they cause us to turn the pages too quickly, it might be time to slow down.

• Ann could keep exploring God's "sea of wonders" even though she was physically limited to a small Welsh farm. Do you ever feel that your circumstances limit your spiritual life or your usefulness to God? Explain your answer. Is Ann's example proving otherwise?

FOR FURTHER RESEARCH

The best treatise of the life and works of Ann Griffiths, which includes English translations of her poems and letters is E. Wyn James, ed., *Flame in the Mountains: Williams Pantycelyn, Ann Griffiths and the Welsh Hymn*, trans. H. A. Hodges (Tal-y-bont, Ceredigion, Wales: Y Lolfa, 2017).

See also the Ann Griffiths website: http://anngriffiths.cardiff.ac.uk.

27

Are These the Beings with Whom I Must Spend the Remainder of My Life?

BETSEY STOCKTON (ca. 1798–1865)

Whatever Betsey had imagined her foreign mission to be, it was not this. The group of Hawaiian men who came rowing in their canoes toward her ship was frightening: "Their appearance was that of half man and half beast—naked—except a narrow strip of tapa round their loins," she said.[1] To a young girl brought up in a conservative American family, this sudden encounter with "the Other" was a sight no book could have prepared her to face.

"The ladies retired to the cabin," she continued, "and burst into tears; and some of the gentlemen turned pale: my own soul sickened within me, and every nerve trembled. Are these, thought I, the beings with whom I must spend the remainder of my life!"[2] The culture shock didn't last long. Her mind, trained to understand reality through the lens of Scripture, found an immediate, steadying response: "They are men and have souls—was the reply which conscience made."[3]

GROWING UP A SLAVE

She had waited long for this moment. Her desire to become a missionary emerged soon after her baptism in 1817, and the opportunity

---

1. Betsey Stockton, *Journal*, April 4, 1823, in *The Christian Advocate*, ed. Ashbel Green (Philadelphia: A. Finley, 1825), 3:39.

2. Stockton, *Journal*, in Green, *Christian Advocate*, 3:39.

3. Stockton, *Journal*, in Green, *Christian Advocate*, 3:39.

arose five years later when some friends of her family, the newly married Charles and Harriet Stewart, were accepted as missionaries to the Sandwich Islands, now known as Hawaii. She asked if she could go along. Her request was unusual. She was single, and the American Board of Commissioners of Foreign Missions had never sent a single woman on a mission trip. She was also a former slave.

Born around 1798 to a slave in the household of Robert Stockton in Princeton, New Jersey, Betsey was still young when she was sent to Philadelphia to work for Robert's daughter Elisabeth. Elisabeth was married to Ashbel Green, a Presbyterian minister. The couple had three sons—Robert, Jacob, and James. Elisabeth died when Betsey was nine years old. Betsey continued to stay with the Green family and was tutored by Ashbel and James. Once she had learned to read well, she took advantage of the Greens' well-stocked library.

As a principal author of the 1818 antislavery resolution of the General Assembly of the Presbyterian Church, Green was opposed to slavery "as totally irreconcilable with the spirit and principles of the gospel of Christ."[4] His emancipation of Betsey, however, came later in her life. She remained a slave at least until the family moved to Princeton, when she probably became an indentured servant.

This delay might have had something to do with her behavior. According to Green, she was "wild and thoughtless, if not vicious," although she always "manifested a great degree of natural sensibility, and of attachment to [the Greens], and a great aptitude for mental improvement."[5]

This behavior might also have been a reason why in 1813 Green sold three years of Betsey's service to a relative and fellow pastor who lived in Woodbury, New Jersey. Later, Green explained his motives as an attempt to "save her from the snares and temptations of the

---

4. From the antislavery resolution of the General Assembly of the Presbyterian Church, as quoted in *The Presbyterian Magazine* 7, 1857: 520.

5. Ashbel Green to the American Board of Commissioners for Foreign Missions, Princeton, New Jersey, September 3, 1821, ABCFM archives vol. 4, no. 210, as quoted in Eileen F. Moffett, "Betsey Stockton, Pioneer American Missionary," *Priscilla Papers* 10, no. 1 (Winter 1996): 1.

city."[6] If so, he might have made the decision awhile before, because by 1813 he had already moved to Princeton, a small college town with limited "snares." Betsey returned to Princeton in 1816, was baptized, and received her independence, although she continued to live with the Greens and work for them for a salary.

MISSIONARY WORK—FROM DREAM TO REALITY

Ashbel Green supported Betsey's desire to join a missionary team. As a member of the American Board of Commissioners of Foreign Missions, he wrote a glowing recommendation. "She has been, for a good while, exceedingly desirous to go on a mission and I am willing that she should. I think her, in many respects, well qualified for this." He listed some of her qualifications. "There is no kind of work in a family at which she is not very expert. She is an excellent nurse. But I think her well qualified for higher employment in a mission than domestick drudgery. She reads extremely well; and few of her age and sex have read more books on religion than she; or can give a better account of them."[7]

Betsey received another recommendation from Michael Osborn, a student at Princeton Seminary who had been her Sabbath school teacher for the past eighteen months: "I would say in general, as the result of an intimate acquaintance with her, that I think her pious, intelligent, industrious, skillful in the management of domestic affairs, apt to teach, and endowed with a large portion of the active preserving, self-sacrificing, spirit of a missionary.... I am of the opinion that few pious young ladies of her age will be found to equal her in knowledge of the Bible, and general theology."[8]

---

6. Thomas French, *The Missionary Whaleship* (n.p.: Vantage Press, 1961), 113.

7. Ashbel Green to the American Board of Commissioners for Foreign Missions, as quoted in Abigail Rian Evans and Katharine Doob Sakenfeld, *Faith of Our Mothers, Living Still: Princeton Seminary Women Redefining Ministry* (Louisville, Ky.: Westminster John Knox Press, 2017), 11.

8. As quoted in Evans and Sakenfeld, *Faith of Our Mothers*, 11.

These testimonies allowed Betsey to fulfill her dream. Her contract stated that she was going to be part of the Stewart family, with the particular task of helping Harriet, who was pregnant at the time of their departure. "In this family," the contract specified, "she is to be regarded and treated neither as an equal or a servant—but as a humble Christian friend."[9] She was also to employ her talents and experience as a teacher in the schools founded by the missionaries.

On November 19, 1822, at twenty-five years of age, Betsey left on board the brig *Thames* with thirteen other missionaries and about the same number of sailors. She was the first Black woman and the first unmarried woman sent by an American missionary society.

AMAZEMENT, FEARS, AND REFLECTIONS

On the ship, Betsey kept a diary and wrote letters to her friends at home. While the originals of these writings have been lost, Ashbel Green published some excerpts in the *Christian Advocate*, allowing us to follow her on her trip to Hawaii. Betsey recorded every aspect of her journey, including her worsening seasickness and her amazement at the beauty of the ocean, with its variety of colors and its flocks of flying fish, playful dolphins, and spouting whales. "If it were in my power," she wrote, "I would like to describe the Phosphorescence of the sea. But to do this would require the pen of a Milton: and he, I think, would fail, were he to attempt it. I never saw any display of Fire-works that equaled it for beauty. As far as we could see the ocean, in the wake of the ship, it appeared one sheet of fire, and exhibited figures of which you can form no idea."[10]

The long trip around South America was a time of discovery for Betsey. She enjoyed tasting new foods and bathing in the warm water of the ocean and was captivated by the work of the fishermen.

---

9. As quoted in The Women's Project of New Jersey, *Past and Promise: Lives of New Jersey Women*, ed. Joan N. Burstyn (Syracuse, N.Y.: Syracuse University Press, 1997), 88.

10. Stockton, *Journal*, December 31, 1822, in Green, *Christian Advocate*, 2:234.

It was also a time of self-examination, particularly during the most frightening times, when water entered her cabin and especially when Harriet gave birth sooner than expected.

While the ship's cramped quarters and the frequent shouts of the sailors were not conducive to personal reflection, she had plenty of time to examine her heart and motives for going on the mission. "I find my heart more deeply corrupted than I had any idea of," she wrote. "I always knew that the human heart was a sink of sin, and that mine was filled with it; but I did not know, until now, that the sink was without a bottom."[11] Each time, however, she found comfort in the promises of Scripture, which she sprinkled in every page of her diary. In hindsight, she was grateful for the toughest times, which kept her dependent on God's mercy. "We have felt our helplessness," she said, "and been made to adore and tremble."[12]

ALL THINGS TO ALL MEN

The natives Betsey had initially feared proved to be generous, welcoming, and eager to learn. They showered the missionaries with fresh fish, potatoes, taro, and coconuts, which Betsey found "very refreshing…after a voyage of five months; part of which time we had no other diet than meat and bread."[13]

There were still local habits the missionaries found questionable and even "disgusting," such as eating baked dog and raw fish, often sitting on the floor surrounded by animals and flies. Shocked, Charles Stewart felt compelled to quote a poem:

> Can this be man?
> Bone of the bone, and flesh of the flesh, of him
> Whose majesty dignifies and crowns creation's plan…?[14]

---

11. Stockton, *Journal*, February 6, 1823, in Green, *Christian Advocate*, 2:564.

12. Stockton, *Journal*, February 9, 1823, in Green, *Christian Advocate*, 2:565.

13. Stockton, *Journal*, April 4, 1823, in Green, *Christian Advocate*, 3:39.

14. Charles Samuel Stewart, *Journal of a Residence in the Sandwich Islands* (London: H. Fisher, Son, and Jackson, 1828), 153.

But these perplexing sights didn't deter Betsey from her vocation, as she learned "to become all things to all men, that we may gain some."[15]

Not all the natives believed the missionaries had come for their good. Some had suspicions about their motives. At a council meeting, they decided to give the missionaries one year to prove themselves. Their suspicions were not unwarranted. There was a large number of foreigners in the island, not all for the best reasons. Some were well-respected merchants or property owners, and others were runaway sailors or fugitives from justice who, according to Charles Stewart, thought they were finally "free from any restraint of God and men" and exercised a negative influence on the natives.[16]

Betsey's diary ends soon after her arrival on the Islands, but Stewart made mention of her as their "humble friend," who "daily proves more and more kind, affectionate, and faithful" and "an invaluable addition to our family."[17] He described her valuable educational accomplishments—first as teacher to the royal family, and later as superintendent of a newly founded school for the local children. She was particularly qualified for this position due to her experience and ability to learn the language. She was also able to put to use her experience in the medical field. Stewart remembered one time particularly when she rescued two infants from conditions that probably would have led to their death.

TEACHER AND PRINCIPAL

Betsey's missionary venture was cut short on October 17, 1825, when Harriet became so ill that her husband decided to return to America. Betsey followed the Stewarts to Harriet's hometown, Cooperstown, New York, where she remained for some time. From then on, her activities focused on education. In 1828 she was invited to Philadelphia to open a school for Black children. Two years later, she accepted

---

15. Stockton, *Journal*, April 4, 1823, in Green, *Christian Advocate*, 3:39.
16. Stewart, *Journal*, 160.
17. Stewart, *Journal*, 46.

an invitation to open a school among the native populations living on the Canadian side of Lake Ontario.

She returned to the Stewarts in 1830, after Harriet's sudden death, and cared for their three children for five years while their father, then a naval chaplain, served at sea. Three years later, she moved with the children to Princeton, where the oldest child, Charles, attended the exclusive Edgehill School. There too she taught both in the local Black community church and in the public school for Black children.

Most accounts of her life fail to report the atmosphere of racism that surrounded her. While the people closest to her were loving and supportive, the idea of spending public funds for a school for Black children received much opposition. What's more, several students at Princeton, particularly those who came from the South, had adopted a condescending attitude toward the Black population, and episodes of violence were not unknown.

There is no record of Betsey's response to these challenges. Her life was devoted to a task she had found essential: the academic and religious education of children of all races. It's probably safe to suppose that she continued to face each new circumstance with the same readiness to draw answers from Scripture and the same humility, honesty, and trust in God's care that she demonstrated in her diary.

She continued to teach until her death on October 24, 1865. Her gravestone reads, "Of African blood and born in slavery, she became fitted by education and divine grace for a life of great usefulness. For many years was a valued missionary at the Sandwich Islands in the family of Rev. C. S. Stewart, and afterwards till her death, a popular and able Principal of Public schools in Philadelphia and Princeton, honored and beloved by a large circle of Christian friends."[18]

---

18. Barbara Bennett Peterson, in *African-American Lives*, ed. Henry Louis Gates Jr. and Evelyn Brooks (New York: Oxford University Press, 2004), 794.

FOOD FOR THOUGHT

- It's safe to suppose that Betsey's belief that all human beings—regardless of appearance or behavior—were created with an immortal soul had much to do with her faithful service to others. How does a view of others as people made in the image of God affect the way that we treat them? Give some practical examples.

- Have you ever found yourself around people who seemed radically different from you and from those you are accustomed to being with? How were they different? How did you react? Did you come to the same conclusions as Betsey? Why or why not?

- Do you think people have a natural tendency to gravitate toward those who are like them? Have you noticed this in your life? Have you noticed it in your church? Give some examples. What are some negative outcomes produced by this tendency? How can it be overcome?

- What did Paul mean when he said, "I am made all things to all men, that I might by all means save some" (1 Cor. 9:22), a verse Betsey applied to her situation? Historically, missionaries have taken it to mean that we should adopt other people's customs, as long as they are not unlawful. What other applications do you see? How can you apply it to people who share your customs but who you still find profoundly different (for example, because of their habits, way of thinking, or emotional responses)? Do you agree or disagree that Paul's commitment included a willingness to understand others by entering into their experience and state of mind and to gain an appreciation of their habits, thoughts, and emotions? Explain your answer.

- We find the greatest example of becoming all things to all men in Christ, "who, being in the form of God, thought it not robbery to be equal with God: but made himself of no reputation, and took upon him the form of a servant, and was made in the likeness of men. And being found in fashion as a man, he humbled himself, and became obedient unto death, even the death of the cross" (Phil. 2:6–8). In her diary, Betsey showed her efforts to imitate this attitude of self-forgetfulness by appearing cheerful in spite of her trials for the sake of those around her and by praying that God would make her a comfort to the Stewarts. Give other examples of how a realization of Christ's love for us can transform our attitude toward others. See chapter 2 of Philippians for context and more applications.

FOR FURTHER RESEARCH

For a short treatment of Betsey's life, see Abigail Rian Evans and Katharine Doob Sakenfeld, *Faith of Our Mothers, Living Still: Princeton Seminary Women Redefining Ministry* (Louisville, Ky.: Westminster John Knox Press, 2017).

For a convenient online reprint of Betsey's journal, see African-American Religion: A Documentary History Project, https://aardoc .sites.amherst.edu/Betsey_Stockton_Journal_1.html.

28

Can True Science Disagree with the Bible?

LYDIA MACKENZIE FALCONER MILLER (1812–1876)

On December 30, 1856, Lydia Miller followed her husband's coffin to the Grange cemetery in Edinburgh, Scotland. With her were thousands of people who loved and respected Hugh Miller, particularly for his thought-provoking writings on a variety of subjects. As Michael Shortland, editor of *Hugh Miller's Memoirs*, aptly said, "In choosing him, readers were choosing a friend."[1]

A question drifted through the crowd: *Why*? On Christmas Eve, after reading some poems to his children and sending them to bed, Hugh had written a suicide note to his wife, Lydia, and shot a bullet through his chest, muffling the sound. Lydia discovered the body the next morning. "Dearest Lydia," he wrote, "I must have walked, and a fearful dream rises upon me. I cannot bear the horrible thought. God and Father of the Lord Jesus Christ, have mercy upon me."[2]

A LOVE STORY

Lydia first met Hugh in 1831 in his hometown of Cromarty, Scotland, where she and her widowed mother had set up a school. Lydia was nineteen, but her delicate features and petite size made her look three or four years younger. Hugh was twenty-nine, six feet tall,

---

1. As quoted in Elizabeth Sutherland, *Lydia, Wife of Hugh Miller of Cromarty* (East Lothian, Scotland: Tuckwell Press, 2002), 111.
2. Sutherland, *Lydia, Wife of Hugh Miller*, 108.

with the rough appearance of "a working man in a Sunday suit." She was attracted by his eyes, of "a deep blue tinged with sapphire." He thought she was "very pretty."[3]

In time, the two became friends and found similar interests in matters of literature, philosophy, and religion. Slowly, friendship turned to love. Aware of these developments, Lydia's mother, Elizabeth, vetoed their relationship. Hugh was a simple stonemason, largely self-taught, with feeble financial prospects. She wanted something better for her daughter. Lydia's tears only confirmed Elizabeth's suspicions that love had already sprouted in her heart.

For a while, Lydia continued to see Hugh clandestinely, but Elizabeth learned about their meetings and talked to Hugh directly. Hugh did his best to respect Elizabeth's wishes, but an unplanned encounter with Lydia in 1833 revealed that their feelings had only grown stronger. They became engaged the same November. To appease Elizabeth, they agreed the engagement would last three years, and if by the end of it Hugh had not found a stable and lucrative occupation, they would emigrate to America.

Hugh's aspiration was to work as a writer for a newspaper or magazine. Since he had no qualifications, he thought of writing a book to attract some attention. Lydia offered to help, both in editing and in financing the publication. Hugh refused her latter proposal, looking instead for pledges.

HANDLING DISAGREEMENTS

Lydia was an able writer and editor. Hugh didn't always concur with her corrections, but it didn't matter. "You know we can differ and yet be very excellent friends," he said.[4] To him, the only element of a marriage in which unity of thought was essential was religion. "However diverse in our tastes, however different in our opinions, however dissimilar in our philosophy," he wrote, "let us at least desire, my own

---

3. Peter Bayne, *The Life and Letters of Hugh Miller* (Boston: Gould and Lincoln, 1871), 1:274.
4. Bayne, *Life and Letters*, 1:300.

dearest Lydia, to be at one in our religion."[5] She agreed, knowing that Hugh was always willing to have honest discussions and was humble and charitable in his judgment.

One example of this willingness to resolve conflicts occurred during a discussion of the necessity of good works in the Christian life. Lydia, who had defended their importance, felt misunderstood by all present and especially offended by the remarks another lady had made. "I was sorry to perceive that you were seriously displeased," Hugh wrote, "and that in consequence of a rather unskillful statement of doctrine on your part, which was I dare say occasioned by the use of language rather bold than correct on mine, Mrs. __ was led to deem your opinion heretical."

Hugh understood that sometimes Christians can agree in heart while it seems as though they disagree because of the way they express themselves. "I am confident that in reality we are at one on this subject," he said. No Christian, he said, doubts that "the law is the rule which God has revealed for our obedience."

He continued:

> On the other, neither Mrs. __ nor you nor I can doubt that the injunction "Do this and live," whether applied to the law as embodied in written commands or as exemplified in the life of Christ, is the now impossible condition of the old covenant, not the glorious watchword of the new; and that under this better covenant the ability of imitating Christ is a grace bestowed, not a condition exacted.
>
> All this, my Lydia, might have been said and agreed to without any angry feeling or personal remark; but we are so weak and foolish, my lassie, that we cannot so much as contend for the necessity of imitating Christ without showing by something more conclusive than argument how impossible it is for us to imitate Him aright.[6]

---

5. Bayne, *Life and Letters*, 1:311.
6. Bayne, *Life and Letters*, 1:311.

WIFE, MOTHER, AND WRITER

Hugh published his first book, *Scenes and Legends of the North of Scotland*, in 1835. Still lacking job prospects in newspapers and magazines, he accepted a clerical job at the Commercial Bank in Cromarty. This provided a steady income, which allowed him to marry his beloved Lydia on January 7, 1837.

The Millers' first year of marriage was crowned in November by the birth of their first child, Elizabeth (called Eliza). But the joy was followed by serious health concerns. First, in the summer of 1838, Hugh contracted smallpox and was so ill that he experienced hallucinations. The following year, Eliza became gravely sick. Her parents thought her fever was connected with teething, but it lasted nine months, until she died in Lydia's arms.

Lydia's description of the scene of the dying child and her weeping father "prostrate in the dust before God"[7] is heart-wrenching. Soon after, Lydia wrote a poem based on the child's last words, which were among her first: "awa, awa," which Lydia interpreted as "away." The last two of the nine stanzas end with a word of hope:

> And does my selfish heart then grudge thee,
> That angels are thy teachers now,
> That glory from thy Saviour's presence
> Kindles the crown upon thy brow?
>
> O, no! to me earth must be lonelier.
> Wanting thy voice, thy hand, thy love;
> Yet dost thou dawn a star of promise,
> Mild beacon to the world above.[8]

The Millers' faith was nurtured weekly by the preaching of the gospel, delivered in the local church by Reverend Alexander Stewart, who had

---

7. Jean L. Watson, *Life of Hugh Miller* (Edinburgh: James Gemmel, George IV Bridge, 1880), 74.

8. *Modern Scottish Poets, with Biographical and Critical Notices*, Third Series (Brechin: D. D. Edwards, 1881), 312, Internet Archive, https://archive.org/stream/modernscots300edwauoft/modernscots300edwauoft_djvu.txt.

become a dear friend of the family. Over time, both Stewart and the Millers agreed with the large group of Christians who ended up dividing from the Church of Scotland in what is known as the Disruption.

Divisions in the church are always painful, but these people believed this was necessary in order to preserve the purity of gospel preaching. The main problem was that local churches were supported by patrons who claimed the right to demote and install ministers. The Millers, like many others, believed the choice of pastors should belong to the churches. Their new branch of the church, known as the Free Church of Scotland, gave a high priority to the preaching of the gospel as it was recovered during the Protestant Reformation.

The Millers' religious convictions permeated their lives and writings. In 1840, Hugh became editor of a new evangelical publication called *The Witness*, second only to the national newspaper *The Scotsman* in circulation. Hugh wrote clearly and forcefully about several religious issues. Since the paper was based in Edinburgh, the family moved there. Lydia continued to help Hugh with editing and suggestions and wrote occasional reviews.

By that time, they had another daughter, Harriet ("Ha-Ha," as she called herself). Three more children followed: William in 1842, Elizabeth ("Bessie") in 1843, and Hugh II in 1850.

In spite of her busy life and frail health, Lydia spent some of her time writing books of her own, something Hugh had greatly encouraged her to do. In 1846 she published a children's book under the pseudonym Mrs. Harriet Myrtle. The name was probably taken from a comparison Hugh used to make of Lydia having "the delicacy of a myrtle" against his "strength of the oak."[9]

The following year, Lydia published a novel, *Passages in the Life of an English Heiress, or Recollections of the Disruption Times in Scotland*. The choice of fiction as a medium to express the social context of the Disruption was both a challenge and an opportunity to portray the variety of emotions that accompanied the event. It was also

---

9. Sutherland, *Lydia, Wife of Hugh Miller*, 43.

a courageous decision because many Christians at that time saw fiction as a lie.

Lydia's convictions are apparent throughout the book. For example, her protagonist, Jane Hamilton Legh, responds to a litany of praises for the Moderates' laissez-faire attitude by saying that those accomplishments "are not the chief ends of a clergyman's life."[10] That's something that Hugh and Lydia might have said.

Apparently, the novel, somewhat too long and unpolished, didn't produce any reviews apart from Hugh's. After that, Lydia focused on children's books, ending with the popular *Cats and Dogs, Nature's Warriors and God's Workers: or Mrs. Myrtle's Lessons in Natural History* (later reprinted as *Cats and Dogs: or, Notes and Anecdotes of Two Great Families of the Animal Kingdom*).

Natural history was one of Lydia's passions, probably sparked by Hugh's interest in geology. In spite of being self-taught in this subject, Hugh became a competent expert on the subject, so much that several scientists sought his views and advice. Like Hugh, Lydia considered science and religion to be complementary, with science as a tool to appreciate God's glory. "An unfailing harmony," she wrote, "runs through all the works of the Creator."[11]

SEARCHING FOR REASONS

Speculations immediately followed Hugh's suicide. A postmortem examination showed "diseased appearances found in the brain." The final judgment was that the suicide had been committed "under the impulse of insanity."[12]

Hugh had not been well for a while. He had complained to his doctor that his brain was "giving way" and had reported terrible nightmares that left him "trembling all over, and quite confused."

---

10. Sutherland, *Lydia, Wife of Hugh Miller*, 79.

11. Lydia Falconer F. Miller (Harriet Myrtle), *Cats and Dogs: or, Notes and Anecdotes of Two Great Families of the Animal Kingdom* (London: T. Nelson & Sons, 1868), 223.

12. Bayne, *Life and Letters*, 2:477.

He had also reported sharp pains like "an electric shock"[13] passing through his brain and leaving a burning sensation on top of his head. Because of these physical symptoms and the visible appearance of a diseased brain, some have suggested Hugh had a brain tumor. Whatever it was, it was entirely unexpected. Like most illnesses of the brain, it was also largely unexplainable.

For a moment, Lydia tried to explain it as an accident—that is, until Hugh's friend Thomas Guthrie showed her the suicide note Hugh had left on his desk. "I shall never forget the face that looked up to mine," Guthrie recalled, "and the cry of agony to which the news, though communicated on my part with all possible delicacy, was received."[14]

After a while, the realization that death might have relieved Hugh of a difficult life of suffering gave Lydia some consolation. The outpouring of support from her church, family, and friends was also a source of encouragement. But her greatest comfort came from God. "Everything that could alleviate the suffering of such a stroke has been given by His loving hand,"[15] she wrote with a shaking hand in a letter to her mother.

FAITH AND REASON

Still stunned by the tragedy and struggling with her poor health, Lydia began to edit some of Hugh's unpublished works and applied his desired revisions to some published ones. Her motives were both to honor his memory and to continue to communicate his passion for geology in the light of God's glorious creation. In order to do so, she had to study pertinent books and seek the advice of experts.

Like Hugh, Lydia believed that serious scientific discoveries could only magnify God's glory. In her preface to his *Footprints of the Creator*, she wrote, "The *fact* of creative power implies an absence

---

13. Bayne, *Life and Letters*, 2:464.
14. Thomas Guthrie, *Autobiography of Thomas Guthrie*; and Rev. David K. Guthrie and Charles J. Guthrie, *Memoir* (Detroit: Craig and Taylor, 1878), 540.
15. Sutherland, *Lydia, Wife of Hugh Miller*, 110.

of *limit* to creative power."[16] In this preface, she had to counter the teachings of Charles Darwin, who, with his 1859 *On the Origins of the Species by Means of Natural Selection*, had challenged biblical teachings. She believed Darwin deserved respect. "In so far as Mr. Darwin bases his reasoning on facts, and not on the absence of them…is Mr. Darwin's work a valuable acquisition to the natural historian."[17]

Like Hugh, she conceded that science might bring up evidences that have not been considered, and as long as these are facts and not suppositions, they deserve some serious reflection. But she was convinced that these evidences would always line up with God's revelation. For example, if science proved by facts that there is an elasticity between species, that would be "an elasticity with which the Creator has, for the wisest purposes, endowed them."[18]

In *Footprints of the Creator*, Hugh had discussed the theory of evolution as a "theory of development" and its contradiction of the biblical teaching of an immortal human soul. The pre-Darwinian proponents of this theory ultimately had to admit that it would lead to a denial of the existence of the soul and—consequently—life after death. Hugh added that it would also lead to atheism and moral indifference (who cares about morals if there is no afterlife?) or—as Lydia said—to a "reign of selfishness":

> The most efficient protest against this blind exclusive theory, which would inaugurate the reign of selfishness throughout nature, is to be found in the human heart. Childhood recognizes a Father in Heaven in the daily blessings of its little life; and the more enlightened the mind unsophisticated by special theory becomes, the more is it brought into harmony with this first lesson of the heart. As the eyes of the understanding are opened day by day, the magnificent adaptations of Nature press forward evermore, as parts of "one stupendous whole."[19]

16. Lydia Miller, preface to *Footprints of the Creator: or the Asterolepis of Stromness*, by Hugh Miller (Edinburgh: William P. Nimmo, 1872), lvi.

17. Miller, preface to *Footprints of the Creator*, lxi.

18. Miller, preface to *Footprints of the Creator*, lxi.

19. Miller, preface to *Footprints of the Creator*, lxi.

Lydia worked on Hugh's writings for six years, allowing readers to enjoy many works that might have otherwise remained unpublished. Little is known of her later years. She also assisted Peter Bayne in writing Hugh's biography. She moved to her hometown of Inverness in 1863, where she continued to write for children.

She died at the age of sixty-four on March 11, 1876, at Lochinver, Sutherland, where she was staying with her daughter Bessie. On her death certificate, Bessie's husband, Rev. Norman N. Mackay, wrote, "Disease of the spine 24 years."[20] Lydia had been suffering for many years, trying different treatments that proved ineffective. Some people have speculated that she might have had osteoporosis, which can cause fatal fractures.

Hugh and Lydia Miller have been largely forgotten outside Scotland. Hugh is often remembered as an anomaly in his efforts to reconcile faith and science, and his death provokes more discussions than his life. In his day, however, his writings were greatly valued, and Lydia's efforts were recognized as essential for a faithful preservation of his legacy.

FOOD FOR THOUGHT

- By promoting science as the proper exploration of God's world, Hugh and Lydia were simply reaffirming what Christians had said throughout history. Some of the greatest scientists had been Christians, and the supposed contention between science and Christianity originated with a few eighteenth-century promoters of natural philosophy. Who were some of these great Christian scientists?

- Far from being narrow-minded, Hugh and Lydia welcomed new scientific discoveries. They were convinced that true science—being an exploration of God's creation—cannot disagree with what God has revealed in Scripture. As Lydia

---

20. Sutherland, *Lydia, Wife of Hugh Miller*, 159.

pointed out, however, this applied to scientific facts, not "absence of facts," or suppositions. What do you think about this idea? What are some areas where Christianity has taken into consideration new scientific discoveries? What are some points on which Christianity has refused to compromise?

- How does the fact that science continues to make new discoveries keep Christians humble?

- How should the fact that we are finite creatures, continually discovering new facts about creation, keep any true scientist humble?

- The death of a loved one is always painful, but for Lydia the news that Hugh had committed suicide was absolutely devastating. Why do you think this is usually the case?

- Hugh's visible brain disorder helps us understand in some ways an act his family would have found harder to explain. In your opinion, what is the church's attitude today toward believers who commit suicide? Do you think there is enough compassion and understanding? Is there enough support for their families? What do you think of Martin Luther's comparison of a person who committed suicide to a man overtaken by a robber in a wood?[21] What are your opinions, and how are they based on Scripture?

- How does the apparent disagreement between Lydia and Hugh on the importance of good works and Hugh's humble answer help us in our discussions with others?

- Do you think Christians can write and read fiction? Explain why or why not.

---

21. Martin Luther, *Luther: Letters of Spiritual Counsel*, trans. Theodore G. Tappert (Vancouver, British Columbia: Regent College Publishing, 1960), 58.

FOR FURTHER RESEARCH

For a complete biography of Lydia Miller, see Elizabeth Sutherland, *Lydia, Wife of Hugh Miller of Cromarty* (East Lothian, Scotland: Tuckwell Press, 2002).

For an early, lengthy biography of Hugh Miller, complete with some of his letters, see Peter Bayne, *The Life and Letters of Hugh Miller*, 2 vols. (Boston: Gould and Lincoln, 1871).

For a shorter, newer biography of Hugh Miller, with interesting comments, see Michael A. Taylor, *Hugh Miller: Stonemason, Geologist, Writer* (Edinburgh: National Museums of Scotland, 2007).

For the most popular of Lydia Miller's children's books, see Lydia Falconer F. Miller (Harriet Myrtle), *Cats and Dogs: or, Notes and Anecdotes of Two Great Families of the Animal Kingdom* (London: T. Nelson & Sons, 1868). Other writings by Lydia are available online.

29

Can Christians Have Disturbing Thoughts?

SARAH SERGEANT MILLER (1777–1861)

When Samuel Miller married Sarah Sergeant, he didn't know the extent of her pain. Emotional anguish and religious skepticism were not a proper topic of discussion. At least that's what Sarah's mother had taught her. She had told her daughter that doubting was normal, and "especially that [Sarah] should avoid making it a subject of conversation, or even of thought, as much as possible."[1] And that's what Sarah did. "I took her advice and began a violent struggle," she wrote, "which continued many years afterwards, and so far succeeded, as to enable me to put on the appearance of peace, when all was panic within."[2]

A LONG-STANDING BATTLE

In a detailed autobiographical confession written to her husband six years after their wedding, Sarah explained that she had been constitutionally "prone to melancholy." To aggravate this tendency, a host of deep-seated religious doubts crowded her mind.

Before doubt, there was indifference—youthful disinterest in formal religious instruction. "The peculiar doctrines of the gospel, as a system, had never been presented to my mind and formed no part of the education which was given me," she wrote. "The Bible I read at

---

1. Samuel Miller, *The Life of Samuel Miller, D.D., L.L.D.* (Philadelphia: Claxton, Remsen, and Haffelfinger, 1869), 1:163.

2. Miller, *Life*, 1:163.

school as children generally do, and in the same unprofitable manner, without retaining in my mind, or having my heart engaged in any truth contained in it."[3]

Sarah's father, Jonathan Dickinson Sergeant, attorney general of Pennsylvania, was conservative but not particularly religious. The family maintained weekly church attendance, and Sarah's mother pointed her children to God's providential intervention—both habits Sarah came to appreciate later in life.

But Sarah's mother died in 1787. Two years later, Jonathan Sergeant remarried and sent eleven-year-old Sarah to boarding school—the first in a series of schools where she was exposed to "the sentiments and practices of the world."[4] It could have happened in any school, but she found it particularly so in boarding schools, "where children are constantly together."[5] She mentioned being influenced by the new ideals of the French Revolution.

These new "sentiments" shook Sarah's weak religious convictions. The violent epidemic of yellow fever in 1793 unmasked her religion for what it was: "a superstitious dependence on the Bible." She turned to it automatically but "read it formally, and felt as if there was a righteousness in the mere perusal. It was certainly not the seeking to which the promise 'ye shall find' is annexed. And it remained a sealed book to me."[6]

She had a similar reaction to her father's death the same year. She worried about his eternal state but "found relief only in hoping that he had been prepared for this change in some manner by his later works."[7] It was years later when she shifted her hope to God's mercy, taking his good works as evidence—not means—"of a better preparation."

---

3. Miller, *Life*, 1:150.
4. Miller, *Life*, 1:151.
5. Miller, *Life*, 1:151.
6. Miller, *Life*, 1:153.
7. Miller, *Life*, 1:153.

ADDICTION AND DEPRESSION

Sarah's best friend "M." was an avid reader of theistic works. "She seemed to have become herself persuaded that the Bible was her worst enemy," Sarah wrote, "and seized with eagerness, and read with avidity, every plausible work which had a tendency to weaken, or subvert, its influence."[8]

Sarah followed suit, "more for neglect of thinking, and the desire of being thought of having an independent spirit, than from knowledge or inquiry."[9] In reality, she was mostly interested in having fun, whether at the theater or at parties. She loved fashionable clothes and became addicted to card playing. She didn't call it gambling because the amount of money she bet was just enough to keep the game interesting. The habit was particularly deceiving when she played cards at home with relatives in a seemingly innocent environment: "Three of four nights every week were employed at the fascinating table; and hour after hour passed away, each one finding us more unwilling to leave it. It was becoming quite indispensable to my comfort. Every evening not thus employed was vacant and tedious."[10] Finally, "conscience imperiously said, 'This is a ruinous consumer of time.'"[11] She prayed and made a resolution to stop, only to break that promise a few months later.

Breaking her resolution had a devastating effect on her spirits. "I lost all dependence on my own resolutions, since I had failed in my engagements to him who was my only resource against myself."[12] This loss of self-confidence caused fun and games to lose their appeal, although Sarah kept them up, this time not "for gratification, but for relief."[13] Even the Bible gave her no comfort, in spite of her frequent attempts to read it.

---

8. Miller, *Life*, 1:154.
9. Miller, *Life*, 1:155.
10. Miller, *Life*, 1:156.
11. Miller, *Life*, 1:156.
12. Miller, *Life*, 1:159.
13. Miller, *Life*, 1:159.

"As long as you pore over the Bible so, you will be miserable," M. warned Sarah.[14] She remembered a neighbor whose signs of mental illness were attributed to the influence of Methodists on her life and wondered if M. was right. She mentions laudanum, a tincture of opium that was popular at that time, and her quick discovery that it increased rather than relieved her distress.

MARRIAGE

Around this time—the lowest point in her life—a friend and student of her father began to visit her. He was twice her age and owned considerable wealth. He was obviously pursuing marriage, even though he had not yet made a formal proposal.

She had no feelings for him but wondered if married life could offer her some relief. She thought of charitable activities she could pursue as a married woman—something to give meaning to her life. She didn't give much thought to her suitor's religious beliefs, even though he was reading some of the same books M. was promoting.

Before this man could act on his feelings, Samuel Miller made a similar round of visits to Sarah's home. He was curious to meet her after overhearing a tribute to her virtues. She was, to all who knew her, a kind and pious woman. Since Miller proposed marriage before the other man, Sarah felt free to accept. Miller was from a different world: a minister, professor, and author, he offered her something unlike anything she had experienced before. "Instead of the riches of this world, the Word of Life was presented in every form that could heal a wounded spirit such as mine," she wrote.[15]

This didn't mean instant healing. Five years after her wedding, she was still experiencing feelings of despair. In fact, they "increased in bitterness." She often went to bed praying that she might not get up again. She envisioned herself performing "some horrid act." "The bare idea almost drove me to desperation and, after rising a little

---

14. Miller, *Life*, 1:160.
15. Miller, *Life*, 1:162.

above the suggestion, the thought of such a possession again reduced me to agony,"[16] she wrote.

Eventually, however, the gospel worked in her heart, and she came to see her mental and emotional confusion as a preparation "for that strong hope which, notwithstanding all my sins and my infirmities, I now cherish."[17]

SLOW BUT SURE

Anticipating her husband's surprise at her long and silent anguish, Sarah explained her reticence to speak. Besides her blind trust in her mother's instructions, she feared the possible stigma. She explained, "I was afraid that the result of my agitations would be insanity, and was sure that if my state of mind were known I would already be considered as an insane woman, and become a spectacle."[18]

Her spiritual progress was gradual—learning to distinguish between "a legal and a childlike fear" of God and to place her confidence in Christ instead of in human beings took time. "How to believe the gospel was the question," she wrote. "I have sometime of late been inclined to doubt my hope, because my exercises did not reach the popular standard, but I am directed to the fountain for relief, and always find it there."[19]

Sarah wrote this confession in 1807, after a breakthrough the previous spring. If Samuel had been unaware of her mental distress, in 1802 he knew her faith was still struggling. But he was confident. "A variety of appearances inspire me with hope that the time is not distant when she will be able to unite with her husband in the hopes and joys, as well as the duties, connected with membership in the Redeemer's kingdom,"[20] he wrote in his diary.

---

16. Miller, *Life*, 1:164.
17. Miller, *Life*, 1:163.
18. Miller, *Life*, 1:163.
19. Miller, *Life*, 1:165.
20. Miller, *Life*, 1:169.

Forty-five years later, he could attest to the fulfillment of his expectations. "She is better qualified than many ministers to instruct the inquiring and to answer the perplexed and anxious. Hundreds of times I profited by her remarks on my sermons, and other public performances, more than by the remarks of any other human being."[21] Her progress had been slow but sure.

Besides raising nine children (the couple had ten, but one died in infancy), Sarah kept busy with the charitable work she had dreamed of doing. She was particularly active in the field of education, convinced as she was that a gospel-filled environment would have spared her from much pain. She died in 1861, eleven years after her husband, leaving her candid story as a testimony to God's faithfulness and mercy.[22]

FOOD FOR THOUGHT

- Can Christians suffer from mental illness? Explain your answer.

- Sarah's mother told her not to talk about disturbing thoughts. Have you known Christians who give the same advice, and why would they think this? What is the danger of doing so?

- Besides remembering her mother's advice, Sarah kept quiet for fear of consequences. Can fear of treatment or stigma prevent some people from seeking help? What are the results when this happens? Which other fears produce the same results?

- Sarah's friend told her, "As long as you pore over the Bible so, you will be miserable." Give examples of people today who blame religion for some people's mental anguish and fear.

---

21. Miller, *Life*, 2:496.

22. Sarah's autobiographical writing is preserved in the above-quoted biography her son Samuel wrote about his father.

- How could Sarah's life have been better if she had told Samuel about her anguish? What can Christians do to encourage those around them to freely express their feelings and concerns?

- Sarah eventually recovered. Not everyone can do this without help. In some cases, particularly with serious mental illness, medical intervention is necessary. In any case, however, a supportive family and meaningful work, such as Sarah found after her marriage, is conducive to good mental health. Discuss how you have noticed this in your life or in the life of someone you know.

- Sarah's strong resolutions didn't help her overcome her addiction to card playing. In fact, not being able to keep them only worsened her depression. How do you think the gospel helped her later? Name some promises of the gospel that offer hope to the struggling and support their fight against sin more than any resolution ever can.

FOR FURTHER RESEARCH

The full story of Sarah's life is recorded in Samuel Miller, *The Life of Samuel Miller, D.D., L.L.D.*, 2 vols. (Philadelphia: Claxton, Remsen, and Haffelfinger, 1869).

30

Can We Sing in Heaven
If Our Loved Ones Are Missing?

ANNE ROSS CUNDELL COUSIN (1824–1906)

The name of Anne Cousin is largely unknown today. It might sound familiar only to people who take the time to read the names of the authors of the hymns they sing. To most of them, Anne Cousin is known for one of her hymns, "The Sands of Time Are Sinking," a beautiful song on the sufficiency and beauty of Christ based on the letters of the seventeenth-century Reformer, Samuel Rutherford. "I wrote it as I sat at work one Saturday evening," she said in a letter forty years later, "and though I threw it off at that time, it was the result of long familiarity with the writings of Samuel Rutherford, especially his Letters."[1]

Familiarity is the correct word. While readers might recognize in her poem many of Rutherford's words, her work is not a patchwork of his quotations but a synthesis of a book that had become part of her life. Rutherford's letters, written in the seventeenth century, were particularly popular in Anne's time for the comfort they provided. They were, in fact, written for that purpose, to provide the same comfort Rutherford received from God while exiled in Aberdeen, Scotland, "for his non-conformity to the acts of Episcopacy and his work against the Arminians."[2]

---

1. As quoted in "Irvine Cross Trail: Anne Ross Cousin," North Ayrshire Heritage Trails, https://www.naheritagetrails.co.uk.
2. Samuel Rutherford, *Letters of Samuel Rutherford*, ed. Andrew Alexander Bonar (New York: Robert Carter and Brothers, 1863), xii.

In her long poem (nineteen stanzas), Anne imagined Rutherford on his deathbed expressing his joy in approaching heaven. The poem's refrain, "Glory, glory dwelleth in Emmanuel's land,"[3] is a direct quotation of Rutherford's dying words.

The poem was first published in 1857 in the *Christian Treasury* but didn't become widely known until 1863, when J. Hood Wilson of the Barclay Church, Edinburgh, introduced a version of five verses (only the fourth and fifth of which correspond with the now popular version) into a hymnal, *Service of Praise*, in 1865. This was not her intent because she didn't consider her poems suitable for congregational singing.

A full collection of Anne's poems was published in 1876 with the title *Immanuel's Land and Other Pieces*, listing the author as A. R. C. Some of these poems were later turned into popular hymns, including "King Eternal! King Immortal" and "O Christ, What Burdens Bowed Thy Head." This last one, with its sharp contrast between Thee and me (God's supply and my lack) was put to music by the American Ira D. Sankey and became a favorite among missionaries.

ANNE'S LIFE

Anne wrote most of her poems while she raised her children and assisted her husband, William Cousin, pastor in the Free Church of Scotland. Born in Hull in northeastern England on April 27, 1824, Anne lost her father when she was three, and she and her mother relocated to Leith, Scotland.

As an assistant surgeon in the 33rd Regiment, Anne's father, David Ross Cundell, left the family enough means to allow Anne to receive a good education under the tutelage of Rev. Wyer, an Episcopal clergyman. From him Anne learned English, French, and Italian. She also took piano lessons from John Muir Wood, who operated a successful music publishing company. Later, she learned German and enough Greek to read the New Testament in its original language.

---

3. Thomas Murray, *Life of Samuel Rutherford* (Edinburgh: William Oliphant, 1828), 322.

Although raised as an Episcopalian, Anne became drawn to the preaching of the Free Church of Scotland, particularly that of Horatius Bonar and Alexander Neill Somerville. The secession of some preachers from the established Church of Scotland and the subsequent birth of the Free Church occurred in 1843, when Anne was only nineteen.

The main reason for the secession, known as the Disruption, was a disagreement about patronage, the right of patrons to establish ministers of their own choosing. But the demand that a church be free to appoint its own ministers included the desire for the pure preaching of the gospel, and many preachers of the Disruption were known for their strong defense of the teachings of the Reformation. This obviously attracted Anne.

When Anne and William Cousin were married in 1847, William was minister of Chelsea Presbyterian Church in London, which was part of the Free Church of Scotland. She followed him there. Later they moved to Irvine, Scotland, where she wrote her famous hymn. Together they had six children: four sons and two daughters.

HARD QUESTIONS

In her poems—quite varied in subject—Anne doesn't shy from hard questions, no matter how painful. "The Burden of Dumah" is based on the question a man of Seir asked in Isaiah 21:11, "Watchman, what of the night?" This inspired Anne to describe this night in a long lament over those who seemed to willingly ignore any thought of divine judgment. Her sorrow came from knowing that their earthly mirth and mocking of God will soon come to a painful end:

> Long hath the noon of pride and wrong blazed high,
> And Satan reigned,
> And men blasphemed, and sin sent up its cry.
> And earth complained.
> But none were looking for the day of doom—
> None prayed the year of the redeemed might come.[4]

---

4. A. R. Cousin, *Immanuel's Land and Other Pieces,* new and rev. ed. (London: James Nisbet, 1896), 242.

The night doesn't spare the church:

> For the sad Church, morn hath not broken yet,
> To chase her fears.
> Her path to glory hath been dark, and wet
> With blood and tears.
> Her eyes have failed with looking for the day,
> It seemed so fair, but still so far away.

In the case of the church, however, there is a happy ending: "The Bridegroom cometh! Hark! He calls thee home."

But what if we arrive home and our loved ones are not there? This realization was a cause of distress for one of Anne's friends, and Anne wrote a poem in reply, titled "Thou Shalt Know Hereafter." After Anne described the joy of a person who arrived in heaven, she wondered how she would react to the conspicuous absence of a loved one:

> If then our glance falls on an empty place,
> If there's a jewel lacking in love's ring,
> If seeking for the welcome, warm embrace,
> We meet but empty silence—could we sing?
>
> Could the heart beat without a pulse of pain?
> Would not a cloud o'ercast the beaming eye?
> Would one sad string not mar our harpèd strain?—
> One shadow on our sun-bathed spirit lie?[5]

Anne had no definitive answer because Scripture has not provided one, and she underscored this with the verse she placed under her title. "What I do thou knowest not now; but thou shalt know hereafter" (John 13:7). As we read in Deuteronomy 29:29, "The secret things belong unto the LORD our God." But the verse doesn't end there. "But those things which are revealed belong unto us and to our children for ever, that we may do all the words of this law." The things that are revealed are sufficient for us.

---

5. Cousin, *Immanuel's Land*, 250.

O God! we know, though yet we see not how,—
We know that none shall feel bereaved in heaven;
But oh! we are not asked to see it now,
While friends we love, not yet to prayer are given.[6]

In encouraging her friend to be content with what we know, Anne was not dispensing some complacent formula aimed at dismissing uncomfortable thoughts. The rapid succession of five piercing questions in her poem tells us that she had immersed herself into her friend's agony. It might very well have been an agony she had experienced herself. And it might be from personal experience she learned that the scriptural assurance that God is wise and that our joy will be full is sufficient for those who have experienced God's goodness.

We know Anne's life was not free of doubts. In another poem, "The Clouds Are the Dust of God's Feet," she revealed her own struggle when clouds seem to hide God's face. Even here, her comfort rested in remembering that the works of God's providence, both holy and wise, are motivated by His love.

Thou'rt holy in Thy providence, Lord God,
If I but understood!
I dwell in doubt and sick suspense, Lord God,
Confounding ill with good.
One dawn-streaked opening leads to light above,
Christ alway loved Thy will,
and proved Thy will is love.[7]

Anne's scriptural intuition of the love, goodness, and beauty of God sustained her all her life. Her last years, after William's retirement in Edinburgh, were rather painful, with the successive deaths of her twenty-two-year-old son George, her thirty-two-year-old daughter Isabella, and William, who died before his seventy-first birthday.

---

6. Cousin, *Immanuel's Land*, 250.
7. Cousin, *Immanuel's Land*, 180.

In her sorrow she might have remembered the words of comfort she wrote for another friend who walked through a dark valley, wondering if she had strayed.

> So we, sweet friend, one pathway tread,
> Whether we walk 'neath light or gloom,
> With sun or star above our head,
> Around us, blight or bloom.
>
> May our own God but grant to me
> An evening time of mellow light.
> And bid the dawn soon rise on thee.
> Thou Pilgrim of the Night.[8]

Anne continued her pilgrimage in good health until December 6, 1906, when she died at her home at the age of eighty-two. Four years later, her son John William included her in his *Short Biographical Dictionary of English Literature*.

FOOD FOR THOUGHT

- Trusting that God's promises are true, even when we can't possibly see how, is one of the most challenging parts of the Christian life. Describe a time when you may have experienced a similar struggle. What do you find comforting about Anne's reply to her friend? What else would you add?

- In John 13:7, Deuteronomy 29:29, and many other passages of the Bible, God states that what He has revealed is sufficient for us in this life. When have you experienced this in your life? List some similar verses that express this truth.

- When we try to figure out God, heaven, or His providential intents in this life, we usually miss the mark because God is so much bigger, wiser, and more loving and good than we are.

---

8. A. R. Cousin, "To a Pilgrim of the Night," in Cousin, *Immanuel's Land*, 177.

Just think, could any creature have ever imagined God's solution to human sin? How did Anne's contemplation of God as He reveals Himself in Scripture help her to trust in His care?

• Trusting in God's providence can be difficult if we don't have assurance of the goodness and love of God. How are the closing lines of Anne's poem about her struggles, "Christ alway loved Thy will, and proved Thy will is love," helpful to someone who faces similar trials? How did Christ prove that God's will is love?

• In the poem "To a Pilgrim of the Night," Anne comforted a friend who believed her doubts and trials were a sign that she had strayed from the path to heaven. Anne told her the path is still the same. God keeps us on the straight path because of Christ, whether the path is smooth or rocky, dark or sunny. All Christians walk in it together, in spite of different outward experiences. How can this realization keep us from comparing ourselves with others? In what other ways is it comforting?

FOR FURTHER RESEARCH

Anne's poems are collected in A. R. Cousin, *Immanuel's Land and Other Pieces*, new and rev. ed. (London: James Nisbet, 1896).

31

Can the Church of Christ Be Destroyed?

JEANETTE LI (1899–1968)

Jeanette's birth in 1899 was a disappointment to her family. Like most Chinese parents at that time, You Zhong and his wife, Taai So, wanted a son to carry on the family name. Since they already had a daughter, a relative suggested the new baby should be left at the foundling house for abandoned children. But You Zhong knew that many children died in foundling houses. He decided to keep his daughter and gave her a cheerful name, Li Mao Ya (Jasmine Bud). Taai So, instead, was afraid of a name that could make the spirits jealous. She called the baby Zhao Ya (Noisy Baby)—a name that stuck within the family. The girl's name changed a few more times throughout her life. Today, she is best known as Jeanette Li.

BECOMING CHRISTIAN IN A HOSTILE LAND

Jeanette's family was poor but loving, and the girls grew up relatively happy. In 1905, however, You Zhong died of a sudden illness, leaving the family with a large debt and no means to pay it. Deaf to Taai So's protests, the creditor took her older daughter as payment. Jeanette and her mother were now alone.

The next year, Jeanette became seriously ill, and a relative brought her to the local mission hospital for treatment. Initially her mother was afraid of foreign doctors but allowed Jeanette to stay when she realized they took good care of her. Jeanette's doctor, Jean G. McBurney, led the young girl to Christ and invited her to enroll in their school. To make things easier, the mission offered Taai So a job.

Taai So was baptized in 1908 into the Reformed Presbyterian Church. As for Jeanette, the elders of the church wanted to wait a while before baptizing her, but she insisted. She was baptized the following year at the age of ten. She had never believed in the religious superstitions of her country anyhow, and the gospel provided reasonable and comforting answers to her many questions.

In 1911, due to a strong nationalist movement, the Qing dynasty came to an end and a republic was established. This brought on intense internal conflicts. Foreigners were no longer welcome. The mission closed, leaving the local Christians to fend for themselves.

Jeanette and her mother returned to their ancestral home in Tang Hin (Deqing), only to find that their relatives had taken over their property and refused to let them in. As Christians, Jeanette and her mother were considered a disgrace to their family. But Taai So called the village elders for help and was able to vindicate her right to her own house. When the missionaries returned in 1912, Jeanette was able to continue her education.

WIFE AND TEACHER

Jeanette was only fifteen and a half when her mother arranged her marriage to a Christian boy six months younger, Li Yong Guan. Jeanette wanted to wait, but her mother insisted. The marriage was performed by a Presbyterian missionary, Rev. A. I. Robb. From then on, Jeanette became commonly known as Mrs. Li.

As was customary, Jeanette moved into the home of her husband. There were no feelings of love, nor were they expected. The toughest part of the marriage, for Jeanette, was getting along with her mother-in-law, a domineering woman who disliked her and had no qualms about letting her know.

Since the marriage was not producing children, Li Yong's mother urged her son to get a concubine, which was a common Chinese custom at that time. But after Jeanette spent the night crying and praying, Li Yong never brought up the subject again. In 1919, four years after their marriage, the couple had a son, Min Ch'iu, also known as Timothy. By then Li Yong was gone most of the time, first to complete his studies in Canton, then to work as a teacher in Tai Po, Hong Kong.

Since her husband barely made enough money to support himself, Jeanette began teaching at Oi Lei Hok Tong, a Christian school for girls, in Tak Hing. She gave birth to a daughter named Man Shi, but the baby died after eighteen days. Eventually, Li Yong married another woman.

Realizing that she needed further education, in 1923 Jeanette enrolled in the normal school in Canton, graduating as a teacher three years later. Her aspiration of entering the government college in Nanking was crushed when the college demanded membership in the Nationalist Party, which required its members to renounce foreign religions. Thanks to a friend, she was able to find a job at a government school in Canton. After this, she was offered a position as substitute principal of the Chan Lei School for boys in Tak Hing and was soon promoted to principal.

SPREADING THE GOSPEL IN A DANGEROUS COUNTRY

Throughout this time, Jeanette felt called to greater involvement in evangelizing her country. With this purpose in mind, she took a two-year course at Ginling Bible College in Nanjing. From there, she was sent to the Reformed Presbyterian Mission in Tsitsihar (Qiqihar), Manchuria—a place far from her home where people spoke a different language.

Her work there was fruitful, in spite of the strict supervision of the Japanese forces who had occupied that part of the country. There, she benefited from the teachings and leadership of J. G. Vos, son of the more famous Geerhardus. Her son, Timothy, joined her there.

The 1941 attack on Pearl Harbor brought another interruption to the Americans' stay in the Japanese-occupied territories of China. Once again, the Chinese Christians continued their work alone, and Jeanette opened her home for meetings. But the government watched her carefully, and she had to weigh her words. At times they sent spies to her house to trick her to say or do something that would incriminate her.

Since they couldn't find anything against her, the government tried to employ Jeanette as a spy to find out information about a Roman Catholic Church in the area. In exchange, she would receive money and protection—two things she greatly needed at that time. Knowing that a flat refusal would be dangerous, Jeanette told the officer that as a Christian she couldn't do anything deceitful and asked him what he would do in her place: "Would not your conscience ever after reprove and condemn you?"[1] The officer didn't reply but left her alone.

The Russian invasion of Manchuria in 1945 marked another time of great upheaval. At that time Timothy had finished his studies at a medical school and was working as an intern at Shenyang Medical Hospital, about six hundred miles away. His wife, Pei Deng, and their son, Ch'I Chen, were staying with Jeanette, but since communication between cities was almost impossible, Jeanette thought it would be best if the family could reunite. To do so, she traveled with them to Shenyang.

When returning to Qiqihar proved unfeasible, she accepted a call to do evangelistic work at the hospital in Changchun, almost two hundred miles northeast of Shenyang. In the meantime, Timothy moved to America to specialize in immunology and bacteriology. The unstable political situation in the country forced Jeanette to move several times—first back to Shenyang, then to Shanghai, and finally to her hometown of Tak Hing. When in 1949 the Communist regime once again forced all foreigners out of China, Jeanette took over the orphanage in her town and managed it through many calamities and trials.

---

1. Jeanette Li, *Jeanette Li: A Girl Born Facing Outside*, trans. Rose Huston (Pittsburgh: Crown and Covenant, 2014), 181.

PRISON AND BRAINWASHING

But the "cleansing" started by the Communist regime was not over. After expelling all foreigners, they required all churches to register with the government so they could keep Christians under close scrutiny.

In January 1952, Jeanette was arrested and locked in a prison for seventeen months in awful conditions, sleeping on the floor in a damp cell infested by mosquitoes, with hardly any food, and forced to perform hard labor. When she became ill—first with a serious fever then with hemorrhaging dysentery—she was refused medical treatment.

During one interrogation, she was finally told the reason for her imprisonment: as a Christian with some connections to Americans, she was—in their eyes—a tool of imperialism, and they wanted to know how she had promoted it. Her protest that the church and imperialism are two different things didn't help.

The authorities produced as proof the report of a prayer by a missionary in Hong Kong who asked God to bless President Chang Kai Shek, then leader of the Republic of China in Taiwan. Chang Kai Shek had become a Christian and was opposed to the Communist regime. Jeanette was a suspect because she was in Hong Kong at the time of that prayer. She explained that the missionary was just obeying the Bible, which teaches Christians to pray for those who rule over them. But her explanation didn't help.

The interrogations continued week after week, at all hours of the day and night, followed by indoctrination against the Bible. Finally, in May 1953, unable to prove the validity of any of their charges, the authorities had to release her. She left only after they produced a paper saying she was "freed as an innocent citizen and not as a pardoned criminal."[2]

---

2. Li, *Jeanette Li: A Girl Born Facing Outside*, 290.

SHARING HER STORY

After this she moved to Canton, where her daughter-in-law, Pei Deng, lived. By this time Jeanette's health was so poor that she wished to die. Eventually, she recovered and resumed her work evangelizing Canton. In 1958 she was allowed to travel to Hong Kong, where she cared for children and ministered to refugees. As she crossed the border, an inspector noticed her Bible and asked her why she insisted on being a Christian when so many had abandoned their faith. "I cannot, as many have done, reject the grace of God for me," she replied. "I cannot refuse his love to me which is like the love of father and mother."[3]

Finally, in 1962 she obtained a visa to the United States, where she reunited with her son, who was working for the National Cancer Institute as a pioneer of chemotherapy. She spent the rest of her life in Los Angeles, ministering to the Chinese community, writing her autobiography, and sharing her story with the help of translators.

One of these translators was Rev. Samuel E. Boyle, a missionary to South China who traveled around California with Jeanette. Once, he asked her if she thought the church in China would endure in spite of the anti-Christian indoctrination. Jeanette looked surprised. "The church of Christ is his body," she said. "He purchased the church with his own blood. He has promised that the gates of hell shall never overcome the church. You ask me if the church of Christ will be destroyed? How could it be, in the light of all these great promises?"[4]

This answer sums up her convictions. She died of a stroke in 1968 while she was working with a translator on an account of her imprisonment.

---

3. Li, *Jeanette Li: A Girl Born Facing Outside*, 302.
4. Li, *Jeanette Li: A Girl Born Facing Outside*, xii.

FOOD FOR THOUGHT

- Jeanette's conviction of the truthfulness of God's promises allowed her to survive terrible circumstances. Tell of some times when God's promises have sustained you in your life.

- Jeanette had to constantly pray for wisdom in dealing with the authorities' questions. She was eventually released because they had no proof against her. She had always been a law-abiding citizen. Find some Bible verses that show that Christians must maintain a good testimony in front of others.

- In 1 Timothy 2:2, Paul says to pray "for kings, and for all that are in authority; that we may lead a quiet and peaceable life in all godliness and honesty" (1 Tim. 2:2). Why is this an important injunction for Chinese Christians both in the past and today? Explain why it is also important for American Christians.

FOR FURTHER RESEARCH

Jeanette's autobiography is available in English as *Jeanette Li: A Girl Born Facing Outside*, trans. Rose Huston (Pittsburgh: Crown and Covenant, 2014).

Time Line

249 First general persecution of Christians in the Roman Empire under Emperor Decius.

303 Emperor Diocletian starts the worst persecution against Christians.

312 Emperor Constantine puts a legal end to the persecution of Christians.

ca. 325 **Marcella of Rome** is born.

325 Constantine calls the first Council of Nicea to discuss, among other things, whether Jesus is fully God.

ca. 327 **Macrina the Younger** is born in today's Turkey.

ca. 331 **Monica of Tagaste** is born, probably in today's Algeria.

354 Augustine is born to **Monica of Tagaste**.

370 **Monica**'s husband, Patricius, becomes a Christian.

371 Patricius dies.

379 **Macrina the Younger** and her brother Gregory of Nyssa have a long discussion on the human soul and the resurrection. She dies soon after, and Gregory publishes the account.

380 Emperor Theodosius I makes Christianity the official religion of the Roman Empire.

385 **Monica** joins Augustine in Italy.

386 Augustine is converted and baptized.

387 **Monica of Tagaste** dies near Rome.

405 Jerome finishes the official translation of the Bible in Latin.

410 **Marcella of Rome** dies after suffering abuses by Visigoth soldiers.

410 The Visigoths' raid on Rome signals the collapse of the Western Roman Empire.

622 Considered the first year of the Islamic era.

636 Jerusalem falls to the Arabs.

730– Byzantine emperors forbid the
787 use of images of Jesus (first iconoclast period).

732 Charles Martel stops Islamic invaders at the Battle of Tours.

ca. 800 **Dhuoda of Uzés** is born.

800 Pope Leo III crowns Charlemagne as emperor—the first emperor in the West since the fall of Rome.

ca. 810 **Kassia** is born in today's Turkey.

814– Second iconoclast period in
843 Byzantium.

843 **Dhuoda** completes her
manual for her son William.
She dies soon after.

865 **Kassia** dies.

1054 Western and Eastern Churches
officially divide.

1095 Pope Urban II calls for the
First Crusade in the Holy
Land.

1337 Beginning of the Hundred
Years War between England
and France.

1347– The Black Death devastates
1371 Europe.

ca. 1364 **Christine de Pizan** is born in
Venice, Italy.

1369 **Christine de Pizan** moves to
France with her family.

1390 **Christine** becomes a widow.

1393 **Christine's** first book of
poems becomes public.

1399 **Christine's** *Epistle to the God
of Love* argues against the
misogynist views expressed in
a popular book, *Le Roman de
la Rose*.

1405 In *The Book of the City of
Ladies* and *The Treasure of
the City of Ladies*, **Christine**
insists on the importance of
showing respect for women as
created in God's image.

1430 **Christine de Pizan** dies.

1452   Johannes Gutenberg produces the first printed copy of the Bible.

ca. 1492   **Argula von Grumbach** is born in Germany.

1492   Christopher Columbus discovers America.

ca. 1505   **Elizabeth Aske Bowes** is born in England.

1510   **Renée of France** is born at Blois, France.

1513   **Giulia Gonzaga** is born in Italy.

1517   Luther's posting of Ninety-Five Theses on the church door in Wittenberg is often considered the beginning of the Protestant Reformation.

1521   Pope Leo X excommunicates Luther.

1523   **Argula von Grumbach** endangers her marriage and reputation to defend a student who is accused of being a Lutheran.

1526   **Olympia Morata** is born in Italy.

1528   **Renée of France** marries Ercole II of Este, Duke of Ferrara.

1530   Emperor Charles V summons the German Lutheran nobility to Augsburg to describe their views. **Argula** attends and promotes harmony among differing Protestant views of the Lord's Supper.

1534 The English king Henry VIII
      breaks with Rome and is
      declared head of the English
      church.

1541 **Giulia Gonzaga** contributes
      to the publication of gospel-
      filled books in the Italian
      language.

1542 Pope Paul III allows the
      reorganization of the
      Congregation of the Holy
      Office of the Inquisition,
      mainly against Protestants.

1545– The Council of Trent
1563   condemns Protestant
       doctrines.

ca. 1546 **Charlotte de Bourbon** is born
          in France.

ca. 1550 **Charlotte Arbaleste
          Duplessis-Mornay** is born
          in France.

1550 **Olympia Morata** moves
      to Germany to escape
      persecution.

ca. 1553 **Argula von Grumbach** dies.

1553– Mary I of England attempts
1558   to reverse the English
       Reformation and restore the
       Roman Catholic Church.
       She executes three hundred
       Protestants.

1554 **Elizabeth Aske Bowes** and
her daughter, Marjorie,
leave England to be with the
Reformer John Knox. Marjorie
marries Knox. **Renée of
France** is forced to deny her
Protestant beliefs. **Olympia
Morata** barely survives the
Siege of Schweinfurt during
the Second Margrave War.

1555 **Olympia Morata** dies in
Heidelberg, Germany.

1555 Emperor Charles V signs the
Augsburg Settlement, allowing
each prince to choose the
religion his subjects should
follow.

1558 **Olympia**'s poems and
rendition of the Psalms are
published.

1558 The Roman Catholic Church
publishes a list of banned
books. Elizabeth I of England
brings her country back to
Protestantism.

1559 **Renée** moves back to France
and helps refugees from the
French Wars of Religion.

1560 The Scottish Parliament
declares Scotland a Protestant
nation.

1566 **Giulia Gonzaga** dies.
Pope Pius V finds her
correspondence, which
incriminates other Italian
dissenters.

ca. 1572 **Elizabeth Aske Bowes** dies.

1572 A Roman Catholic mob
kills thousands of French
Protestants in the so-called
St. Bartholomew's Day
Massacre.

1572 **Charlotte de Bourbon** flees
from her convent.

1575 **Renée of France** dies.
Charlotte de Bourbon
marries William of Orange.

                1576 Spanish troops massacre seven
thousand people in Antwerp,
Holland.

                1581 William of Orange leads
a confederacy of Dutch
provinces to freedom from
the Spanish.

1582 **Charlotte de Bourbon** dies
while nursing her husband
after an assassination attempt.

                1598 With the Edict of Nantes,
French king Henry IV grants
French Protestants some
freedom of worship.

ca. 1600 **Bathsua Makin** is born in
England.

                1603 James VI of Scotland succeeds
Elizabeth I as King James I
of England. He continues
Elizabeth's policies.

1606 **Charlotte Arbaleste
Duplessis-Mornay** dies.

                1607 The first English colony in
America is established at
Jamestown, Virginia.

                1611 Completion of the King James
Bible.

1612 **Anne Bradstreet** is born in
England.

1616 **Dorothy Leigh** dies. Her
book of advice to her sons is
published.

1618 **Elisabeth of the Palatinate** is born in Heidelberg, Germany.

1618 Start of the Thirty Years War between the Catholic Habsburg rulers and the Protestant powers of Germany.

1620 **Lucy Hutchinson** is born in England. A crucial loss at the Battle of White Mountain ends the rule of Frederick V in Bohemia and forces him and his family, including **Elisabeth of the Palatinate**, into exile.

1620 A group of Puritans leaves England on a ship named *Mayflower*. About a hundred of them land in Plymouth, Massachusetts, where they found a colony.

1630 **Anne Bradstreet** moves to North America with her family as part of the John Winthrop fleet of Puritan emigrants. She arrives at Salem, Massachusetts.

ca. 1637 **Mary White Rowlandson** is born in England.

1642 Start of the first English Civil War.

1648 The Peace of Westphalia puts an end to the Thirty Years War and to the eight-year war of Dutch independence against Spain.

1649 The British Parliament votes to execute Charles I for treason.

1650 **Anne Bradstreet**'s collection of poems is published, making her the first published poetess in North America. **Mary White Rowlandson** and her family arrive in Massachusetts from England.

1660 **Lucy Hutchinson**'s husband is imprisoned for his role in the execution of Charles I.

1662 Charles II of England orders all pastors and preachers to follow his government-mandated rules of worship. On August 24, about one thousand pastors preached their last sermon to their congregations. Many left England.

1672 **Anne Bradstreet** dies.

1673 **Bathsua Makin** establishes a school for gentlewomen and publishes a pamphlet arguing for the education of women.

1675 **Bathsua Makin** dies.

1676 **Mary White Rowlandson** is captured by Native Americans.

1680 **Elisabeth of the Palatinate** dies.

1681 **Lucy Hutchinson** dies.

1682 **Mary White Rowlandson**'s account of her captivity becomes a best seller.

1685 King Louis XIV of France revokes the Edict of Nantes, ending religious freedom for Protestants. Thousands of French Protestants flee the country.

ca. 1692 **Anne Dutton** is born in England.

1700 **Kata Bethlen** is born in Transylvania (Hungarian territory).

1702– After years of abuse, some
1703 Huguenots fight a war of rebellion and self-defense against the government.

1711 **Mary White Rowlandson** dies. **Marie Durand** is born in France.

1717 **Anne Steele** is born in England.

1730 **Marie Durand** is imprisoned for her faith.

1737 Start of the Welsh revival, which will affect the poetess **Ann Griffiths**.

1742 **Isabella Marshall Graham** is born in Scotland.

ca. 1753 **Phillis Wheatley** is born in West Africa.

1759 **Kata Bethlen** dies.

1761 **Phillis Wheatley** is purchased as a slave in Boston, Massachusetts.

1765 **Anne Dutton** dies.

1768 **Marie Durand** is released from prison.

1773 **Phillis Wheatley** publishes her collection of poems, becoming the first published African American poet.

1775 Start of the American Revolutionary War.

1776 **Marie Durand** dies. **Ann Griffiths** is born in Wales.

1777 **Sarah Sergeant Miller** is born.

1778 **Anne Steele** dies.

1784 **Phillis Wheatley** dies.

1789 **Isabella Marshall Graham**
      moves to America and starts
      to establish schools and
      charitable societies.

ca. 1798 **Betsey Stockton** is born in
          Princeton, New Jersey.

1801 **Sarah Miller** marries Samuel
      Miller.

1805 **Ann Griffiths** dies.

1812 **Lydia Mackenzie Falconer
      Miller** is born in Scotland.

1814 **Isabella Marshall Graham**
      dies.

1822 **Betsey Stockton** leaves
      as missionary to Hawaii,
      becoming the first single
      woman missionary and first
      African-American woman
      missionary in the modern
      mission era.

1824 **Anne Ross Cundell Cousin** is
      born in England.

1843 A group of Christians,
      including Hugh and **Lydia
      F. M. Miller**, leave the Church
      of Scotland to start a new
      denomination, the Free
      Church, independent from the
      state. This event is known as
      the Disruption.

1856 **Lydia F. M. Miller** begins
      her work of editing and
      completing the scientific
      writings of her husband,
      geologist Hugh Miller.

1789 Start of the French Revolution.

1807 The British Parliament votes to
      abolish the slave trade.

1861	**Sarah Sergeant Miller** dies.	1861	The American Civil War begins.
		1863	President Abraham Lincoln issues the Emancipation Proclamation.
1865	**Betsey Stockton** dies.		
		1871	Charles Darwin publishes *The Descent of Man*, suggesting that human beings evolved from other species.
1876	**Lydia Mackenzie Falconer Miller** dies.		
1899	**Jeanette Li** is born in China.	1899	Start of the Boxer Rebellion in China, when many Christians are killed.
1906	**Anne Ross Cundell Cousin** dies in Scotland.		
		1914	World War I begins.
		1939	World War II begins.
		1946	Beginning of the Chinese Communist Revolution.
		1949	Proclamation of the People's Republic of China.
1952	**Jeanette Li** is imprisoned for her faith by the Chinese Communist regime. She stays in prison for about sixteen months.		
1968	**Jeanette Li** dies in America while writing her autobiography.		